The South of England

The South of England

AN ARTIST'S JOURNEY THROUGH ENGLISH LANDSCAPES

SYDNEY R. JONES

SENATE

The South of England

First published in 1948 as *England South* by
The Studio Publications, London & New York

This edition published in 1998 by Senate,
an imprint of Tiger Books International PLC,
26A York Street, Twickenham,
Middlesex TW1 3LJ, United Kingdom

ISBN 1 85958 526 4

Printed and bound in the UK by
Cox & Wyman, Reading, England

CONTENTS

PREFACE

Some of us now and again experience feelings of sentiment, and even melancholy, on turning the pages of diaries and sketch-books filled by ourselves once upon a time. We may think the jottings pleasant, decent, or silly, or perhaps quite out of date. Reviewing such records of auld lang syne could be likened to a body-snatching performance of ransacking one's own sarcophagus. All these shades of notion occurred to me when I sorted out the matter for this book from the accumulations of a longish lifetime.

For ages and ages England's green and pleasant land has been changing. It has changed a good deal since I first knew it. Now it changes faster than ever before. One day the whole show may be blown up. Some of the subjects of my drawings and words have vanished already; many of them are still to be seen. They mostly relate to periods and systems which caused men and women to ply the crafts and create beauty everywhere, before the Dissolution of the Monasteries, after that event, and until the Industrial Revolution set in motion the materialistic wonders of avarice and catastrophe. Though I have noticed the grand and expressive monuments of the newer order, represented by powerful power stations, aerodromes, cinemas, horizontal flats, chromium-plated saloon bars, sleek by-passes and so forth, my limited space does not permit me to dwell on them at this moment. Thus I am forced to keep to the old strain, to concentrate on Salisbury spire, Wells, Bodiam Castle, Hammoon, Lacock, and other out-of-date objects.

Artists gather collections of the sort now presented. What is done to-day may be needed at once, to-morrow, or many years hence. Topographical subjects especially have a chance of being useful by keeping the present for the future in a kind of preserve flavoured sweet, bitter, or horrible. Artists also like doing these things. They belong to the last remnants of craftsmen not assassinated by mass production and trades unions, are able to work long hours, can receive low wages, and are allowed to enjoy pleasant tasks. Rightly or wrongly, some of them think they contribute to the public weal. A Prime Minister—nameless of course—said as much when he urged a number of us to keep at it in these jaded years. He may have talked through his hat, for it is widely realized that politicians are very clever people quite able to speak splendidly about nothing. But I hope he was right, to clear me of blame for following his advice. And I trust this book will amuse some of my readers and not annoy too many of them.

S. R. J.

1. WILTSHIRE AND LONDON

Pale blue scabia, tufted yarrow, and brown knapweed nodded prettily in the breeze as I walked along the downs in Wiltshire. The lines of weathered hills spread in curve beyond curve and pointed to old remembrance. Liddington Castle and Barbury Castle stood out plain and clear. Their crowns of earthworks veiled forgotten secrets. The wild flowers in the grass at my feet kept the ageless pageant of Nature fresh and vital. I reached Barbury, climbed to the summit, 879 feet high, and found the sarsen stone fitted with two lettered tablets. One inscription read, "Richard Jefferies, 1848–1887." Faced to Liddington the other tablet gave the words, "Alfred Williams, 1877–1930."

> "Still to find and still to follow
> Joy in every hill and hollow
> Company in solitude."

These memorials of two Wiltshire natives, raised on their own beloved Hill, blended with earthen relics left by unknown men in lost ages. The past met the recent in the lovely present.

The views from Barbury were wonderful. Panoramas gave the pattern of the land. The rises and falls, fields, woods, trees, and distances, the cottages, farmsteads, villages, and churches mingled in colours of green, golden, and blue. The lookout commanded old haunts of customs and rural industries, now as extinct as the dancers with bells and ribbons or the festivals of scouring the White Horse perched beyond Liddington. The eye surveyed marks made by centuries of toil and ploughing and harvesting. Imagination swept farther. It ranged through the Vale of the White Horse to King Alfred's birthplace at Wantage; it lighted on Athelstan's Malmesbury, Roman and eighteenth-century Bath, the Avebury circles, Wans Dyke and Stonehenge, Old Sarum, Salisbury, and Silchester; Winchester, once England's capital; and a great deal else gathered within a radius of 30 miles round Barbury Castle. Excursions with vision and mental flight sent my fancy roving over the beauty, story, and legend that is the heritage of England.

But this hill on which Richard Jefferies and Alfred Williams had stood commanded other things either to be seen or thought of. Villages marred by convenient and ugly new dwellings, Swindon smoky with railway shops, unlovely Didcot in the Vale, pretty little Imber ruined by the Army, acres of aerodromes, atomic bomb activities at Harwell, and like suggestions, disturbed the tranquillity of the lovely scene. Mean and gloomy sights, symbols of modernism, threatened the spiritual supplies of Nature without which peoples perish. Harry Batsford's words in *The National Trust* book crossed my mind: "It does not look as if the present age is capable of creating beauty, but there is no doubt of its ability to obliterate and destroy what has come down to us from earlier times." Nothing seemed to be safe from exploitation and spoilers, and those atomic bombs round the corner augered very nastily. These unpleasant ideas sent me away from Barbury in a hurry. I jumped into a car sent to meet me, and took a fast train from Swindon to London.

In the fog of the City bright and beautiful I sought my publishers' offices at *The Studio*, and found the hive complete with bosses, swains, and nymphs. Greeted as "old Adam without Eve from Eden," I apologized for my intrusion by offering a résumé of the flight from Barbury Castle via Swindon, the bomb area, and Didcot. Then I hinted at inviolate years before the era of atomics, when a pound meant a golden sovereign and a silver bob went quite a long way; years of the hospitable manor-houses before taxation; village craftsmen, whiskered faces, smocks, rosy cheeks above big aprons, all long since decayed; inns and hotels with unrationed sirloins; walking, bicycling, driving tubs behind ponies, steering high motors that often wouldn't go; when old towns and villages looked more like themselves; and so on about the carefree years merrily recalled by Sir Alfred Munnings in *The Studio* magazine for September 1944.

To my surprise one of the nymphs exclaimed, "Ah! Those must have been the days!"

"Goodness my Guinness!" I responded. "Had no idea you young sprites thought anything good of us and our baggy old times."

"Figs for that!" she retorted. "We reckon it was just a golden age. We were born in war years, have lived through war, hear of war to follow and nothing but regimentation. We've also noticed that other people besides Hitler have ruined town and country."

"Why not do a book on what you have picked up and can remember, early and recent?" said one of the sage beings.

"That's an idea," I answered. "If you are game I will, or rather will try. Scenery and architecture, and their relation to history and people—those would be my main themes. There's too much in England to pack into one volume. I've tackled *London* and the *Thames* already. We will continue with south of the Thames from the Straits of Dover to Land's End, and pick up the Weald, Salisbury Plain, Somerset, Devon, and all sorts of places on the way. That is more than enough for a beginning. I'll start at once, go about, rub up old memories to adorn or spoil your paper ration; see what is left in the counties before the promised functional triumphs knock the old relics into a cocked hat or the atomics get in first and remove the lot."

Turning to one of the nymphs I requested, "Do be an angel, Venus, and look up a train for Tonbridge in the morning. And please telephone the *Rose and Crown* for a bed—name of Sydney Jones, single room of course."

I left London on the morrow to begin *England*.

A village in Hampshire—WHERWELL

A village in Wiltshire—CASTLE COMBE

A village in Devon—SAUNTON

A village in Kent—CHIDDINGSTONE

2. THE DOWNS AND THE WEALD

SURREY, KENT, SUSSEX

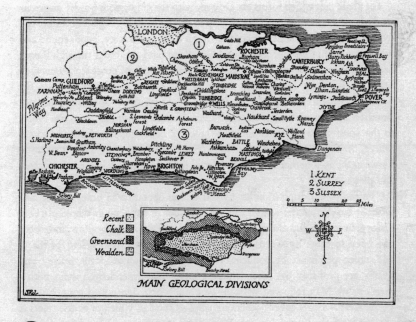

MAIN GEOLOGICAL DIVISIONS

On clear days at Leith Hill, Westerham, Chanctonbury Ring, Mount Harry, and other points nearest to heaven in south-eastern England, the wide panoramas visible include great expanses of the green and fertile country indicated by the map above. Standing on one of these heights you see the rounded hill forms of the North or the South Downs extending in smooth curves from east to west. Above cultivated fields the steep banks and ridge tops are covered with old grassland, soft in colour and good to look at, good to walk on, and good for sheep that roamed over it in thousands for centuries. Here and there light faces of chalk pits shine out, and lanes and tracks emphasize the prevailing notes of green and white. Or, particularly in Surrey and western Sussex, great woods and heaths clothe the hills, affording lovely miles of glade and shade, vistas between trees, and almost untrodden ways. From the Downs in the north or the south the opposite line of downs can be traced, forming the end of distant landscapes. Between and below the two ranges of hills lies the Weald. Patterned with fields and hedgerows, old forests, and woods, it is diversified by hilly stretches and many parks of flourishing, decayed, and over-taxed gentry. Orchards, market gardens, climbing hops, and chalk workings, tell of to-day's provision. Oak trees, cinder heaps, and hammer-ponds recall the dead iron industry. Downs rising in places to more than 700 and 800 feet, wooded hills beneath them, miles of rich pastoral acres, pretty river valleys, a border of coast and sea—such is the face of the Downs and the Weald country.

The chalk belt which forms the Downs, with the contiguous border of greensand, shape a curved figure on the map in the form of a rough and unfinished oval. It traces from the Dover coast through Kent and Surrey, bends round and down the Hampshire border beyond Guildford, and continues through Sussex back to the sea at Beachy Head. Except for the length of coast from Pevensey Level to Romney Marsh, this curve of chalk and greensand encloses the wealden formation of the Weald. It was not always thus. Once, probably one hundred million years ago, the high mass of chalk continued from the North to the South Downs. When most of the chalk departed, somehow and somewhere, the brave north and south hills remained with a wide weald stretching between them, together forming a delectable land for man's life, conquest, toil, and pleasure.

The geological disposition left by this ageless operation of time, climate, and weather has carried the weight of a vast number of happenings whose places in history, in scenes, and along the moving tracks of old and new years, have been presented so often by words and pictures that nothing fresh is left for me to add, unless perchance by accident. For of English counties, Kent, Surrey, and Sussex are probably the most widely known. Nature endowed them with a lavish hand. Man followed with his best and worst. Unspoiled country some of the areas are now called; others are labelled spoiled, which of course refers to the deeds of the human species. Wide tracts, far from the madding crowds, offer peace, quiet, and solitude. In out-of-the-way parts, particularly in Sussex, objects and natives seen may suggest the Saxon heritage. Often in circling between Canterbury, Chichester, and Farnham the fringe of medievalism is touched. A strong array of castles rouses up visions of knights in shining armour, the days of old, dark deeds in dungeons, and that sort of thing. The appearance of fields and boundaries, woods, sylvan domains, the hill shapes, and the place-names, help to piece together the course of ordinary life and endeavour which flowed full and steadily here from early beginnings. Memories of those who set it going from generation to generation are kept green by numerous great, manor, moated, and yeomen's houses, and by quarters and dwellings in ancient towns, ports, and villages such as Midhurst, Petworth, Lewes, Rye, Sandwich, Biddenden, Groombridge, Betchworth, and Chiddingfold. These, with dozens more, have a charm and quality remarkably choice even for England. The few remaining tiles deposited on the ground of The Pantiles at Tunbridge Wells through the generosity of Princess Anne introduce this district's place in a giddy social round that twinkled lights brilliant and lurid on the features of ladies, gentlemen, and rogues from the seventeenth century to Victorian years. For all one knows, shades of Regency bucks and their girls may yet lurk behind the terraces at Hastings and in the Old Steine at Brighton.

But the period of Georgius VI Rex undoubtedly is dominant in much of this country and its seaboard. The London and urban sprawl has altered the character of places favoured by people who hurry away by the eight something in the morning and reappear at night. A good deal of searching for simple beauty is sometimes needed where holiday-makers with or without pay congregate, to brighten verdant greens and the sad sea waves with the conventional town vivacity. It is a section of England streaked with many contrasts. A big jerk in time and idea separates the cottage over the mouth of the Southern Railway tunnel at Clayton and the earthworks on Wolstonbury up above. It's a strange mixture to leave the Pilgrims' Way at St. Catherine's Hill and join in the motor crawl through Guildford for London on a Sunday night; to drop down from Kit's Coty House into clouds of cement on the Medway; or to head from old Chiddingstone into Peacehaven! Yet it is still possible to get lost in the lovely woods around Worth before Crawley is manufactured into a satellite town, and to find beauty unalloyed far and wide.

This downland, vale, and sea-girt strip of country, I suppose, has been con-cerned with more doings of mankind than any other part of England. The natural features and the yields explained by geology tell of a full and storied past. Almost everywhere scenes belong to the stuff of unrecorded times and of history, suggest big happenings, denote the placid and lively motions of town, social, and country life in all the ages. Since human scheming as yet has not removed the hills, grand views are visible. The same main outlines must have been seen by those early comers who shaped flints gained from the chalk, piled up mysterious relics such as the Coldrum Stones, toiled at Holmbury, Thurn-ham, Ditchling, Cissbury, and many other strategic points to make camps and earthworks, centuries before the tangled Weald was drained, cultivated, and decked in ordered beauty. Here, always, was a front line of England facing the Continent from a moat of sea. The earliest explorers and traders from abroad came that way. In the year 596 St. Augustine and Christianity flowed in. Cæsar's landing at Pegwell Bay in 55, the beginning of English history with the victory of Hengist and Horsa at Aylesford in 455, and the Norman invasion at Pevensey, Hastings, and Battle in 1066, gave the island kingdom three of its most vital dates, equalled in our own time by yet one more, 1940 and the Battle of Britain, fought over this same front line.

Time, ever thrusting onward, liberally bestowed moving pageants on this south-east corner of England as it urged along peace and war, faith, endeavour, toil, and pleasure, deeds good and bad, and long, long years when country traditions grew strong, village kindliness glowed, and good shepherds tended their flocks. Closely settled, the counties developed a wealth of incident in the affairs of ordinary workaday folk seated in the many towns, villages, and hamlets. Situated between London and a commanding stretch of coastline, the ground made settings for figures big and little, noble and otherwise, who dominated, brightened, or darkened numerous passages in the national story. Along came all the kings and queens, variously engaged—John very glum at Dover for surrendering the crown to the Pope; Henry III to Lewes for a fall to De Montfort; a fatter Henry through Otford, mounted on a white horse bound for the Field of the Cloth of Gold; Elizabeth to Northiam for a feast under the oak tree yet standing; the last Charles in flight from the battle of Worcester along still secluded tracks over the Sussex downs; the last James on the Medway outward bound for ever. In fact, the area bristles with scenes and places associated with the whole collection of crowned heads up to one thing and another.

Crowds now remembered or almost forgotten garnished the hurly-burly of years through every royal reign in this important section of England. Nobles, statesmen, and clerics, squires, yeomen, and villagers, town and seafaring folk, and all sorts and conditions of men and women kept life flowing either vividly, steadily, or slowly, yet always in continuous motion. The passage of time brought to these parts its galaxy of famous names. Sidneys of Penshurst, Sackvilles of Knole, Norfolks of Arundel, Howards of Reigate Priory, Waller of Groombridge, John Evelyn of Wotton, and many another reminder of great families and renown claim home quarters in this full and rich inheritance. The three cathedral cities of Canterbury, Rochester, and Chichester hold their own particular stores for tracing anew the ways of grand churchmen who led the people and showered goodness through the old years of prelatic pomp and circumstance. Becket of Canterbury, John Fisher of Rochester, Richard Woodman of Warbleton, and noble victims of faith burnt at Lewes, place the district high on the roll of martyrs. William of Wykeham, great founder and builder, will always keep his place at Farnham Castle, even though in these lean days it is too big for any bishop to occupy. Jack Cade's end is told by a tablet near Heathfield; memories of illustrious personages abound in the Cinque Ports; and visible traces of Charles Dickens at Gad's Hill, Blake in Felpham, Richard Jefferies and W. H. Hudson in Broadwater Churchyard, Kipling at Burwash, with scores of signs elsewhere, show how these lands have been patterned with the names of innumerable individuals who left their marks on their times. "In sooth a goodly company" to quote the words of Richard Barham (*Thomas Ingoldsby*), himself a native of Canterbury.

Less radiant lights, though of much importance to the years of long settlement, left their time of day by evidences of themselves in populated centres, on lonely heights, among the fields and the trees, and by the sea. Quarters and haunts they once knew revive memories of squires and families settled on paternal acres. Sights and scenes recall country workers and their masters, shepherds with Pyecombe crooks, and the solid stocks that kept things going in charming towns and old ports such as Steyning and Rye. Past accumulations point out the ways of monks and summer pilgrims. Weavers from Flanders, natives who learned from them, and iron workers whose centuries of labour ended when Ashburnham furnace died out in 1828, all made particular contributions to the face of the land by which their presence now can be recognized. Some sly spots and shady corners dimly illuminate activities of a darker hue. These carry the dubious fame of smuggling, of the Hawkhurst and Alfriston gangs, and of gentlemen who nourished genius for contraband behind highly respectable exteriors. Other departed saints and sinners, ghosts of the pleasure resorts and "the Wells," still can be fitted into their earthly places. Evidences here and there spin the record of human antics to Regency sprites, Victorian families, paddling children, and a sad little Dombey who wondered what "the waves were always saying" at Brighton. Indeed, this division of England never seems to have failed in supporting plenty of action. The characteristics it presents tumble the ages of the human procession down from a remote past to the years before yesterday.

The diversity of performances staged through many periods in this busy downland, weald, and coastal country obviously needed a varied collection of stage properties for the use of the actors. And as the human species is rarely satisfied and always on the shift, a process due to an attitude of mind sometimes miscalled progress, the dwellers throughout this locality continuously looked about for means to forward their exploits and to provide for shelter and requirements. In their amblings onward through the centuries people wanted vantage points, earthworks, cromlechs, castles, palaces, cathedrals, churches, town and country houses, cottages, market places, cloth factories, forges, villas, balconies, and all sorts of paraphernalia, ranging from the thirty-three iron grave slabs at Wadhurst to the ducking-chair at Fordwich. In this direction the land and its yields served well. Primitive arrivals and their followers, consumed with the idea of fighting each other, found capital high spots for their purposes ready made by nature all along the crests of the North and South Downs, and only in need of the ditches and earthworks which now mark this series of fortified sites. Wonderful viewpoints are these, proving that ancients with clubs and javelins had keen eyes for country and lookout. Illimitable supplies of chalk in the hills offered materials for lime and building. Flints scattered through the chalk, after serving prehistoric tribes for tools and nasty weapons, were logically developed into the walls of churches and houses which sparkle in towns and villages. In the greensand lay ragstone ready to be fashioned into hard, greenish-grey masonry, and destined to give Maidstone the second half of its name. Sandstone cropped out in various directions. There was marble at Bethersden. The Weald had sand and clay suitable for making bricks and tiles. Iron ore could be won from below ground. Abundant oak trees supplied stout wood for all kinds of purposes.

The inhabitants, whether temporary or permanent, therefore had a choice of local products with which to further their schemes. After the first experimental years of finding out how to live, they used the natural resources so remarkably well in building up what was wanted for the round of life and incident that Kent, Surrey, and Sussex are among the richest of counties for displaying the effective use of a number of materials turned to the needs of man. Masonry, brick construction, chequered flintwork, timber framing, surfaces of plaster, tiled roofs and walls, thatching, stone tiles, and weather-boarding, all were employed in creating large and small buildings. The wide range of accomplishment that resulted from using the supplies of the earth to meet demands is strongly evident in all directions. It is shown by remains of palaces, ecclesiastical edifices reminiscent of royal and monastic splendour, the churches and a fine series of monuments within them, and by the crop of castles needed for the south-eastern defences, numerous great houses, and communal quarters in towns and country. Stonework at Rochester, Leeds Castle, Cowdray, Battle Abbey, Penshurst, church walls of ragstone, sandstone, and flint, spires covered with shingles, the timbers of Ightham Mote, a squared stone and flint gatehouse at Sandwich, Chichester's stone cross, Sackville College, East Grinstead, Petworth's almshouses, brickwork of Abbot's Hospital and a timber and plaster town hall at Guildford, Horsham stone roofs, and a boundless store of subjects, demonstrate this application of local provision to local needs. But the middling and toiling people of the settled and progressive community achieved some of the most notable results by applying the handy materials for their requirements of work, hearth, and home. In so doing they wrought truly and effectively within modest limits, infused the spirit of themselves into their work, and beautified their surroundings while turning nature's provision to good account. Thus came into being the famed and numerous yeomen's dwellings developed on the "hall-house" plan, the houses and cottages grouped in lovely compositions of timbering, plaster, stone, flint, brickwork, tile-hanging, and weather-boarding, the noble roofs and the characteristic chimneys. In the things built up traditional influences can be traced. Earlier examples are medieval in construction and character, while the workmanship of later date exhibits the Renaissance feeling, which is often admirably conceived and rendered. But whether of early or late date and whatever the type of local material, the charm of this phase in domestic and home building continually urges the explorer onward from Witley to Burwash and Elham, from Midhurst to Chilham, and through all the villages, towns, and countryside of south-eastern England.

Ways and means for exploring and getting about, very necessary for our present purposes, always were important in this part of the land that knew so many travellers from earliest times. High above the marsh of the Weald the chalk hills offered good and dry going. Primitive and later peoples therefore blazed and used the trackways along the North and South Downs, for these led to the harbours of Kent and Sussex, with the promise of the wide world beyond. To-day stretches of these hoary routes of grass on chalk, reclaimed by nature, wild flowers and birds, serve for the means of escape from a world still troubled by alarums and explosions. The other communications developed in due time, gathering particular character and fame as the years rolled on. The Romans drove Stane Street from London Bridge to Chichester. Now we can survey their glorious sweep over Bignor Hill, move on to Billinghurst for a suggestion of the possible constructor, Belinus. Up from the Kentish coast the legions marched through Canterbury and Rochester, but their Watling Street also became the route of Chaucer's pilgrims, of Marlowe, Prince Hal, Falstaff, Bardolph, the immortal Dover Road of *A Tale of Two Cities* and *David Copperfield*. Through the Weald miry routes directed right and left and to the coast. On these Horace Walpole bestowed suitable language after losing his horses and tramping ignominiously on shanks. But a wave of the hand by the first gentleman in Europe and the sprouting of a Royal Pavilion worked wonders. The routes of pleasure developed—there were several of them—and the Brighton Road, "nearly perfect, and certainly the most fashionable," shone with Regency lustre and pranks as it carried along the processions of Vanity Fair and W. M. Thackeray. From the lights and shades of other communicating ways Thackeray again is spotted piloting Madam Bernstein, Lady Maria Esmond, and Harry Warrington through Farnham and Reigate to the diversions of Tunbridge Wells.

Less known to fame, the network of lanes and footpaths represent the joggings of centuries made by the sons and daughters of the soil born of even and long settled years. Sequestered and lovely at all times and seasons they trace over hill and dale, through woods, old forests, and meadows. Perfect pictures they yield, amplified by clustered cottage roofs, church towers, cones of oast-houses, farms in the fields. Stores of scenic wealth are offered, such as the glades of Ashdown Forest, the views from Holmbury Hill, Graffham Down and Ditchling Beacon, distant Bodiam in the Rother valley and the fairy castle of Leeds. Other routes served particular people. Lonely and hollow ways used by smugglers for conveying booty inland from Cuckmere Haven and other retired spots pass old hiding-places and houses with great cellars and concealed receptacles, which remind that smuggling was an extensive local industry not too long ago. The coastal communications and cliff walks gathered their special history and stories of land and sea long before the brave backward march of progress added the villas, bungalows, shacks, and sundry human provisions to compete with nature's bounty round from east Kent to west Sussex. Even a William the Conqueror nowadays might hesitate to face the close formation of pointed roofs and chimney-pots on guard at Pevensey Bay. It is a mercy to know that the Seven Sisters Cliffs and the cliff land at Fairlight are secure with the National Trust. There is also consolation in the thought that, as far as one can tell, the Shakespeare Cliff at Dover will shine for a long time yet as a white wall of old England.

Harking back again to the oldest of routes, and straining at the leash to be on the move, I invite my readers to the North Downs for—

A PILGRIMAGE TO CANTERBURY

"Whanne that April with his shoures sote
The droughte of March hath perced to the rote,"

my youngest cousin Margaret, and her most senior cousin, myself, decided to walk to Canterbury. We had reduced Chaucer's opening passage in the prologue to "after the beastly winter." Spring was prancing along. Green sprouts sprouted, primroses peeped, daffodils nodded. The larks rose high and thrushes sang on orchard boughs. Muddy puddles were drying up. Warm breezes made gay circles of dust dance and dance again in the sunlight shining from blue skies flecked with little white clouds.

Our walking feat about to begin, with no certainty that our feet would permit its conclusion, we had dipped into various books concerned with that part of the country and had reread word by word Hilaire Belloc's masterpiece, *The Old Road*. We also quickly romped through *The Canterbury Tales* in an edition shorn of archaic words for the benefit of infantile minds, and though we gleaned that "sote" meant sweet and that times and human nature had changed a good deal for the worse since the year 1386, this light labour left us not much richer in topographical information. Not being near the Tabard Inn, Southwark, at that moment, but under the hospitable roof of Margaret's home, a dozen miles south of Winchester in Hampshire, it was decided to forgo the route taken by Chaucer's celebrated company until we reached it, and to keep more or less on the way known to prehistoric gentlemen and their ladies long before medieval pilgrims thought of following in the same tracks from Winchester to the shrine of St. Thomas at Canterbury.

Not needing to consider a couple of palfreys, we donned shoes sufficiently strong yet light, remembered the thermos, and buckled on our armour of knapsacks and sketch-bags. Margaret, tallish and well set up, looked just right for the part in a Bradley tweed suit, the period then being an old-fashioned one when shorts were not usually visible on the outside of females. We thought motoring to Winchester might be allowed, did so, got on our feet in the cathedral close, left the long length of grey walls, passed where the north gate used to be, and followed the path to King's Worthy. There, leaving the Roman road, we went east along the highway which marks the ancient route as far as Itchen Stoke. From that village a turning directing past Ovington introduced the first thrill of the genuine antique article, obvious by the ruts cut in the chalk and yew trees standing like sentries on guard (129). The lane, after mounting the hills and giving long views over watered landscapes, led down into Bishop's Sutton, where the primitive trace and the modern highway again unite as one.

At this point, favoured a long time ago by sporting bishops of Winchester addicted to hounds and the chase, our first fall from high purpose happened. A man in a car drew up and proffered a lift. We thanked him, but said we were walking. He said he was driving solo and felt lonely. He could take us all the way to London, would be grateful for our company, and explained he was an army gent hastening from some benighted military establishment to S.W.3. "Besides," he added, "walking is silly in these days," a remark which made us contemplate the lone soul with pity. After noting his second-rate contrivance on wheels, we refrained from suggesting a ride in a Rolls might be preferred. Still, here was an offer—doubtless devised by the devil to tempt weak humanity from playing the game. The pros of it, however malignant, battled in our thoughts against the pure cons. Almost a dozen miles had been covered conscientiously on foot. Daylight would not last for ever. Night quarters must be found somewhere. Alton was a good way off, Farnham farther. The old road, too, corresponded with the modern highway, or ran close to it right into Surrey. And Surrey, not Hampshire, was the real point for starting our adventures. An ill wind blew down the old adage, "Never refuse a lift."

"Come," said he born to command, "do let me take you on. Jump in!" So we obeyed the order, squatted on rear seats behind the gregarious major.

From the opening of the throttle, never can such a racket have been known since the rides of Dick Turpin and Wild Darrell, or the race of the three from Ghent to Aix with the good news of nobody knows what. We shot along, overtook everything moving, scorned all road signs, and swerved with hair-breadth escapes through imminent deadly breaches. Alton speedily gained, a graze along a lorry damaged our near wing, which the major, without stopping, said did not matter. A collision with a bus, narrowly averted, aroused dreadful language between the two drivers most horrible to hear; but this, nor a police-man, arrested the acceleration. Onward we fled. Margaret and I bounced up and down like marionettes on strings. Though we laughed and did not experience fright, there was a common foreboding between us of the last ride together and no to-morrows. We also managed to remember that the old road lay on our right from Ropley to within three miles of Alton and thence continued as the highway into Surrey. If Providence permitted our arrival alive in that county, we made a whispered agreement to forsake the military lunatic at Farnham.

Running into Farnham, I leaned forward to inform the speed merchant of this intention of dropping off. "Absurd," he bawled over his shoulder; "I can take you right through."

"But we don't want to go on," I replied with an effort to be firm.

"Much better go on," was the answer. "Sleep in London and come back here to-morrow with me. I will pick you up anywhere after two o'clock." And very likely, we thought, not stop again short of the benighted military establishment.

"But we must have something to eat after walking miles," I said, with a bright idea of feinting from frontal attack.

"All right. I'll wait," sounded back, and the car drew up in front of a likely establishment in Farnham. "Will half an hour be enough? You will find me parked round the corner when you are ready." The combustible combination then disappeared into Castle Street.

We took care to keep to our armour, did not go in to eat where the major indicated, warily sneaked off in another direction, and found a nice lodging within the picturesque courtyard of the *Bush Hotel*. Margaret breathed freely again. She patted her hair before a mirror, slyly twinkled her eyes, then turned and merrily said, "The major can wait!" Hampshire, about which we knew a good deal, faded in the sunset glow. Surrey and Kent lay before us. Though saints, very perfect gentle knights, good wives of Bath, or even murderers might not be met, and with a compact made to consign motoring to future days, we eagerly prepared for any mild diversions offered in this prosaic age to a pair of new pilgrims on the old Pilgrims' Way.

On a fresh spring morning such as we found, or at any other time of year when the elements behave themselves, Farnham exhibits one of the pleasantest in a group of attractive towns that have flourished for many a long day in the neighbourhood. Neither too large nor too small, too noisy nor dull, it must be the very spot for pleasant life. It has the River Wey to water the meadows, a castle on a hill with a park, a busy thoroughfare of age and associations, quiet streets and byways, a good collection of inns, houses, doorways, and knockers to summon a lot of periods, and vistas of greenery and hills beyond lines of mellow roofs. In fact, this is just the sort of place that always gives me the notion of forsaking my present abode, wheresoever it may be at the moment, and settling down afresh in a little Queen Anne or Georgian retreat with a garden, accompanied by two cats, a trusty domestic not too young, a stock of candles to dine by, and sundry old books in original bindings. These last, if destined for Farnham, might include the *Angler* of Izaak Walton, who wrote something else at the castle; a medley of poems by George Wither and Sir John Denham, if only to recall these Roundhead and Royalist defenders of the castle during the Civil War; Temple's *Miscellanea* and the *Journal to Stella*, for a thought of Sir William Temple and Jonathan Swift over at Moor Park with Esther Johnson handy in "Stella's Cottage"; *Rural Rides*, of course, because William Cobbett was born in the town at the *Jolly Farmer* public-house; to which appropriately could be added *The Virginians* with a sprig of rosemary at Chapter 20 to locate a stay at *The Bush*; White's *Selborne*, penned not far away, a worn hymnal for Sunday singings of *Rock of Ages*, composed by the town's clerical native Augustus Toplady; Jane Austen's six novels to enliven country walks to the lady's home at Chawton a few miles distant; and the eight volumes of *The Spectator* in faded brown bindings for dipping into at any time. Properly housed in this wise, fitted out with faithful service, cats and candles, and saturated with the right books, one would naturally sense greetings of poke-bonnets, long wigs, short wigs, lavender, roses, etc., etc., among the old brick walls, hooded doorways, and white window-frames in the progress to morning coffee and other lubricants, now on offer in abundance, which permit past healths to be drunk in present liquids.

And it is the present of Farnham, a solid present, that is so remarkably good. The Georgian mood in Castle Street (25) and West Street, and buildings old and new here and there give pictures of an ancient town keeping up to date in sturdy age. This is due to the inhabitants themselves. Ably led and by combined effort in preservation and fresh construction, they have united judicious regard for past years with provision for to-day. The general effect of these laudable actions presents a notable example of what English people in town and country might do for themselves if prompted by the requisite enthusiasm, purpose, and pride of place; this result contrasts with the plannings of a despotic age framed to shove docile mortals and everything else into a common and soulless melting-pot.

To my surprise many inquisitive visitors fail to discover one of Farnham's best sights at close quarters. This is the castle on the hill, visible to all and sundry. Those who may see it from afar assuredly should penetrate the quiet oasis standing above the town. The castle buildings there and the views from the mound offer ample rewards.

Two pilgrims, then, sheltered at *The Bush*, determined to attack this stronghold without delay, for I knew it of old. In between looking at Georgian doorways, shops, and all the pretty things in Castle Street, I paraded scanty information of a—yes, I thought a Saxon place in the ninth century, which certainly became the castle residence of the Bishops of Winchester from the eleven hundreds until this century, except for a gap during the Civil War when held in turn by George Wither, Sir John Denham, and Sir William Waller, poets all three, who, with Commonwealth fanatics, knocked the structure about.[1] These particulars, with the mention of building by King Stephen's brother Henri de Blois and William of Wykeham, the Tudor brickwork and fine tower in view standing for Bishop Fox, impressive Carolean interiors, and the sum of thirteen thousand pounds nine shillings and elevenpence three farthings for repairs after the Restoration, could not be expected to excite Margaret overmuch. When she feigned politeness to cloak boredom on my adding, "Isn't it clever of me to remember all that?" I did not disclose a study of the local guidebook at the hotel after bacon and eggs for breakfast. But on reaching the trees, the way in, and the opening beyond, her spirits began to bubble up, for a castle mound and romantic surroundings are liable to play the tricks of sentiment on anyone anywhere.

The mode of attack called for no consideration of lance and helmet, the crossbow, trebuchet, and weapons of the good old days. "Admission 3*d*."

---

[1] Farnham Castle ceased to be the residence of the Bishops of Winchester in 1927.

painted on a notice-board indicated the only ammunition necessary for storming the fortress; yet such terms of current nomenclature, scurvy though they may appear, are heralded often enough, with variations of 6*d*. and 1*s*., to summon knights and ladies to arms in this mundane age of easy chivalry. Even two threepenny-pieces could be dispensed with here in opening the assault, for no sentry barred the way. We forthwith carried the barbican, secured the crest of the upward climb, and apparently advanced to sole possession of the summit of the earthen mound enclosed by its twelfth-century wall. It was lovely on the top. Bright morning light shone on near objects below, the park lay in grand stretches of green and trees, and over the hills and far away views expanded to distant haze. Not a sound was heard; no bugle note told of our victory.

"Well," I said, flushed with conquest, "we have done quite as well as Waller did, and without the help of beastly Roundheads."

"We've also saved sixpence," Margaret lightly added in voicing a sentiment much too mercenary for an occasion of valour.

This appreciation of a bargain, occasionally obvious in the fair sex, happened to be premature. Though we seemed to be alone, a counter-attack developed immediately, and from an ambush concealed in plants and flowers that thrived in peace on the high earth of war's sieges. Out of the camouflage the official keeper advanced with a pleasant "Good morning," at which I acknowledged defeat by presenting alms with two threepenny-pieces. These were accepted on behalf of His Majesty's Exchequer and with a charm of thanks unknown in departments of Inland Revenue. The splendid veteran of past sea fights then meditated on the promise of the flower-beds, led over to the deep well-shaft of the keep, explained relics of masonry and fireplaces, pointed out landmarks on the hills, indicating always the true enthusiasm of a trusty custodian. Leaving us to wander where we would, he returned to work in the flower borders.

"There is something curious about this castle, almost unique for England," I remarked as we circled round the earthwork. "A long time ago it is supposed to have belonged to the Saxon Swithin, Bishop of Winchester, the man of the showers because his reburial, arranged for a July 15th, had to be postponed for forty days on account of the wet. The mound was a small affair, not one of the great strongholds. Towards the close of the twelfth century, about the year 1180 in fact, the owners fancied looking grander, but this top space was rather limited for medieval capers that required lofty walls, towers, great halls, and all the accompaniments of pomp and pageantry. So the builders merely added the wall round the mound, and down below beyond the barbican they developed the real castle, which grew into what it is now. This arrangement is very rarely seen."

We were then standing on the edge of the mound looking downward from the height into the castle forecourt.

THE NORTH DOWNS. *The line of heights from Box Hill through Surrey towards Kent. Below:* FARNHAM. *Castle Street leads down from the old fortified residence of the Bishops of Winchester. The town, birthplace of Cobbett in 1762, is remarkable for the care bestowed on the early, Georgian and modern buildings.*

GUILDFORD. *The ruins of the early tower-keep, rising over tile-hung houses and roofs, command the River Wey.*

"Isn't it a perfect picture?" I said. "All sorts of periods, twelfth-century and Wykeham's stone, Tudor brickwork, and the Restoration part done by Izaak Walton's friend Bishop Morley, who lived the simple life in a stone cell to the tune of eighty-seven years and content with one meal a day. And it is quite wonderful to think of William of Wykeham being down there entertaining Henry Yevele, William de Wynford, Sir Edward Dalyngrigge, and many a master thinker of a great age, and of them talking together of Canterbury, Winchester, Bodiam, and all the works they created for the delight of their own times and posterity." We agreed that Farnham Castle mound and the looks from it could change a threepenny-piece into something more glistening than gold.

Pilgrims in a mechanized age who now go by the big highway along the Hog's Back from Farnham to Guildford may continue from thence on good and fast roads through Dorking, Reigate, Westerham, Maidstone, and Charing, for Canterbury and the Straits of Dover. And if one thinks with the Preacher, "there is no new thing under the sun," it is odd to speculate on how many millions of people have gone much the same way through ageless time. From the beginnings of man's travels, and long before Winchester and Canterbury were shrines, Farnham must have been an important junction of communications. It was accessible from southern harbours and the Thames valley at a point on the east–west cross track of indefinable origin that led from Cornwall, the Mendips, and Salisbury Plain to the ports of Kent. The Pilgrims' Way, coming up from Winchester, here joined this primitive route, and as one and the same for mile upon mile traced along the southern slopes of the North Downs, here and there mounted hill crests and crossed river valleys, and finally reached the eastern goal. To-day as we speed over smooth surfaces from Farnham to Canterbury the old, old road is never far away.

Though medieval pilgrims deviated from the old road and followed more tracks than one, the original route that came to be known as the Pilgrims' Way is still obvious through about two-thirds of its course. Sectors lost and doubtful gaps, never of great length, have been pieced together by authorities, to mark the trace generally complete. It leads along hard roads and lanes, on tracks and paths, points a line over hillsides, directs through woods, coppices, fields, and between wild hedgerows, ever offering harvest to the eye with the luxuriance of near beauty, venerable churches and villages, dark yew trees, rural domains, and expansive views. Through these scenes old-time devotees moved onward to the great shrine of Canterbury. Pursuing their way in leisurely fashion, they halted and paid homage at churches, wells, ancient stones, and landmarks which long custom and antiquity had made sacred and mysterious to men's minds. Not only was this done at the commemoration of Becket's murder in December and at the anniversary of the canonization of St. Thomas in July: the stream of pilgrims passed to and fro at all times of the year. Particularly in summer sunshine the mixed "compagnies," such as Chaucer immortalized, took to the hills. In holiday mood and under open skies they found the joys of pleasant days, bodily good, and spiritual devotion.

This way of travel and its variants, largely defined up to the present day, therefore offer the interests and jumps of ages always to be met with in following tracks of predecessors. Though but the polished highway from Farnham to the Hog's Back ascent, the route then takes to the southern slopes for Seale, Puttenham, and St. Catherine's Hill, that memorable point of antiquity supporting the ruined chapel. Over the valley of the Wey St. Catherine's is answered by the hilltop stones of St. Martha's, once St. Thomas's Chapel, now solitary in a wonderful stretch of the trail and dominant over wooded and wide scenes (31). The pilgrim traces beckon ahead, through the lime avenue and pretty village cluster of Shere, and keeping to the contours above Dorking, Reigate, and Westerham, they sweep from hill to hill along the escarpments of the North Downs right across Surrey into Kent (25). Hundreds of sights spur the body and stir the mind. Friendly yew trees give signs of direction and, marshalled as at Hackhurst Down, they stand in dark ranks like sentinels of immortality. There, at Burford Bridge, are the stepping-stones in the River Mole marking one of the ancient crossings. Round Box Hill, and glorifying many another expanse, the beech trees rise in the splendour of pale branches and foliage over carpets of leaves. Byways and tracks, such as those up to Denbies Park, along Buckland Hills and Quarry Hangers, are shaded in greenery or strike across open land. They continue past Chevening, Otford, and Wrotham to the pilgrims' ferry point over the Medway. Ever and always, the impressive outlines of chalk promontories jut towards the Weald, seeming poised as cliffs of dreams over the oceans of memory.

Pointers to old dreams and memories crowd and border the route. The geographical position of the track, its very age and long use caused the large accumulation of relics and memorials round it to be no trick of chance. Human events and settlement naturally centred about this important way of communication. It became a lifeline of work, faith, peace and war, of manifold doings and impulses. It therefore keeps the stuff of unrecorded times and years of history, directs to past haunts and homes of big people, middling people, and those of ordinary stature that represented the salt of the earth of this England. These evidences stand for milestones to those who march bravely on. They transform the roads, lanes, and tracks into living volumes of man's progress, with chapters of old years and history opened at page after page.

The promise of sights and reminders, then, can urge modern pilgrims onward in expectation from Farnham. North of the town is the Roman entrenchment of Cæsar's Camp. To the south Sir William Temple's home of Moor Park upholds that philosopher's words, "The greatest advantages men have by riches are, to give, to build, to plant and make pleasant scenes." Here a young man came as secretary, one Jonathan Swift, and wrote *A Tale of a Tub*, a copy of which William Cobbett carried in his knapsack to cheer soldiering days in Nova Scotia. Down the vale the ruins of Waverley fix the site of the first Cistercian abbey in England. The church of Seale, on its mound, introduces a fine example of the timber porches so famed in Surrey, and Puttenham, where we stayed at *The Jolly Farmer* plumb on the Pilgrims' Way, lies prettily amongst elm trees with slopes whitish and green for a background. At this point Canterbuty pilgrims deviated to Compton and saw, as we did, the treasures in the church with the Norman vaulting; they arrived too soon, however, for visiting the home and public picture gallery of G. F. Watts, an artist hailed in my youth as a branch of the old masters, now probably reduced to a splinter by the wiseacres, but a grand old Victorian for all that. In addition to the ancient bridges at Elstead and Eashing, the neighbourhood also holds Sir Thomas More's house of Loseley, built with the stones from Waverley Abbey into Tudor gables, bays, and shining windows from which Queen Elizabeth, King Charles, and Shakespeare's Earl of Southampton looked out. Over the passage of the River Wey St. Catherine's Hill looms up. There we halted, to catch the scene in mood romantic against the afterglow. Then, for the dozenth time, we moved into Guildford, a port of call for refreshment and beds with pilgrims old and new.

Cobbett's description of "the most agreeable and most happy-looking" capital town of Surrey is so often quoted that I need not repeat it. Nor shall Mr. Pepys be resurrected again, mixed up in a crowd and a wedding at the *Red Lyon* on August 8, 1668, prior to the inevitable benediction, "and so to bed." Yet in spite of all that has happened since the arrival of these two and other past worthies, and with London encroaching nearer yearly, incessant traffic, and the presence of sundry low apparatuses to administer the accessories for the higher standards of living, Guildford has triumphed over the punches of progress, to keep secure some of the most picturesque of town sights. Whenever I go there the ways up and down always seem so gay, human, and ancient, abounding in all sorts of appeal. True, the end of the great coaching days on the Portsmouth Road gave the town a quiet span. But the motors altered that; and sometimes it is heartening to see an old place freshening to the current of new breezes whilst retaining a good deal to keep ancestry in mind and just round the corner. Guildford, beautifully situated among hill and dale, has managed to do this. The thoroughfares are busy enough, yet streets and odd narrow ways offer all one could wish in Georgian brickwork, tile-hanging, pointed gables, great chimney-stacks, and bay windows and casements from which pretty faces looked out on the changing fashions of the passing years. High Street alone is a joy. It shows the common lapses of modern shop fronts, but otherwise this is

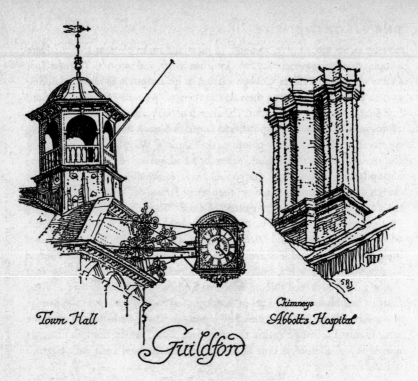

Town Hall

Chimneys
Abbott's Hospital

Guildford

surely one of the most cheerful of main highways in England. The Town Hall, a bright combination of sparkling windows, pediments, cornices, and a charming bell turret high up, overhangs the pavement with a balcony carried on carved brackets, specially devised to support the frames of mayors and corporations in "good capon lined" on august occasions. From a flourish of curly ironwork the clock juts out, shining a jolly golden face over the hurrying and scurrying below. Altogether this is a delicious little town hall. Period, 1683 and Restoration of course, the exact article for Nell Gwynn and King Charles. His Majesty's portrait and that of brother James reside inside on canvases painted by Sir Peter Lely. Round about are the inns, gabled and square frontages, good interiors and staircases of various dates, all to be noticed while making purchases and consuming refreshments. Even the granite surface of this old street represents almost the only type left on earth capable of withstanding a stream of cars and lorries on a hill climb.

On the crest of Guildford High Street stands the Hospital of the Blessed Trinity, looking very much as it must have done in 1622 when completed for the town's native, George Abbot, Archbishop of Canterbury. There, just as good as ever, are the founder's brick walls, turrets, and gables, the massive oak doors carved and emblazoned, beautiful lead spout-heads dated 1627, and the dining-hall, fireplaces, contemporary furniture, and rarities inside that are

THE PILGRIMS' WAY at St. Martha's in Surrey, between St. Catherine's Hill and Albury.

CANTERBURY, *shrine of pilgrims ancient and modern,*
stands proudly in the green lands of Kent. A view from
the north-western uplands. The German raids caused
dreadful damage round the Cathedral and in the city.

Sydney
R JONES
Canterbury

ROCHESTER. *The great Norman keep, begun about 1128, dominates the River Medway. Facing the castle, the modern tower and spire rise over the fine Norman nave of the Cathedral founded by St. Augustine in 601. The riverside walk in front of the castle is lined with balustrades from old Rochester bridges, demolished in 1857, and from which Mr. Pickwick contemplated the scene while waiting for breakfast.*

courteously shown to ardent visitors. One visitor, lodged in the upper room over the entrance gateway in 1685, had little ardour for the rarities in this peaceful home of brethren and sisters. He was the Duke of Monmouth, very melancholy indeed on the way from Sedgemoor, and without a semblance of relish for the merry stories of the hare, the hounds, and the chase which his comrade in misfortune, Grey, propounded with great gusto; perhaps lack of humour may be excused in a duke, when resembling a captured hare, with Tower Hill and the block foreshadowed as a dead certainty. The founder of this hospital was buried in Holy Trinity Church opposite, now the pro-cathedral and conspicuous for eighteenth-century brickwork on the site of an older structure. Abbot's tomb is an elaborate work comprising a recumbent figure under a canopy, and mournful reliefs signifying an age addicted to skulls, crossbones, and anatomical débris for symbols of transience and immortality.

Out and about the town lots of other things rivet attention among the old walls, gables, and roofs. St. Mary's Church has the pre-Conquest tower, wall paintings, and various features to make it one of the most interesting edifices in the county. The castle and the Norman keep, built of flint, stone, and Roman bricks, is a hoary remnant of the residence much favoured by Plantagenet kings, who usually did their fighting elsewhere. At Castle Arch the tile-hung house, very attractive, contains an exciting collection of local country imple-ments on view to all comers; and the River Wey down below offers delicious mixtures of piled-up roofs, reflections, high trees and foliage. From the banks of the stream we sketched one of these combinations of houses and water topped by the castle tower (26), in between times taking cups of powerful tea at a haunt patronized by lorry drivers, who entertained Margaret immensely. While at work an old warrior, unshaven and without a collar, came to inspect our efforts; meanwhile he directed on our simple heads a battery of words and phrases made up of psychology, ideals, materialism, awful present, unknown future, and other trifles, launched in a flood of oratory so suggestive of political windbags that we simply gasped on the banks of the River Wey in the presence of this new Touchstone railing on how the world wags. The explosion even caused me to use an india-rubber on my drawing, an unusual procedure. People to be met, in fact, help to furbish Guildford into the cheery town it is. One day long ago in a Quaker's book-shop I chanced on William Hyde, the rare artist illustrator of *The Old Road*. When we visited Abbot's Hospital one of the brethren, born in 1871 and roofed with the picturesque cap of the fraternity, said of his courtyard home and nobly I thought, "This is a real memorial. It goes on for ever and does lasting good." Over coffee at a restaurant in High Street, notable for a richly decorated staircase of seventeenth-century date, we began to hear a most thrilling account of a—but it was time to regain the Pilgrims' Way.

We left the town with Margaret saying, "What a pity to go so soon!" to which I replied, "We will come again"—sound advice for anyone with a kink for the curious in Guildford.

The route of pilgrimage, striking up from Shalford through the Chantries woods to St. Martha's high on the hill, directs for a good many miles eastward through London's playground and "beauty spots," an expanse of country enjoyed by variegated types of human beauty in search of clean air and change, and amply adorned with works of man erected from proceeds accumulated in the metropolis. Such places as Aldershot, Woking, Epsom, and Croydon are not far distant. For all these advantages, which may or may not be the quest of explorers mentally related to Bill Combe and *Doctor Syntax in search of the Picturesque*, these bold stretches of Downs have preserved places of quiet and unalloyed charm, and much that approaches the elevations of grandeur in scenery. Though so near London, chances are offered for detecting the tang of old and even primitive time almost within range of sights and sounds of the present.

The height of St. Martha's crowned with its church, but a few miles from Guildford, is one of these spots for capturing the spirit of age in remote and lovely surroundings (31). Ancient camps are near. The Pilgrims' Way leads down for Weston Wood and Albury. While we sketched and the morning mists faded away, rich distant miles brightened beyond the banks and woods below us. No living soul came near, and the silence, only broken by singing birds, seemed to respond to forgotten years. Elsewhere on the way I have previously indicated across Surrey, this appeal of time, mood, and place can be felt, and quite remarkably considering the nearness of urban cultivations of bricks and mortar lying to the north and about Dorking, Reigate, Godstone, and Westerham. The tops of the hills, too, 700 and 800 feet high and usually above the Pilgrims' Way, afford famous prospects from Box Hill to Tatsfield. In parts, as at Colley Hill near Reigate, the chalk lands drop steeply; or they shape in smooth curves clothed with rough grass. There are the great woods, fern, combes, dells, clear streams hurrying down. Sandy lanes can be seen tracing out to the Weald, and far, far away the vast plain extends, green and blue, bright or golden, from morning till sunset.

It was the hills hereabout that caused a second and last motoring lapse. "Listen to this," I said to Margaret one morning on reading a letter. "A friend offers to motor us about. He lives not far away, knows the district inside out, and will show off great sights from the high points. What do you think?"

"Do you remember the drive to Farnham?" Margaret queried.

"Well, yes," I replied.

"And the vow we made to keep on our feet to Canterbury?"

"Well, yes," I repeated. "But look here. This affair is nothing like the other one. It will be safe, sure, and intelligent. It comes under the name of Iliffe and in the motoring world the name of Iliffe is—well, Iliffe, *The Autocar*, and all that. Besides, free lunch and tea are indicated."

The epilogue made Margaret waver. Finally, without overmuch argument, we went motoring again, this time very comfortably indeed in matters of a Hooper body on a Rolls-Royce coupé, guide, pace, and food, with breaks on foot to keep up a semblance of a walking expedition. Never before or since in so short a time have I collected a more splendid galaxy of impressions. The views we obtained from Colley Hill, White Hill, Arthur's Seat, Oxted Chalk Pits, Titsey, and Tatsfield are surely some of the most wonderful in south-eastern England.

The chalk slopes and the sandy country to the south offer lots of interest. Tangible features range from relics of early and Roman date to the cigarette cartons and modern remains dispersed over popular beauty spots. The Tillingbourne stream winds below St. Martha's between hanging woods and meadows, flowing through the vale famously described by Cobbett when he delivered the peerless invective on gunpowder and banknotes, viz. "To think that the springs which God has commanded to flow from the sides of these happy hills, for the comfort and delight of man; to think that these springs should be perverted into means of spreading misery over a whole nation . . ." and so forth on "the minds of man under the influence of the devil!" Great Tangley Manor is near, timbered, gabled, set in rare gardens, and the interior contains chestnut wood from Spanish ships, John Caryll's reward for helping to defeat the Armada. Aldbury has the Silent Pool, which we thought of seeing but didn't, for it owns the dubious fame of a beauty spot, was sneered at by my antiquarian acquaintance Dr. Charles Cox, and the water is the legendary home of a naked female victim of King John, whose presence might have caused embarrassment to a pair of innocents. The wicked monarch often stayed at Guildford Castle, bent on hunting and chasing mixed kinds of game. Very much on the route of old pilgrimage four villages extend in a line. Shere, the first one, is another beauty spot, pretty in houses and cottages leading on to a Gray's elegy churchyard under the shade of a brooch spire and Norman porch; Gomshall shows more cottages and gabled farmhouses; Abinger Hammer is watered by the ponds of the past iron days; and Wotton marks John Evelyn's birthplace and home. Mossy lanes and woods of pine, fir, beech, holly, and birch lead up to the heights of Hurtwood, Holmbury, and Leith Hill, magnificently wild thirty-five years ago, now beauty spots all and in command of great panoramas over many counties. Leith Hill tower raises this eminence to the Weald's own mountain, the highest point in south-eastern England. The tower, built in the eighteenth century by Farmer Hull for his own tomb, also provided smugglers with a neat sarcophagus for hiding treasure bound for London until, alas, somebody sealed up the openings.

Onward again, between the hills, more of Time's emblems can be sought in pleasant places. Dorking, where we ate, made merry, and slept, as ancient pilgrims used to do, is best remembered for old survivals and inns in the wide main street, and for its traces of the Roman Stane Street in the churchyard pointing north to the Roman crossing of the River Mole at Burford Bridge. A few miles away Betchworth's cottages and big Georgian house keep rural and unspoiled. The next town of Reigate, another bed-and-breakfast point for the Canterbury pilgrims, has the park and fine Renaissance home of the Howards of Effingham on the site of a thirteenth-century priory. A castle once loomed over the town at a strong position on the Pilgrims' Way, long since gone as surely as de Warenne, the owner. Standing up there you can think of another chase of King John in 1216, but with the king himself for the chased, while the stronghold fell to Louis of France; perhaps, too, may be seen the quaint character we met under a cloth hat who said he lived in a Howard house of great beams carved with dates hundreds and hundreds of years old, and left at last saying, "There's nothing like work. That's what we want, and nobody wants to do it," sage words, though we hoped not specially directed to us after miles and miles of foot labour. Last tracks through Surrey bring into the picture the Roman villa at Titsey Park, timbered gables at Brewer Street, pretty Bletchingley shorn of its Norman castle that belonged to Anne of Cleves, Godstone as a London bus stop in front of the *Clayton Arms*, a fourteenth-century foundation and reminiscent of coaches, kings, and coachmen on the oldest of the roads to Brighton.

East of Tatsfield and Limpsfield Surrey meets Kent. The bright fame of the garden county is introduced at once by two homes of national heroes, General Wolfe's eighteenth-century Quebec House at Westerham and the manor-house of Chartwell adjoining Crockham Hill Common, where it would be impolite to intrude on the privacy and bricklaying of the Right Hon. Winston Churchill. Here also begins an enchanted stretch of country, one of Kent's best. It extends in greensand ridges, valleys, and woods from Crockham Hill to Maidstone, and offers so much to delight that one can only mention the rich landscapes seen from 800 feet at Ide Hill, trees in Whitley, Mereworth, and Oaken woods, and the Sackville house of Knole for an architectural climax.

The Pilgrims' Way continues on the face of the chalk downs mostly by used lanes to Otford on the River Darent, an immemorial point both for the stream crossing and a meeting-place of communications from London and the Straits of Dover. From thence onward, to Wrotham, the Medway, Thurnham, Hollingbourne, Charing, Chilham, Golden Hill, and Canterbury, the route insinuates more powerfully than ever its consequential meaning. It follows hard roads, lanes, lonely tracks, and nears relics. The miles imply visible links with unrecorded ages. More than that; they signify a great highway of history, one fraught with incident and directing right and left to traces of weighty circumstances remembered. Kings, prelates, the powerful and the rich, faith, good

CHILHAM, *one of the claimants to be the prettiest village in Kent. A lovely spot of old houses and cottages grouped round the church and castle, and notable for reminders of Julius Cæsar, Britons, Saxons, Normans, and pilgrims bound for Canterbury. Below :* THE PILGRIMS' WAY *at Thurnham on the best preserved stretch of the original route.*

CANTERBURY. *West Gate and St. Dunstan's Street containing fine gabled houses and "The Falstaff" hotel on the site of a pilgrims' hostel. Below: Butchery Lane, one of the narrow streets leading to the Cathedral. Much was completely destroyed in the German raids and valuable Roman remains have been discovered under the ruins in this neighbourhood.*

deeds and pomp, battles lost and won, tyranny and crime, reminders of these are crowded on and about this final sweep of the ancient route. Here are the stones at Trottiscliffe and elsewhere, erected by people unknown; the fortified sites; the legendary battlegrounds of forgotten warriors, of the Tenth Legion at Chilham, Hengist and Horsa at Aylesford, and actual scenes of strife known to historical record. Remnants and standing survivals of castles, great houses, and a succession of palaces and monastic buildings mark out the comings and goings of those who reigned on the Throne and ruled in Church and State. A moated castle at Allington, the Norman and Jacobean walls of Chilham, Leeds Castle in fairyland, Norman towers at West Malling, Maidstone Palace on the Medway, broken palaces at Wrotham and Charing, a decayed home of priors at Godmersham, with many other monuments, all point to the importance of the hillside way when it served as a centre of communications for life, traffic, and spiritual light. On the direct line, above and below it, stand squires' manorhouses and the characteristic yeomen's dwellings. Near and distant are the villages, cottages, fields, and orchard boundaries, abundant in loveliness. Each one locates the haunts of generations of ordinary folk who probably did not bother about the deeds of the mighty while they worked, played, and rejoiced, begat quantities of children (Mrs. Honywood of Lenham accumulated 367 descendants in a Tudor lifetime), worshipped within ragstone and flint walls on Sundays, drank home-brewed in pubs such as *The Bull* and *The George* at Otford and Shoreham, and from decade to decade transmitted home-bred virtues and customs down ancestral lines. During their threescore years and tens, and sometimes more, they added their own quotas of beauty to the rich homeland. They made walls in timber and all sorts of materials, erected fine roofs, chimneys, and barns, many of which now adorn Kemsing, Thurnham, Lenham, and scores of attractive quarters. These things done, the villagers retired to pretty churchyards to rest under solemn shades of the famous Kentish yew trees, obvious at Challock and Molash for instance. There they ended, to share just the same fate and the company of their superior brothers and sisters departed, the Nevills of Birling, Wottons of Boughton Malherbe, Culpepers of Hollingbourne, Sondes of Throwley, and the like, whose faces, figures, and raiment, "the boast of heraldry, the pomp of pow'r," make such splendid shows on tombs and memorials in many of the churches in this locality. And always, when belief was strong and religion meant something real, the pilgrims came along, marking the footsteps of faith yet to be followed from point to point.

Otford itself, I have previously stated, made a point of first-rate importance on the old road. Relics found there prove it to have been a Roman place. Tradition gives it the actual field of Offa's significant victory in 773, and here Edmund Ironside defeated Canute in 1016 and chased the Danes to Aylesford. Though these battles may not interest us much nowadays, the possessions of Otford do. You can, as we did, walk down a wonderful street, see the manor-house and timbered buildings, visit *The Bull* inn if only for the good cheer of panelling and an arched fireplace, and wander round ruins in the meadows, sad fragments of the palace that housed Archbishops of Canterbury from Becket's to Cranmer's time. Once this palace was great and splendid, for Archbishop Warham's building accounts reveal the cost at piles and piles of money. It lodged Henry VIII, the Queen, and 5,000 retainers when they progressed along this old route in 1520 bound for The Field of the Cloth of Gold, and did themselves very well indeed judging by the records of grub and drinks consumed. With his characteristic gratitude for hospitality received, the royal grabber stole the palace in 1537; less than a hundred years afterwards the law of the eighth Commandment operated and the buildings fell to pieces. From here, also, good explorers can divert along the valley to admire the natural charms of the "Silver Darent," and with time plentiful, dawdle on for the magnificent church screen, the *Old George* inn, and Tudor houses of Shoreham, and so to Eynsford for more sights, shown by the fifteenth-century bridge, Tudor houses and cottages again, Little Mote house, ruins of a Norman castle, Roman remains, and the church doorway where William de Eynesford and Thomas à Becket had the row that foreshadowed the murder and the shrine of Canterbury. But this brings us only 20 miles from Hyde Park corner. We must get back a bit, escape from the aeroplanes, and return to the Pilgrims' Way.

Capital walking can be had from Otford to Wrotham and the wide Medway valley. The ancient route changes from road to lane, and to tracks marked white in the grass between brambles, bushes, and trees. Villages, hamlets, churches, and farms lie below, facing luxuriance and grand distances. On one remote bit where the dicky birds trilled joyously in the fresh greenery we found two men, one young, one old, trimming the hedges with hooks and sticks. When we stopped walking they stopped working, and the conversation turned to the weather, the brambles and tangles, and then on our part to pilgrims.

"Yes, this is the Pilgrims' Way," the old man said.

Eyeing our knapsacks the young one asked, "Have you come far?"

"Only from Winchester," Margaret replied.

Age and youth glanced at each other, both looked at their billhooks, and without further comment continued the hedge trimming. They did not utter the words "lunatics" or "balmy," but each seemed to be implied by their resumption of stable and intelligent action.

We continued towards Canterbury. Very soon signs of war appeared, warlike sounds of the kind that perhaps had roused the route ever since Romans camped not far away on the prehistoric site of Oldbury Hill. Violent flappings made a big noise. Close at hand we observed two pigeons fighting in a tree, hopping from branch to branch, feathers flying, and the disputed female watching the proceedings from a comfortable perch. That happened some time ago. Now even birds may have advanced to our easier and less bloodthirsty method of settling matrimonial differences by the ten thousand. The sun, suitably obscured during this interlude of strife, next shone brilliantly for the entry into Wrotham, a village rich for church brasses, yet poor in its remnants of one more archbishop's palace.

The views from Wrotham Hill, where the chalk ridge commences the bend towards Rochester, one is almost tempted to say are the finest in the series of fine prospects to be seen from the North Downs. The wide vale, the river, the great plain, stretches of hills pointing height after height eastward, and the distances faded far away, combine in landscape effects presented in the grand manner. Other views in the neighbourhood are perfectly dreadful. These happen through the presence of bungalows and the people in and outside them, inevitable objects on the landscape all through the Surrey and Kent country of London's borderland. But past inhabitants hereabout may have been even worse. Some of their leavings might cause one to get the wind-up on night and dismal occasions; so at least Margaret and I thought while we relied on birds singing and the sunshine to keep back the creeps. For we walked the land of the ancient of days, mysterious as Stonehenge and Avebury, the home of fierce grizzly men supplied with huge biceps and flint weapons, who if met would cause a flight to the bungalows for help. However, we arrived years too late for frightful experiences. About one million years ago, it is computed, these stalwarts made their flint implements on Oldbury Hill. Others threw about big stones weighing tons apiece, dropped the missiles for funereal and doubtful purposes at Addington, Coldrum, Grey Wethers, and elsewhere, and sent on the wings of Time a mythical story of monoliths in avenues all the way from Addington to the megalithic monument of Kit's Coty House across the valley. We saw these antiquities of unknown warriors, impressive memorials all, the gravestones of lost ages. Their presence seemed to make the air heavy with a something far older than the beginnings of Kent.

We stole on, past the Norman fragment at Paddlesworth and down to Snodland, the point at which real pilgrims adjusted their surcoats, tippets, wimples, and whatnots in readiness for the Medway crossing. Over the water the track led alongside the river's horseshoe bend to the south porch and embattled tower of Burham old church, a pilgrim halt near a temple of the god Mithras, sanctuaries of Christians and Romans now eclipsed by triumphant Mammon performing the rites of—cement! The church of Christ is decaying and the pagan temple has gone. Walls of Roman tiles and medieval stone round a deserted church alone speak silently of far more than a thousand years' worship and pilgrimage.

*   *   *   *   *

Few bodies clothed in the habiliments of to-day, yet with true English blood thrilling the heart, could arrive at these Medway banks without falling for the temptation of turning into Rochester, the city standing on that other route trodden by pilgrims and historical crowds of all ages, the shrine reached with much leisurely story-telling by Chaucer's nine-and-twenty "compagnie," the "Cloisterham" of Charles Dickens, "possibly known to the Druids by another name, and certainly to the Romans by another, and to the Saxons by another, and to the Normans by another." Thus impelled, we turned down the Medway, sent a thought over the trees to the Elizabethan mansion of Cobham, and presently faced the gaunt iron structure of Rochester Bridge, though for some reasons a good many years behindhand. For in 1836, when Mr. Pickwick leant over the balustrades, charmed with the appearance of every object around while waiting for breakfast, the bridge had many stone arches and a wide span in the middle. It also possessed some beauty, to make certain its doom and demolition in 1857. Consequently the majestic view of bridge, castle, and cathedral shown in the old prints became but a memory. Making the best of this iron thing, we still could do much as the illustrious gentleman did—contemplate the scene and, in a minor key of reflection, notice "the ancient castle, its towers roofless and its massive walls crumbling away, but telling us proudly of its own might and strength, as when, seven hundred years ago, it rang with the clash of arms or resounded with the noise of feasting and revelry." Such a falling away from grand days had overtaken this relic that a bandstand with a spiky top alone represented the hilarious revels of those faded times. A quiet corner, near and just below, offered seclusion from the public gaze for sketching the castle and cathedral upstanding from the river, with the Pickwickian balustrade from the old bridge marking the line of the waterside Esplanade (34).

This wreck of a castle certainly was a tower of strength in its heyday, one of the mightiest in the land. Built on the site of an older one and at an angle of the Roman wall, it commanded the river near the crossing which used to be above the present bridge. Now seeming to have had its eyes picked out by the rooks, woebegone of face, and with internals sadly out of order, the big mass of stonework, aided by the softening hand of time, still manages to present a substantial shadow of the bold warrior it has been through the sieges, captures, and exploits of King John, Simon de Montfort, and others who fought to secure this prize, thereby putting Rochester into history century by century. When Gundulf, the designer of the White Tower of London, was consecrated bishop of Rochester in 1076, he commenced work on the castle. Though a great builder, he did not happen to think of the sanitary arrangements we now favour, and the consequences of this lapse alone caused the defenders to surrender to William Rufus in 1088. Improvements in this direction must have been made later, for King John, in October 1215, had to fight something more substantial than an absence of drainpipes. After cursing, eating straw, and bumping his head on a floor in rage for agreeing to Magna Charta, the king attacked the castle, undermined the keep, and down crashed the masonry; the

CANTERBURY. *Christ Church Gate, resplendent and Tudor, leads into the close from Mercury Lane and other ancient ways. It has been restored by the Friends of Canterbury Cathedral.*

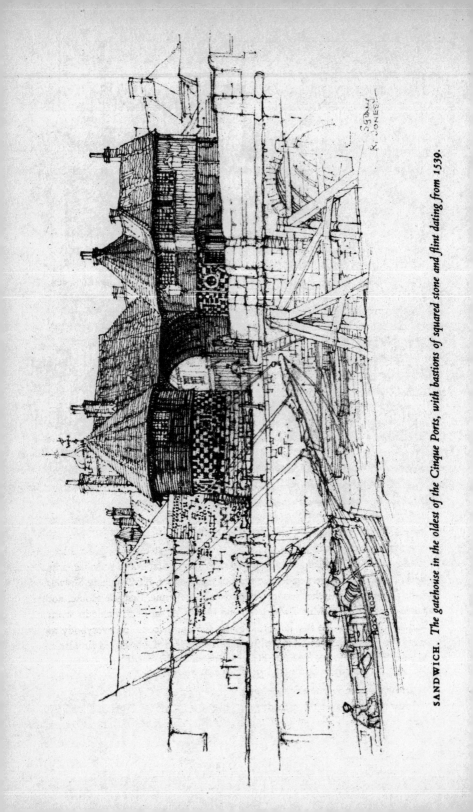

SANDWICH. *The gatehouse in the oldest of the Cinque Ports, with bastions of squared stone and flint dating from 1539.*

signs of the operation are visible to this day. The tower-keep, one of the earliest of the great examples, is the work of William de Corbeuil. Commenced about 1130, it measures 70 feet square and rises to 120 feet in height. Though sizes befog most of us, these represent quite a lot—so much, in fact, that a central wall across the interior was needed to carry the roof. The wall remains one of the most interesting features, with the well-shaft contained in the thickness, and pierced at the level of the great hall by semi-circular arches enriched with mouldings springing from Norman capitals and massive pillars.

Castles had their day. When times changed the life and movement under the arcade in the great hall ended. Floors collapsed, the roof toppled in, misery ceased in the dungeon. The mighty stronghold fell a casualty, and like many another of its once proud companions now "open free to the public" or "admission 3d.," it settled down to be the gnarled old ruin, a mere shell to jog memories of knights and lovely ladies, blazoned coats, waving banners, feasts and revels, the call to arms, assaults, violence, and death. And—but at the safe distance of a great many years—oh! for the coloured days and argent fields of Froissart, when might shone as a castled knight centuries before the lance and the helm of power fell to the bureaucrats, co-ops, and trades unions.

The bridge led us into High Street, which looked just what it is, a very good sample of an old street on the top of Watling Street, bordered on each side with a collection of house-fronts of mixed vintages here and there overflowing round corners into little alleys for the sake of peace from the main thoroughfare traffic; and jaunty gables, too, bent at curious angles by twisted beams a trifle stiff in the joints, yet hearty enough in strength and benevolence for many a year to come. The civic dignity of a city that has owned a mayor since 1460 is worthily upheld by the Guildhall, an excellent covering of 1687 brickwork, cornice, and pediment to shield the notable portraits, staircases, and ceilings within. The covered space below, supported by pairs of columns, might be very convenient for unfortunates to growl in the dry on rateable assessments, and the pretty ship for a vane on the lantern high up perpetually indicates the direction of municipal gusts of wind. Lower down the street more good brickwork at the Corn Exchange supports a clock which juts far out to warn laggards with Time's own fingers under the arms of the founder, Sir Cloudesly Shovel, "the ablest seaman in her service" declared Queen Anne. Eastgate House, not far beyond, without Miss Twinkleton and the young ladies to tickle its worn and picturesque frame any longer, showers a daily welcome on everybody to view the public museum treasures, plaster ceilings, and richly carved fireplaces. Hospitality is offered at many points too; it beams from tea-shops, expands to the *George Inn* above the Early English crypt, and winks from little square windowpanes under the wide opening of the celebrated *Bull Hotel*.

Just off High Street the cathedral occupies almost the same ground used by Bishop Justus for making "the Church of the Blessed Apostle Andrew" after his ordination by St. Augustine in the year 604. That means a very long lease even for Rochester and makes the bishopric, with that of London, the oldest in England after Canterbury. Through the chops and changes of centuries, Puritan spoliation, and restoration, the successor of King Ethelbert's Church has managed to keep especially glorious a Norman nave and sculptured western doorway, one of the finest crypts in the country, of about 1200 date, and the fourteenth-century doorway to the chapter room. College Gate in High Street, Deanery Gate, and Prior's Gate continue in use, and where kings, monks, and laymen reverently approached the shrine in the bad old days, good modern pilgrims keep the ageless procession moving with their tread and tyres.

Many things seen tell that Rochester had its full share of incidents commonly associated with towns of similar character and great age, the usual arrivals and departures of kings, queens, saints, villains, somebodys and nobodys. Among the kings, Henry VIII was rude; he first failed to notice the resemblance between Holbein's flattering portrait and Anne of Cleves trying to look coy at the *Crown Inn*, then exploded with the classic words dear to schoolboys, "A great Flanders mare," and finally decided on divorce before marriage with Catherine Howard to follow. Another king, James II, also did not find the city attractive, bolted from his guard and lodging, took to the river, and bade good-bye to England, home, and beauty. The wily monks of St. Andrew, in search of a saint and envious of the success of St. Thomas farther down Watling Street, set up a murdered baker, who diverted a goodly store of wealth from the shrine at Canterbury. Whether a somebody or a nobody, Pepys did not like the giddy height of the castle ruins when perched on the top, but recovered his nerve sufficiently to kiss a pretty young woman prior to spooning with her in the fields after dark.

And if the streets of "Cloisterham" are "so silent" no longer, it is the feeling of ancientness implied in a hundred ways in Rochester that grips the imagination, even if one does not happen to recall much about Roman Durobrivæ, Justus, Gundulf, and the defunct figures that once lived and moved about the walls, gateways, and houses now in the midst of or near the flow of this century's movement. To leave High Street by College Gate, pass between the mass of the Norman keep and the cathedral, thread between little greens and cobbled ways, finding here and there the home of John Fisher, the martyr, built on the line of the Roman wall; prim frontages in Minor Canon Row; Satis House, named by Queen Elizabeth; The Vines, laid out on the monk's vineyard; splendid brickwork at Restoration House, behind which King Charles stayed after landing at Dover—to light upon such things in wandering about this old city is to experience a sensation of leaving to-day behind and touching the fringe of a strange faded world.

Impressions of the sort above mentioned we gathered; but for Margaret and I, and pilgrims from the great world wherever the masterpieces of imaginative

1 Miss Twinkleton's Seminary

Tope's & Jasper's

Mr Sapsea's & Uncle Pumblechook's

Charles Dickens Gables, ROCHESTER

prose are read, the grey city by the Medway shines perpetually bright with memories of Charles Dickens. Rochester came into the immortal pages almost from the first to the last, from *Pickwick* to *Edwin Drood*. David Copperfield, the child, crossed the bridge; the tired man himself stood before the "old red brick" walls of Restoration House on June 6, 1870. Three days later the voice at Gad's Hill was silenced, and the creator of the wonderful sequence of novels went to rest at Westminster Abbey.

Though Dickens was not buried near de Corbeuil's keep, as he wished, the magician's spirit haunts the mouldering stones and the beauty of old years round about it. Ghosts of figures remembered come and go, radiant still in their local habitations and scenes. Up and down, almost everywhere, the master greets you and his characters come to life again. "Dear me," said Mr. Grewgious, peeping in, "it's like looking down the throat of Old Time," and if no ordinary mortal could think of such a perfect simile, how faultless it is for the cathedral, showing every architectural style since the Saxon foundation. Over the way, instead of admiring the nice brick fronts and hooded doorways all in a clerical line at Minor Canon Row, you tip-toe towards a tall sash window in an effort to catch a glimpse of the Reverend Septimus Crisparkle asking, "Do what, Ma dear?" of a pretty old lady seated at breakfast like a Dresden china shepherdess. College Gate, of course, is Jasper's, and any night Edwin Drood may pierce the gloom, "And so *he* goes up the postern stair." Next door tea is now offered, and not stale either, even if it did happen to be mashed by Mrs. Tope, wife of the "Chief Verger and Showman." You find the good brickwork, the porch, and the curly gable at Restoration House not a bit in ruins, but surely that is Pip in front of it asking, "Is that the name of this house, miss?" and Estella saying, "You have been crying till you are half blind" and contemptuously pushing him out. Eastgate House, ever "a venerable brick edifice" yet perky with gables, bargeboards, fat bay windows, and twinkling casements, introduces splendid fireplaces inside topped with shining oak panels that once reflected the pretty faces of Rosa and the fresh maidens who performed with combs and curlpapers behind the departed courtyard wall and "resplendent brass plate flashing forth the legend: Seminary for Young Ladies. Miss Twinkleton." Meals obviously must be taken at "the Bull Inn, in High Street" to meet the Pickwickians, and Joe, Mrs. Gargery, Mr. Wopsle, and Trabb's boy as well, crowding into the quaint courtyard of the four-hundred-year-old hostelry so wonderfully preserved in Dickensian character. With great expectations we sought tea, and finding Mr. Sapsea's premises still occupied by an auctioneer, Margaret piloted me under an adjoining gable that originally belonged to the same house. There we settled in a back parlour exactly like Uncle Pumblechook's very own. Selecting the best specimen from a plate of cakes, Margaret wickedly imitated the abject hypocrite's words, "May I? May I?" later followed by "Seven? And eight? And six? and so on," when I got into a muddle with adding up the bill. Outside again, and under the stone gables of Watts' Charity, we almost encountered the actual "Seven Poor Travellers" just as the hour struck for leaving Rochester, Charles Dickens, and Watling Street, to resume the other pilgrim route that was hoary and worn ages before Plautius and Vespasian pushed Roman roads into Britannia Magna.

The ferry path past Burham old church starts the Pilgrims' Way on a delightful and adventurous piece of its course. Association with ageless enigmas continues. Chalk workings of to-day, marked out white on the hills, cannot dispel a consciousness of the land's remote antiquity. Bits of primitive trackway appear at the sides of metalled roads. The Countless and other stones deposited by archaic barbarians lie about the ground. Kit's Coty House keeps secrets of unknown times in a lonely field. As we approached its monoliths, three standing up with one on the top, they suggested a huge mushroom on triple legs. Of course, nobody knows when, how, or by whom the blocks were put up, so I could only advance archæological research with a theory that the bulk, estimated to weigh thirty tons, represented far too much for human beings of present size to push about comfortably without derrick cranes; and Margaret, who thought the cromlech nicely placed for a daylight view, decided it would be an uncanny thing to meet in the dark or dim moonlight, particularly by sensitive wanderers haunted with fears of goblins. We looked away from terrific antiquity to the Medway vale of history. Down there lay Aylesford of many memories, centred round the vital ford now crossed by six arches of the fourteenth-century bridge; and Maidstone's Perpendicular church, College, Archbishop's Palace, old houses, and William Hazlitt's birthplace, encompassed by buses, cars, and traffic jams; Boxley, with the once-powerful abbey in the ruins that Tennyson loved when he lived near; and Allington Castle, rising

WARNHAM. *A timbered manor-house of Tudor period roofed with local Horsham Slates. Shelley was born in this village and a Lucas made a fine collection of Wealden ironwork at Warnham Court. Below:* CROWHURST, *notable for a great yew tree below the fifteenth-century spire. The parish contains the old home of the Angell family, and the early Tudor manor-house of Crowhurst Place, surrounded by a moat.*

LINGFIELD. *Old houses, cottages and a village lock-up on the green stand in pleasant Surrey country. The fifteenth-century church, once a college, contains notable monuments to the Cobhams and Howards of Effingham.*

from the moat in Edwardian glory of towers, walls, and a gatehouse. All these we explored, and went onward again with anticipation keyed high.

The Pilgrims' Way, leaving the Maidstone high road near Kit's Coty House sweeps south-east to Eastwell Park, then continues north-east through Chilham to Harbledown and Canterbury. This journeying is marvellous, lovely everywhere. Our expectations were realized. We saw Kent at its best. In those spring days, with the blossom out, here truly was a land of pure delight. From the Maidstone road to Dun Street (significant name) the 17 miles of the route have not been deviated or altered. I think it one of the finest walks in southern England; not the grandest, but one of the most thrilling, and a Pilgrims' Way climax. Richard Wyndham says: "At its best it is a narrow metalled road, at its worst (but pleasantest) a footpath. For fast motoring I cannot even recommend the best"—which is a mercy. I pray that the makers of the brave new England may not pounce upon it with town and country planning or try to further "preserve" it by changing the pure elements into a concoction like a pickle or a jam, with official labels alongside, "For the benefit of the public. Keep off the grass." Fast motoring aforementioned can be taken on the parallel highway from Maidstone through Charing to Canterbury, handy at all points for the Pilgrims' Way.

The scenes, I have said, show Kent at its best. The original route, largely in primitive form, hugs the chalk slopes at elevations of from 300 to 500 feet. It winds through bushy lanes, along green and white tracks, and curves over open turf. Ancient yew trees and thorns make gallant parades in marching along, and thrushes and singing birds tune the old bugle calls. Patches of exposed chalk shine out white. Big grassy spaces, ploughlands, pastures and sheep are there. The vale down below extends in pure pastoral landscapes patterned with orchards, hop gardens, high trees and woods. Roofs, churches, and tapering oasts mark sequestered clusters of habitations. Rounded hills up above, here and there wooded at 600 feet heights and reached by narrow lanes often banked in yew trees, offer great visions of the Weald of Kent spread in luxuriance to the rise of the "hurst" and "den" country at the Sussex border.

These quiet miles contain villages and hamlets of remarkable beauty, both in the vales and placed high. Many of their names ring an antique melody in such strains as Sutton Valence, Wychling, Otterden, and Boughton Malherbe of the Normans. Actually touching the Pilgrims' Way are Boxley, Detling, and Thurnham; just below it the chain is continued by Hollingbourne, Harrietsham, Lenham, Charing, and Westwell, each within a short distance of their original main line of communication. Inquisitive souls can find all kinds of curious and pleasant things—church monuments and brasses at Otterden and Throwley; a lead font at Wychling; views and a windmill at the sandy escarpment of Sutton Valence; a Tudor gateway and dovecote at Detling; Thurnham castle ruins on the hill and Friars Place (39); a Culpeper house, church monu-

IGHTHAM MOTE

Elizabethan Turret
COBHAM

Jacobean Turret
CHILHAM

A Sackville Gable
KNOLE

Edwardian
Gatehouse
LEEDS CASTLE

Archbishop's Palace
MAIDSTONE

Kent Details

ments, and attractive street at Hollingbourne; Harrietsham's timbered houses, Lenham's old square and cobbled ways; remains of Cranmer's great palace and the vivid picturesqueness of Charing; Westwell for a rood-screen; and more than enough elsewhere to keep fancy continuously moving. For a town there is Ashford on the Stour, which keeps enough to show how much nicer it must have been before the days of railways. Prettiness continues along the river past Wye to the bridge, church, and thirteenth-century home of the priors of Canterbury, backed by the wooded heights of Godmersham Park. Eastwards the chalk uplands wind away for the South Foreland, Dover, and the sea.

Stately mansions, manor-houses, and yeomen's dwellings add peculiar grace to this district, famous for structures that developed out of a social system long since dead, buried, and almost forgotten. Continuing in charm, they remind of times when the idea of home meant beauty expressed in good craftsmanship and materials generously bestowed. Celebrated examples extend in line from Knole to Chilham Castle, the strong point on the Pilgrims' Way reminiscent of Romans, Saxons, Normans, Jacobeans, and of Charles Ricketts and Charles Shannon as well, who lived and painted in the keep. The sequence also includes Leeds Castle; the Tudor wing of Sir Henry Wotton's birthplace at Boughton Malherbe; medieval Godinton, framed in 1628 curved gables; Godmersham, built in 1732, at which a frequent visitor, Jane Austen, experienced frightful doubts on the suitability of five bob or half-a-guinea for a servant's tip—but hers were days when money meant gold and not paper. Nor can the gem of Ightham Mote be forgotten. Edwardian stone, Tudor timbers overhanging the water, a hall, buttery, and a chapel, decorative roses, pomegranates of Aragon, linen-fold panelling, clipped yews, gardens, and the complete make-up, embody everything desired for the moated fantasy of romance. It is so secluded, hidden in a glen of high trees, seems so remote from this cheap and noisy age, that any day one might expect to meet past owners, Sir Thomas Cawne (*circa* 1340), Sir Richard Clement (*temp.* 1520), or Sir William Selby (died 1611), risen from resplendent tombs in Ightham Church and clanking about in armour. While sketching there a native wag said, "Don't make it too beautiful," to which I replied, "¡That could not be done." The house shows well from the road; now I think it may be visited on certain days for a humble shilling, but to pass under the fifteenth-century gateway into the medieval courtyard is a privilege worth much more than to-day's inflated pound.

Smaller homes, dwellings of the sturdy breed of yeomen, rank quite foremost among the achievements in local domestic building. Sundridge, Loose, Egerton, Molash, in fact almost every parish, can show at least one of these charming houses of the Men of Kent celebrated in rhyme and story. Most of them belong to the Tudor period; a few, like Wardes at Otham, are earlier; and many have the internal alterations of later days. Typical specimens are easily recognized by the timbered walls, the wide hall in the centre, originally open to the roof inside, overhanging upper storeys at each end, angle-posts and brackets at the corners made of trees turned upside down, with a steep roof over all, supported across the hall space by big curved braces. The example from Battle illustrated on page 78, though in Sussex and traditionally associated with pilgrims, gives an impression of this effective arrangement. Yeomen's dwellings are very numerous not only between Westerham and Canterbury but throughout Surrey, Kent, and Sussex. Aymer Vallance, who rescued Stoneacre at Otham from decay, told me he could account for quite fifty of these old ancestral homes in that immediate neighbourhood.

Pilgrims twain, we deposited ourselves at the inn of Chilham to sleep and refresh for the last lap of the course from Winchester to Canterbury. Outside we saw the square, houses faced with timbering, plaster and brick, the coloured roof tiles, castle gates, the flint church tower, and the trees of this Kent show village (39). It was peaceful. The tranquil scene gave little hint of fights staged there by Britons, Romans, Saxons, and Danes, who had battled to secure the commanding hill-tops of the Stour valley. We proceeded on along lanes and pathways. Near at hand lay the barrows and burial grounds of early strife. In the vale the riverside highway carried Canterbury traffic through Chartham, but lorry-drivers did not stop, as we did, for the pretty green, the timbered houses, and one of the oldest English brasses in the church. Singing "Under the greenwood tree" we pushed through Bigberry Wood. The narrow track beyond led up Harbledown, "the blee in Canterbury way," gained by pilgrims after days and nights of story-telling. There they beheld with joy the majestic sight of fretted stone glittering over the shrine of "the holy blisful martyr." Many of them espied the golden angel shining on the Norman steeple and echoed the praise of Erasmus, *Tanta majestate sese erigit in coelum*. Others gazed in ecstasy on Bell Harry, the perfect slender tower risen 235 feet high in 1503 to replace the original spire. Enraptured, no doubt they knelt down in worship and to pray, according to the custom of godly times. We too eagerly mounted Golden Hill, stood within the fence. Yet without violent emotion, for we observed—surburban villas, shrubs, tidy gardens, and little else beyond. Only by walking round the villas to Watling Street could be seen the unique view of Christendom's priceless heritage. Golden Hill is protected now by the National Trust, a preservation accomplished many years too late.

Following in the trail of Chaucer's company, we joined the buses and cars on the descent, passed the flint church of St. Dunstan, where Sir Thomas More's severed head rests, waited at the drab railway crossing for a train to go by, and from St. Dunstan's Street went through the West Gate (40), though not on bare feet, as Henry II did when he walked through to be scourged for the murder of Thomas à Becket. Every kind of frontage imaginable—gabled, overhanging, stone, timbered, plastered, tiled, Tudor, Georgian, and nasty modern—cheered us along St. Peter's Street, High Street, and into Mercery

Sidney R. Jones

GROOMBRIDGE, a village just in Kent with cottages round the green. Groombridge Place, opposite the green, is a perfect moated house of Restoration brickwork in a perfect setting. It marks the site of the home of Sir Richard Waller who captured the royal French prisoner at Agincourt.

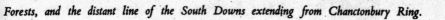
Forests, and the distant line of the South Downs extending from Chanctonbury Ring.

Sydney R
JONES

TONBRIDGE. *The Edwardian gatehouse of the Castle adjoining the relics of the keep built in the reign of Henry I by Richard FitzGilbert de Clare. The Castle was dismantled in the Civil War. Below:* TUNBRIDGE WELLS. *Church of King Charles the Martyr, dating from 1676, and the entrance to The Pantiles.*

Lane, six feet wide in the roadway, with a resplendent vision beyond of the Christ Church Gate, erected in 1517 for the ceremonial way into the close (45). Centuries ago the enriched oak doors opened for Henry VIII and Queen Elizabeth. Without crowns or waiting for more royalty we threaded the gateway, crossed the close, and entered the great cathedral of Christ Church, our goal from Winchester. Moulded piers and Perpendicular arches soared upward to the clerestory. The lofty vault seemed to lead to the very fringe of heaven. We crossed to the north transept, followed the footprints of Richard the Lionheart, Henry from Agincourt, Charles of Spain, Louis of France, of the illustrious and prosperous, the poor, the sick, and the crowds that had flocked to this famous shrine of England and Europe.

Steps led up to the Martyrdom. It was beautifully lit in the glow of old painted glass from Edward IV's superb royal window. We looked about. The space was empty. Of tangible remembrances of St. Thomas no trace remained. The walls seen by Becket and the four murderers in candlelight on December 29, 1170; the jewelled shrine of the Trinity Chapel, which yielded Henry VIII twenty-six cartloads of treasure; pilgrims of the old faith, their worship and their prayers—all had gone. Even the solitary stone supposed to mark the site of the murder was probably the wrong one. The place and signs of the martyr had vanished as surely as Joseph Pennell, Elizabeth Pennell, and their showman, who in life intoned, "'Enery the Heighth, when he was in Canterbury, took the bones, which they was laid beneath, out on the green, and had them burned. With them he took the 'oly shrine, which it and bones is here no longer!"

Nowadays devotees are wisely left in peace to look, think, and meditate on whatever this hallowed spot may suggest. Our own speculations on things that were and things that are came to an end in a final idea of things gone from bad to worse and almost to the devil. We then left the ghosts, if invisibly present, in their calm and beautiful seclusion, and walked through the evening air to an establishment which claimed a seat outside the West Gate since 1403. This being the *Falstaff Hotel*, we went inside, dined well, and in something fizzing with water out of a Canterbury syphon, drank to the health of old-time pilgrims, our predecessors at the same hostel, long since retired either upstairs or downstairs in the heavenly home of many mansions. Margaret added, "I hope they all got there, and not to the other place."

Canterbury remains wonderful, continues unique. It speaks volumes. But not all the good books it has evoked, or yet will inspire, can ever completely capture the story, the significance, and the loveliness of this corner-stone of the Christian faith and history that still calls pilgrims from the corners of the earth and wheresoever the English tongue is spoken. Old stones, buildings, and handiwork convey better than words can tell the charm, interest, and meaning of this city of the world. The cathedral's eastern arm, reconstructed by William of Sens and William the Englishman in 1184, consummate beauty of the late fourteenth century in nave and transepts, the glorious tower over the delicate fan vault, the fifteenth-century screen, England's richest treasure of early stained glass, and exuberant craftsmanship displayed in chapels and monuments from the western towers to Becket's Crown; the spacious close with courts and ruins bordered by stonework and Georgian clerical homes; the Norman stairway of The King's School; impressive town walls in Broad Street, that were marked out before Romans and Normans strengthened them; a fine hall and chapel in the Norman castle keep; St. Augustine's abbey gateway; a pilgrims' refectory hall and chapel at the Hospital of St. Thomas; picturesque Grey Friars astride Stour Street; St. Mildred's, St. Peter's, and other quiet churches made of Roman, Saxon, and medieval walls; fascination everywhere in domestic buildings created from Tudor to Georgian years; and Mercery, Burgate, Black Griffin, Friars, and Watling, amplified by a collection of ancient names, to point out the highways and byways trodden by Geoffrey Chaucer, Christopher Marlowe, Richard Lovelace, Thomas Ingoldsby, Charles Dickens, Agnes, David Copperfield, and the throngs of all centuries—these, and wonders beyond count assembled in sight of the green lands of Kent, open richly decorated pages of past years for all to read anew. It is not necessary to dwell on them here, nor to cite the architectural wealth connected with events, legend, romance, pageantry, the kings and queens, and every type of humanity. Such particulars are widely understood and appreciated.

Nor need I write on other well-known details of historical, ecclesiastical, and lay import—the colour of the Roman cat that left a footmark in cement against the existing tessellated pavement of Durovernum, what St. Augustine said to Ethelbert's Queen Bertha at the Saxon church of St. Martin in the sixth century, the age of quaintly named tea-lounges and their edible contents, the blatant brick and stone cinema in contrast to antique black and white, the approximate dimensions of the surplice of one archbishop, the brand and quantity of tobacco smoked by another, the convenience of the Maison for a hair-cut before Mother Church matins, and so forth. Everybody is fully acquainted with these matters. I will merely add these personal impressions. The city is a very nice one for feeding and sleeping. My note of July 1920, "Streets hung with bunting and festoons—such a gay picture like a stage scene in *Die Meistersinger*," means that Canterbury Cricket Week is great fun. And an intelligent railway official, most obliging, directed me to the tunnel mound over the old Whitstable line for perhaps the best general view of the spiritual home that was, and I trust may be spared to remain, incomparable Canterbury (32–33).

To-day, alas, parts of Canterbury are rubble and wreckage made by the Germans. My last visit there caused me to weep. North and east of the cathedral was battered and flat. Most of Burgate Street and Butchery Lane had gone (40). The West Gate stood in an empty space. Beautiful houses in St. Dunstan's Street and elsewhere had suffered. The *Royal Fountain Hotel*, reckoned the finest in Europe by a German ambassador in 1299, was no more. Yet the old shrine shone in a new light. Its desecration gave grim warning for a renewal of spiritual faith.

At Canterbury our pilgrimage was not quite completed, a fact that may cause distress to my readers after this long expedition. But courage! the end is near. The eastward country urged us along the other routes used since goodness knows when by mixed assortments of pilgrims outward or inward bound from the Straits of Dover, and engaged on diverse missions dictated by particular fancies for marauding, conquering, trading, progressing royally, riding steeds bravely, footing it humbly, and even carrying from Richborough samples of oysters that once upon a time tickled Roman palates. Crack legions in shining helmets marched over the ground from Rutupiae (Richborough), the chief Roman port on their coastal front line flanked by Reculver and Dover. They also stepped up and down Stone Street, which now scarcely touches a village between Canterbury and Hythe. Other visitors, like Hengist, Horsa, and St. Augustine, followed much the same way as the Eagles on landing at Pegwell Bay. Canute, and Richard the Lionheart back from doing time for fourteen months in Austrian jails, both advanced from Sandwich, England's premier harbour, until the salt water decided to recede for the encouragement of a premier golf club and bad language in place of mighty deeds done with the clubs of war. Henry V, "gallantly armed" in victory from Agincourt, young Henry VIII (before he put on weight) courted by Charles V, monarch of half the world, and a great many more bigwigs in peaceful and turbulent years, preferred to travel via Dover and Barham Downs. Those splendid high lands, on the final sweep of the chalk to the white cliffs of Dover and Folkestone, provided fresh air for King John's 60,000 untrustworthy warriors in 1213; they accommodated noble Simon de Montford and his companions faced towards France, and troops prepared with hot welcomes for Napoleon and Hitler, all of whom camped and waited for invaders that never came.

This corner of England sent Crusaders of the Cross onward to Palestine. Knights Templars named Temple Ewell. Knights Hospitallers knew Swingfield, a fact made clear by the remains of their preceptory at St. John's farm. Queen Ethelburga and less royal notables founded religious houses at Lyminge, St. Radigund's Abbey, and elsewhere, to be duly knocked down as all may see who look; nevertheless Queen Ethelburga's Grove still offers a delightful trackway towards Canterbury. Wool merchants travelled these parts, bound from the Cotswolds to the Staple at Calais that operated from 1363. Weavers and wool manufacturers began to arrive from the Low Countries in the fourteenth century, and refugees, escaped from the clutches of the infamous Duke of Alva, settled in Sandwich, Deal, and neighbouring places; with thoughts of home sweet home, they brought the character of Flemish and Dutch brickwork and gables to Queen Elizabeth's realm. The roads and tracks served strings of pack horses and wagons laden with merchandise of export and import, and in the round of the years the coaches and chaises bounded along to the sounds of horns and the sharp taps of hoofs. And from the twelfth century until Henry VIII instigated vandalism, the stream of pilgrims never ceased to flow to the shrine of St. Thomas. The Pilgrims' Way yet continues over the hills from Dover to Canterbury. Within hail of it runs the first and last 15-mile section of the great Dover Road, that highway of humanity during much more than fifteen centuries, THE road of Mr. Jarvis Lorry, Sydney Carton, and Charles Dickens.

Arrivers, departers, settlers, foreigners in and out on all sorts of jobs, the traces and reminders of them, and a host of matters quite beyond mention in my limited space, made these miles of south-eastern land some of the most interesting and historical in the kingdom. We sought the places and scenes, went to and fro over downlands, flat country, and by the seashore. The chalk hills from Wye and Chartham Down to the coast offered the graciousness of slopes, woods, and dells in magnificent profusion. The lower stretches of land from Canterbury to the seaboard gave a suggestion of being in Flanders or Zeeland without the trouble of crossing the water. Villages and hamlets everywhere abounded in lovely and interesting features. Good groups embraced Littlebourne on its green, Wickhambreaux with a stone and flint shop completed with corbie-stepped gables, Ickham, Ash, and the charming street of Wingham. Bishopsbourne, where Richard Hooker and Joseph Conrad both lived and died, and Elham, built round a square, each had enough to delight for this world and the next; and for remarkable Norman church work Patrixbourne shone with the south doorway tympanum, and Barfreston with its perfect little nave and chancel, no larger than a drawing-room for scandal in secular domains. Out in the fields pretty farm groups had numerous oasthouses gathered round them, like soldiers in cocked hats, and stood out all the prettier for their promise of national beverage. The many parks in this Kentish tract gave us the locations of numerous big houses—a developed priory at Monks Horton, 1638 brickwork at Broome Park, the Queen Anne front of Bourne Park, Goodnestone figured in Jane Austen's letters. These and similar ample establishments sent our thoughts back to lost years when they made backgrounds to cultured and spacious life; such quarters demonstrated how nicely houses could be built before politicians, designated by all the letters of the alphabet from A and B to Z, invented the pastime of soaking the rich to bribe the populace. Anywhere between Sturry Court, Postling Court, and Northbourne Court, comfortable largish houses dated Tudor, Elizabethan, seventeenth century, and Georgian, added distinction and charm to almost every village; and Tappington Farm, Denton, the old manor-house of the Barhams fitted with a splendid staircase, looked just the thing for an *Ingoldsby Legend* of "Sir Thomas the Good":

MISSING!! Stolen or strayed, Lost or mislaid,

WARBLETON. Priory Farm, of the true Sussex character. It incorporates fifteenth-century remains of an Augustinian priory. The neighbouring village, once in the heart of the iron country, was the home of Richard Woodman, iron master and martyr.

CRANBROOK, *in the hilly Weald of Kent, contains weather-boarded buildings*
This market town was a centre of the weaving industry famous for broadcloth

GOUDHURST, *one of the " hyrsts" among the woods and hills on the borders of Kent*
and Sussex. This high village has a fine collection of tile-hung and boarded houses and
the church contains forty Culpeper memorials and a splendid Campion tomb of 1642.

Littlebourne

Ickham

1 667
I W

Reading Street

Wickhambreaux

East Kent Details ~ Continental Patterns

We found the weathered guardians of the coast—Henry VIII's artillery forts at Sandown, Deal, and Walmer, schemed in 1539 to "keep the Downs"; the embattled walls of Lympne above the ruined fortress of Roman Portus Lemanis; Dover's Norman keep, upstanding at England's gateway throughout history. Two ancient towns bore marks of their long ago, for Sandwich was the oldest of the Cinque Ports and Fordwich served Canterbury monks with a quay to land Caen stone for building the cathedral. The stone and flint barbican gate at Sandwich (46) led us to the 1579 guildhall, surrounded by old houses of English and foreign character in quaint streets; and the timbered and tiny town hall at Fordwich, recorded since 1216, with a ducking-chair and crane handy for the River Stour, indicated that wives sometimes used to be more talkative than they are to-day. We looked out for reminders of the settlers and refugees from the Low Countries, traced their influence in stepped, curved, and pedimental gables, curious flint and brickwork, and the iron wall ties. Deal, Sandwich, and little places near the coast contained these Dutch and Flemish patterns. Reading Street on Thanet had quite a collection of them, and when we inspected a specimen at a house agent's premises in Broadstairs, dated 1676, the proprietor came out with an eye on clients for houses and seemed disappointed to find us only interested in Flemish brick and flint gables.

At Deal we gleaned a tragic tale of the sea, told to us by a widow in her home. Her husband, a fisherman, prospered early in life and became the possessor and captain of his own boat. But the first voyage out was the last one. He never returned. No news came and it was thought that the captain, the crew of twelve, and the boat perished on the Goodwin Sands. Every night afterwards the widow trimmed her lamp and placed the beacon in the window facing the sea to guide the wanderer home. We saw the lamp ready trimmed, as it had been for the past thirty years, and with womanly instinct Margaret sympathetically touched the mourner's hand. My thoughts went back to Frank Bramley's picture of 1888, "A Hopeless Dawn." Is it surprising that seafaring folk so often speak of the cruel, relentless sea?

There came a bright morning when neither wind nor foul weather threatened land and water, a day of dappled lights on smooth sea and sunshine over cliffs and fields. Then it was that the last stage of this pilgrimage began. We left Julius Cæsar's first landing-place at Deal to walk along the shore to St. Margaret's Bay. Warned not to loiter lest the incoming tide should terminate ourselves and our proceedings, we avoided that fate and reached St. Margaret's little beach. The majestic shapes of great chalk bastions rose high, facing the Straits and France. We looked at the white ramparts, and in them recognized the seaward end of the downlands that had led us from Magdalen Hill, Winchester. Up the ascent to the strong Norman tower, a cliff walk past the South Foreland, then Dover with the Shakespeare Cliff beyond filled the picture, the guardians of "This precious stone set in the silver sea." A Roman lighthouse, Saxon tower, Norman keep, medieval church, de Burgh's Maison Dieu, a Cloth Hall, modern dullness in streets, and the busy harbour of happy and unpleasant memories, fittingly bunched the nation's years together at the finale of our marching days.

Had we not arrived so abominably late we might have witnessed a defeat of the Spanish Armada quite near the castle, or administered a few words to plundering Romans and Saxons; we might have spotted Edward III back from Crécy, Henry VIII dressed up to meet Francis I, Henrietta Maria on the lookout for a husband, Charles II ditto for a throne, and a lot of other people who happened to pass in and out at this gateway of England. But we did see the beginning and the finish of the Dover Road. Away it directed for Canterbury. There was the ancient route whose coloured centuries served "Merrie England" for life, love and devotion, honour, pomp and pageantry, crime and death, the tramp of feet, the glory of horses, until the whirl of the industrial, money-getting, and scientific age knocked the bottom out of picturesqueness with mechanized peace, mechanized war, and mechanized everybody and everything mechanically driven on an endless chain round and round an Ixion's eternal wheel. Ah! the old road had got into a very bad way before we appeared. Gone were the merry sounding horns, the mettlesome steeds, the bravery of armour and banners, the blazon and the artistry. A hundred years ago, when stage coaches gave up the ghost before the new railways, the last relics of romance and the old order were scurvily put up for cash and dissipated to the highest bidder, viz:

DOVER MAILERS.—To be sold by Auction, by MR. DIXON, at his Repository, Barbican, on Friday, Feb. 14, at 12 o'clock precisely. TWENTY-FIVE superior, fine-shaped, fast, powerful HORSES, that have been working the Dover Royal Day Mail.

The Times, February 11, 1845.

THE WEALD, SOUTH DOWNS AND THE SUSSEX COAST

A further mention of the Weald sends my thoughts all the way back to Surrey again. Hopeful of suggesting the kind of general assemblage in this country bounded by the North and South Downs, I made the drawing of the view seen from Deepdene Temple on the sandy ridge near Leith Hill, now illustrated on pages 58 and 59. Behind my perch, though not in sight, I well knew the Hurtwood ridge, Holmbury Hill and Pitch Hill, the Surrey highlands centred round Hindhead, Blackdown's Cap reared more than 900 feet over the Sussex border. I recalled that district of pines, thick woods, valleys, commons, bracken and gorse, Thursley, Witley, Chiddingfold, and more pretty villages of warm and homely character, all of which bound the western end of the Weald. Beyond near trees I could see the North Downs for the Weald's northern limits, standing shoulder to shoulder and pointing a formation to Kent and the Straits of Dover. Chanctonbury Ring and a line of downs in the distance marked the Weald's southern borders; and far away, quite beyond my vision, earlier observations told me that the Weald ended in the east by meeting the marshes of Romney and Walland, and the submerged forest on the coast between Bexhill and Winchelsea.

This piece of England I saw from Deepdene, a sample of the tract contained within the boundaries mentioned above, gave a good impression of the Wealden landscape. But at scores of points elsewhere—some of them are noted on previous pages—I could have viewed Weald prospects just as good and typical by looking from the North Downs or the parallel heights between the Hurt-wood, Sevenoaks, and Maidstone, from the South Downs, or from the ridges in the Weald about Ashdown Forest, Wadhurst, Ticehurst, and Goudhurst. This lie of country permits the character of the Weald to be comprehended whole in large and full perspectives. As a conqueror or a missionary saint might spy out chances with a single sweep of the eye, you espy vales and hills, contours and shapes, expanded in great visions near and far. You trace the old forests, relics of the Weald's original dense covering, finely displayed in a 30-mile belt from Horsham to Hawkhurst, with the Forests of St. Leonard's, Tilgate, Worth, and Ashdown, all in a line to the forest's ridge at the Sussex and Kent border. You look over hilly stretches clothed in greenery, big woods and little woods, winding courses of streams, patchwork fields, shingled spires and stone towers, secluded farms, ricks, timbered barns, blossom and fruit in orchards, vines in hop gardens, country houses in parks, the locations of picturesque towns, villages, and hamlets snug amongst trees. And colour, yes, the real English colours delight everywhere. They glisten bright over fields, are toned deep and rich in woodlands; they softly tint open expanses, and lead from full greens, luxuriant and variegated, to blue and purple distances. Travel through these scenes, meet them at close quarters, and you find just the sort of pictures that

PENSHURST PLACE
Long Gallery Tower & Q. Elizabeth's Rooms

Cottage Chimney

Churchyard Gate

Notes in Penshurst

true-blue Britishers, doomed to murky towns or marooned in far countries, might conjure up for thoughts of the native land. "The charming friendly English landscape. Is there any in the world like it? To a traveller returning home it looks so kind—it seems to shake hands with you as you pass through it." Nobody with a seeing eye could fail to realize the truth of Thackeray's words while travelling through the Weald.

In all directions stand the oaks of England. They belong to the breed that built Queen Elizabeth's ships, kept the iron furnaces going, and yielded timber from Whiligh to Master Hugh Herland, King's Carpenter to Richard II, for the grand roof of Westminster Hall. These are the trees that named pubs "The Sussex Oak" (I spent a nice week in one of the woody establishments). Catsfield owns a trunk more than 40 feet round, and Northiam has the oak under which Queen Elizabeth removed her green silk shoes with heels three inches high, forgot to put them on again, so they have remained near by ever since.

Lanes and roads under the chequered shadows of trees ran past greenery and gardens, old halls and parks. They lead to pleasant little towns such as Horsham, Cuckfield, Battle (78), and Cranbrook (66); to large villages almost towns and true rural villages. Clustered round spires of shingles or stone church towers, these centres of old life are graced with houses, cottages, and inns built in the endless patterns of timber and plaster, seventeenth- and eighteenth-century brickwork, hanging tiles and weather-boarding, and exceptional brick chimneys rise from fine roofs of tiles and Horsham stone. Warnham (51) and Crawley, Crowhurst (51), Lingfield (52) and Lindfield, Chiddingstone (12), Penshurst, Groombridge round a green (57), vivid streets at Burwash and

BODIAM CASTLE, *one of the most perfect relics of an elusive and romantic past. Built by Sir Edward Dalyngrigge, late in the fourteenth century when the prime period of castle building had ended, it was devised more for the display of domestic life than purposes of war.*

Bodiam Castle

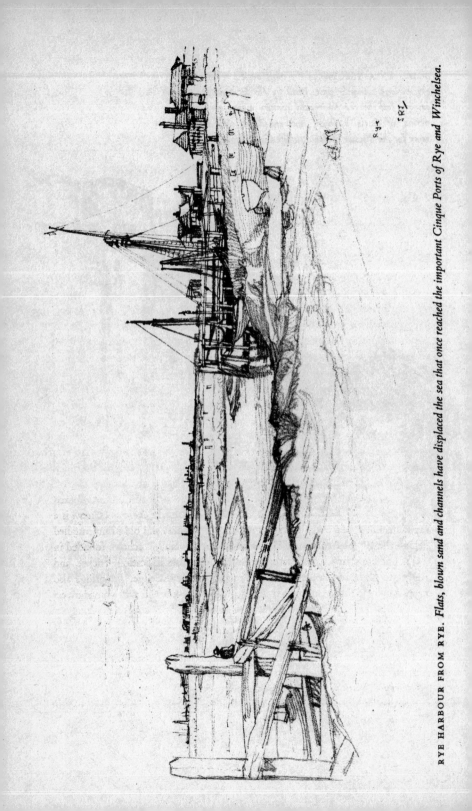

RYE HARBOUR FROM RYE. *Flats, blown sand and channels have displaced the sea that once reached the important Cinque Ports of Rye and* Winchelsea.

Brenchley, Goudhurst (66) and the neighbouring "hursts," Biddenden, Tenterden and the other "dens," with towns, villages, and hamlets galore, tell of these quarters famed for beauty.

Of castles and fortified residences the Weald had its crop. Walls of some of them sat down long ago when people wanted a change from days of knight-errantry, tournaments, mighty feasts of unlimited rations, and the most horrible deeds and dire consequences that preceded our own elegant years. Other walls kept upright, or nearly so. They still rise in the soft and still air to charm passers-by. You can, for example, stop to wonder at Bodiam (71), Hurstmon-ceux (78), Tonbridge (60), perhaps imagine the sounds of Queen Elizabeth's 1591 festivities at Cowdray, look across enchanted water to Scotney's Edwardian tower, and if very lucky, cross the moat to the fourteenth-century gatehouse and timbered quadrangle of Hever, Anne Boleyn's home and one of the many consolation perquisites for Anne of Cleves from dear Henry. Notable houses; the Weald has scores of them. There are the big and famous houses, manor-houses, and manor-houses turned farms; good village houses; yeomen's houses by the dozen, of the kind we have met already on the Pilgrim-age to Canterbury; houses decked in every period and fashion of home, often tucked out of the way as at Slinfold, Cowden, Small Hythe (a retreat of Ellen Terry), and Warbleton Priory (65); and rare Penshurst, set in walled gardens, long flower borders and yew trees, the pride and crown of them all, the great hall-house owned by the fourteenth-century Pulteneys of London E.C. and by the Elizabethan Sidneys.

Midway across the Weald are Tonbridge and Tunbridge Wells. The former town stands as a great-great-grandpapa, and the skittish offspring smirks at a respectful distance of 4½ miles. Tonbridge is ancient. De Clare's ruined Norman castle mound proves that, and the gatehouse is in the best manner of Edwardian days (60). The church has Norman and Early English features, the timbered gables in High Street figure in every guide-book, and the *Rose and Crown* is a capital example of a coaching inn, with all conveniences and old prints installed behind the Royal Arms and a Georgian front. The famous school, founded in 1553, but built largely in Victorian Gothic, dispenses education, cricket, and rugger to small and larger fry as preliminaries to knowledge. Tonbridge also keeps a cheerful little chimney-sweep, a great philosopher to wit, who showers good luck by shaking hands with willing and unwilling victims. He seized my white hand with his black one and shook it for nearly five minutes. This act was not especially lucky for me while engaged in sketching on white paper. But anyone wishing for luck or good fortune beyond the dreams of avarice, will find no difficulty in tracing the whereabouts of this lively black gentleman, for he is very well known in the neighbourhood.

To write on the old beauties of Tunbridge Wells, relative of course to visible objects and not people, is a task beyond my lean powers of description. Remnants of the earlier strain need a good deal of finding, and later signs of the times are very insistent and not inspiring. Words of the Saxon monk Eadmer suggest that the success of the town must be ascribed to the Devil, who, humiliated by having his nose pulled with red-hot tongs by St. Dunstan at Mayfield, leapt at one bound to cool at the spring which ever afterwards bubbled with chalybeate qualities. That first royal visit, the forerunner of many subsequent ones, fixed the site for a pump room dedicated to the noses and other portions of jaded ladies and gentlemen. But after the departure of the Devil and before the consecration of the pump room, Lord North arrived from Eridge Castle in 1606, drank at the spring, and improved in health. Other people followed and did likewise. Soon it was discovered that doses of pungent water could rouse up a good deal of fun and gaiety while relieving the joints and unseen parts of the human apparatus. Tunbridge Wells thus became one of the earliest exponents of the activity devoted to maladies and pleasure which flourished at watery inland resorts, reached an aristocratic zenith, and descended through democratic years to spa mixtures of bandstands and noises of the vulgar disposed round insignificant backgrounds of pump rooms.

The Wells rose to fame with visits by Queen Henrietta Maria in 1630, Charles II, the Court, and a smart society versed in a number of matters even more exciting than chalybeate springs. The descent of the fashion on a rural domain furnished with only grass, trees, rocks, and water caused a housing problem. But instead of bleating "We want houses" to politicians with no bricks, the homeless wisely fended for themselves. They planned a self-contained economy, squatted on the greensward in tents, huts, and anything handy, bought local produce at booths, flirted with farmers' wives and daughters, plucked various grades of the cherry ripe, danced on the turf at night to the music of fiddles, and drowned signs of dyspepsia with high jinks, fresh air, and the Devil's own water. Soon the houses appeared. Royal bodies stayed in them, sat in the pew in the new Chapel. Between the visits of Queen Anne and of the princess who was crowned Queen Victoria, the yearly processions we all know of brought in the fashion, the wealthy, the hangers-on, the brilliant men and women of Georgian and Regency years—William Pitt, Doctor Johnson, Mrs. Thrale, Garrick, Richardson, Goldsmith, Sir Joshua Reynolds, in fact all the celebrities, and Thackeray's characters live perennially on the pages of *The Virginians*.

A good deal has happened since then. Not much architectural beauty survives to suggest the day and night lights of past days. Now the town has a brand-new Ritz cinema, new and sleek public buildings, rows of dull edifices, noisy buses and cars to hush echoes of bygones. Soon, perhaps, one of our town planners will knock down a lot of the buildings, make a fresh start, and leave everything ready for future planners to do just the same when fashions change again!

One visit to Tunbridge Wells keeps vivid in my memory because it gave a hint of "The Wells" that bowed, scraped, and thrived on royalty for a couple of centuries. The experience occurred years ago, and with Margaret, who then lived a good deal in Kent. I intimated my presence with a bicycle at Edenbridge, requested her appearance there likewise mounted; we met, made a lovely ride through Hever, Chiddingstone (12), Penshurst, and along the beautiful upper Medway vale, achieved a climax in viewing Groombridge green (57) and the Place, a perfect moated Stuart home, and continued by the prettiest way imaginable past Eridge Warren, pines, bracken, the High Rocks, and oasthouses into Tunbridge Wells.

The town seemed a trifle mouldy after the freshness of the approach. We looked about, spotted bow windows, weatherboarding, and stucco spa fronts above modern shop premises, inspected Decimus Burton's lay-out of Calverley Crescent, observed the deportment of the notable *Castle Hotel* without going inside. Settled on a seat on The Common we thought the town showed best from there. The church of King Charles the Martyr and white Regency houses leading to The Pantiles spread below, and roofs piled up to the wooded background (60). We then walked down to the church, attracted by the pleasant exterior capped by a bell turret perched not quite upright after many services and long sermons once endured by the most fashionable congregations in England. The building entered, we noted Ionic columns, an elaborate plaster ceiling in high relief, ascended to the galleries, and read from framed parchments accounts of the money spent in erecting the structure between the years 1676 and 1684. I had just checked the figures down to the last sixpence when Margaret touched my elbow. She whispered that the pews in the nave were filling up, and immediately tilted her hat to a Sunday angle. From the gallery we saw numerous and elderly worshippers kneel down in silence. Then the date occurred to us, May 29, Oak Apple Day, the anniversary of the Restoration of the Martyr's son, Charles II. Ever afterwards the day and the episode have remained with me, to hint of the old Tunbridge Wells of the Stuarts, past queens and celebrities.

We quietly withdrew and went outside. Time's shadow on the south wall taunted with the sundial's maxim, "Ye may waste, but cannot stop me." The warning spurred us into the present again, represented at the moment by The Pantiles over the way. But in no time we pushed Time back by imagining elegant crowds and grandees in wigs, satins, and brocades under the promenade and the lime trees; and by meditating on a few square tiles trodden by the said crowds and grandees, the last relics of the paving provided in 1700 at the expense of Princess Anne before she ascended the Throne. Forward once more in this century we found tea behind the colonnade. A very good tea it was, for in this department Tunbridge Wells continues to uphold the past prestige of "tee" and "tay" without wasting any time; and as for the Romary biscuits, they have the true flavour of the grandee days.

Lack of space now forces me to leave the Weald country, which long ages wore down from the chalk and man transformed into a demi-paradise of Eden without introducing the wicked serpent. This fair ground below the downs of Kipling's "Sussex by the Sea" is a tricky land to cover, in spite of all its loveliness. It is well served by railway lines and main roads that spread like a spider's web towards London. These indicate a profusion of human beings. The presence of human beings means houses and, in the modern sense, nasty ones. Urban penetrations in many parts are liable to greet the wanderer with exhibitions of ugliness. They crop up unexpectedly when you least wish to make their acquaintance. Yet in the right places, away from the surplus congregations of the metropolis, the Weald is ever its own true self, quiet, homely, loving, a land richly endowed with present beauty and graceful accumulations of old years. Wandering about, you may pick up all sorts of impressions, absorb little cameos for memory to keep. For more than forty years I have been crossing the Weald. It has given me remembrances of cherry and apple orchards in blossom, the glow of hop-pickers' fires in twilight, sunset over the deep woods of Balcombe and Worth; a Tudor home beautifully renewed at Sissinghurst Castle, Crowhurst Place reflected in the moat, Lamberhurst's Jacobean pulpit; a medieval cloth factory at Smarden and the Cloth Hall gables at Biddenden; Ashburnham, Huggett's, and more furnace names of the old iron industry; Horsmonden and other furnace ponds that kept the forge hammers throbbing with water-wheels; a wonderful Lucas collection of firebacks, andirons, and iron implements at Warnham Court; dancing on the lawn between clipt yews at Hever Castle; and Sir Frank Brangwyn under a very wide hat painting at Ditchling. Such and sundry recollections of many shades and colours await all those who go in quest of the Weald.

The South Downs sweep through Sussex from the Hampshire border to Beachy Head. Magnificently wooded are the western ranges, and the eastern sections stretch away smooth, green, and open in curves and graceful outlines. Choice river valleys made by the Arun, Adur, Ouse, and the Cuckmere cut through the chalk. The hills rise to 700 and 800 feet—Duncton Beacon reaches 837, Chanctonbury Ring 783, Ditchling Beacon 813, Firle Beacon 718. These South Downs offer altitude, space, clear air, lights and shadows over slopes, combes, and hollows; they are magic at sunrise, serene in evening and afterglow; their range of appeal is infinite under shine, cloud, or mist, in summer and wintry weather. The big, characterful shapes suggest repose, immutability, the everlasting; they look likely to keep constant until the last trump, unless civilization obliterates their dignity and quiet or bull-dozers begin to remove mountains. Wonderful solitude reigns over these hills. In the loneliest section, between Beacon Hill, Westdean Woods, Charlton Forest, Graffham Down, Bignor Hill, and the River Arun you can feel as lost to the world as King

HASTINGS. *Ruins of William the Conqueror's castle on the great rock between the new and old towns. The stronghold probably occupied a Roman Site, had a keep built by Henry II and a collegiate church. It is now a grand viewpoint for a thriving resort, notable for Regency architecture and a picturesque old town.*

HURSTMONCEUX CASTLE *before the restoration. In its day the largest Commoners' house in Sussex, the castle was built of brick in 1440 by Sir Roger Fiennes who fought at Agincourt. No military events happened here. Below:* BATTLE. *The pilgrims' hostel at the gateway of the abbey founded by William the Conqueror on the site of King Harold's fall.*

Charles hoped he was when he escaped that way after the Battle of Worcester and drank a tankard of home-brewed at Houghton's inn on October 14, 1651. Views? Where can better be seen? High points all along the ridges command tremendous expanses of downlands, the Weald, luscious distances and the sea. Very many positions show British entrenchments, tumuli, Roman camps; and the Iron Age hill fort and neolithic flint mine at Cissbury Ring make one shudder to think of the eons that separate unshaven Sussex primitives from the built and human beauties of Worthing 4 miles away. It is exhilarating to follow the east and west down trackways, to trace the Roman Stane Street over Bignor Hill, to get a hundred years or so back by fancying Regency ladies and gentlemen crossing the hills from Lewes, Clayton, and Poynings in search of Brighton.

Within reach of the Downs, and on them, are the towns and villages true to the cheerful Sussex type; pretty collections of houses and cottages bright in the textures and colours of timber, tiles, brick and thatch, with gardens and trees to show them off. Near Beachy Head, for example, East Dean (83), West Dean, and Litlington (83) lead to Alfriston, spread round its green and church. At the other end of the hills South Harting might be a candidate for heavenly charm on earth, Graffham hugs Graffham Down (89), and Bignor's timbered village shop under a thatched roof competes with its Roman villa. Between these eastern and western limits scenes and buildings continue the homely theme. They call for a halt at many an interesting house, such as the Tudor survival at Hangleton, the Anne of Cleves house at Southover, and West Dean manor farm and priest's house. Bigger things are shown by the towers and gateway of Amberley Castle, Bramber's Norman motte and keep, and Arundel Castle piled extraordinarily round the Norman origins that Sir W. Waller blew to pieces in the Civil War. A string of towns keeps old tunes fresh. Lewes, ever fascinating with a castle and hilly streets (84), begins the series which fittingly ends at venerable Midhurst and the *Spread Eagle*. A halfway point is made by Steyning, prized for Church Street and High Street (85). Arundel, nearer the coast, yields fine silhouettes and perfect eighteenth-century façades; while Petworth, beyond the River Rother, abounds in picturesque groupings, gathered feudally under the many peep-holes of the 1696 mansion filled with artistic treasures (85).

The peace and quiet of the South Downs and borderlands can hardly be claimed for the neighbouring coast, where sometimes a dampness descends over human spirits. For one thing, the sea is always about and it is permanently wet. And piers, crowds, promenades, pavilions, concrete and glass, villas, bungalows and shacks, and such emblematic words as cinema, dance hall, ice rink, happy-drome, fish and chips, winkles, milk bar, and pie shop, noted in my diary on the spot, all represent higher aspects of life beyond my limited range of appreciation. But millions and millions of people enjoy these things, loudly sing their

Grenville place BRIGHTON

Brunswick Terrace HOVE

The Old Ship BRIGHTON

Wellington Square HASTINGS

Sussex Details ~ Regency Style

praises. Long may they flourish—but not for the likes of me. To my unimaginative eye some of the dreariest sights of our island are presented on the coast route drive through Bognor, Littlehampton, Worthing, Brighton, Peacehaven, Bexhill, and St. Leonards. For a view of pagan England, I think one of the best can be enjoyed from the seaward end of Brighton pier. The landscape of buildings, too well known for present description, appears to be limitless, gives the impression of extending east to Moscow and west to New York. Such prospects doubtless inspire the planners and wise men of our age; they accurately indicate current ideals, tendencies, and tastes, just at Canterbury's Bell Harry and the Chain Gate at Wells tell of wicked monkish years and Bath and Blandford illuminate the depravities of the eighteenth century.

Yet for old-fashioned parties this section of South Coast still offers scraps of cheer. Rye and Winchelsea continue superb, redolent of their grand days. The gates, the houses, Watchbell Street, Mermaid Street, the fourteenth-century canopied tombs of the Alards, Admirals of the Cinque Ports, byways, and gems of architecture, combine in pictorial array. Rye Harbour meets the golden sands (72), and mystery and legend haunt the Marshes. The cliff lands at Fairlight have been saved for the nation. All hail to Mrs. Eves! I well recall the late Reginald Eves, the portrait painter, telling me of his lifelong efforts to preserve this land from speculators and marauders of English soil. The majesty of Beachy Head so far has defied man; and the grand chalk pile is majestic indeed when seen from the shore below. Birling Gap and Cuckmere Haven keep their loveliness, though half-naked bodies lie about on the beach in place of kegs, casks, and smugglers departed. The Seven Sisters show seven pretty white faces, but only by the grace of God and preservation have their upper storeys and permanent waves been saved from spoliation. And so on, with thoughts of such curiosities as Shoreham bridge and churches, a Saxon tower at Sompting, Climping church, and all the way to Pagham old harbour, conquered by the sea and recently threatened by county council planning. Everywhere scenes are associated with famous names, lights of history from early years to the Pre-Raphaelite days of Burne-Jones at Rottingdean and Dante Gabriel Rossetti's marriage in St. Clement's Church, Hastings, a foundation of 1040, rebuilt after a French raid in 1381 and blasted by Germans in 1943.

My maudlin lookout spots Hastings for the most pleasant and attractive of the seaside resorts. It has the old town of winding ways, fishermen's drying sheds, and jumbles of houses; all new conveniences are handy for those who like them; and the Conqueror's castle on the high bluff guards ye ancient from the modern, and vice versa (77). Also for those who fancy it, the town possesses some of the best of the Regency architecture, offered by charming domestic examples in Wellington Square, on the sea front, and up and down the hills. These structures of course indicate that the South Coast, for all its new bravura, is still the quarter par excellence for showing off the achievements of the Regency. Terraces, squares, and crescents at Hastings and Hove, relics in the Old Steine at Brighton, and varied stucco collections dotted here, there, and everywhere point to the years of George III's young Georgy at Brighton, sister Amelia at Worthing, and Princess Charlotte in pursuit of invigoration at Bognor. In quiet hours, which are rare, the classic and bow windows and the iron balconies perhaps become animated with the shades of the Earl of Barrymore, Colonel Hanger, the bloods of fashion and folly, with Mrs. Fitzherbert as well, and the frisky and risky ladies who were dipped in the briny by celebrated Martha Gunn. But the busy Old Steine of to-day carries little suggestion of the hair-raising feats, the pickaback rides, and the escapades once staged along its promenade; only in fancy can be seen H.R.H. shooting doves and upsetting chimney-tops in between diversions at the fantastic Pavilion. At my last dinner, with scores and scores of consumers, at the reconstructed *Old Ship* at Brighton, it needed a good deal of imagination to re-create Thackeray's little party of the Osbornes and the Crawleys at the open balcony windows on that brilliant moonlit night before the Battle of Waterloo:

"Gad, what a fine night, and how bright the moon is!" George said, with a puff of his cigar, which went soaring up skywards.

"How delicious they smell in the open air! I adore them. Who'd think the moon was two hundred and thirty-six thousand eight hundred and forty-seven miles off?" Becky added, gazing at that orb with a smile.

Perpetually emitting 1066, the South Coast offers the one and only historical date retained in memory by all inhabitants of the British Isles who are not Americans. The fact that this is my only safe date without the aid of a primer quite recently prompted me to go and furbish these figures of 1066; to fight anew, and even without an adversary, the battle that completely upset the English story and did not happen at Hastings. At Pevensey Bay my landing passed unnoticed. Nor did I slip on the beach and fall flat on my face like William, to provide future chroniclers with an episode. The absence of heavy artillery defeated the desirable possibility of removing the close formation of bungalows ; I just walked through this objectionable objective to the Roman walls of Pevensey secured by the Conqueror, and admired the spectacular ruins of his own castle. Craving blessings on my adventure in correct warrior fashion at the thirteenth-century church, seeing the tiny Court House, and provisioning near the ancient Mint House took very little time. I did not dawdle for two weeks, as William did while an undefended England lay open to him, pending the arrival of Harold from hammering Norwegians at Stamford Bridge. Hastening onward, I passed every known form of villa, bungalow, and worse, read wayside appeals to "Keep Death off the Road," wished someone also would exhibit "Keep Death off the Landscape," and called a short halt at Bexhill between the gloom of Victorian bricks and a big white something with decks, shaped like a ship half sunk on dry land and messed about at one end by a bomb, an ominous emblem at that point for speeding along my campaign. More dreadful sights, some fifty odd years old, others quite in the new fashion, and all prime for a casualty clearing station, bravely urged me to the capture of Hastings, my own and the Conqueror's base for operations. The state of the castle indicated a draughty place for a bivouac, so a departure from historical exactitude ended in a comfortable billet under the high-sounding and warlike name of Warrior Square.

Winning or losing a Battle of Hastings is simpler now than in 1066. And as the original scrap was not fought at Hastings, a new victory is easily gained by simply walking into Battle, the sweet little town with Abbot Ralph's church, delightful streets, early buildings, Georgian hoods and shop fronts, amongst which invasion is welcomed rather than opposed. The battlefield presents the scene complete. Telham Hill, the Conqueror's H.Q., is studded with oak trees and gorse grows there as the Normans saw it. Down below lies the marshland, drained a century ago. Harold's hill, later called Senlac, and now exquisite with the abbey ruins, joins the town. To tread these hills and the vale

EAST DEAN, *in the downland country near Beachy Head.*

LITLINGTON, *one of the pretty villages and hamlets in the Cuckmere Valley, behind the chalk cliffs of the Seven Sisters.*

LEWES. *The fourteenth-century barbican gate
with the arch of the Norman gatehouse beyond.
This ancient town between the hills, famed for the
battle between Henry III and Simon de Montfort, is a Sussex prize for charm of past and present.*

PETWORTH. *Dominated by the great house of Lord Leconfield, this feudal town abounds in picturesque groupings of varied architecture. Below:* STEYNING. *An attractive High Street in one of the small towns that distinguish the Sussex country.*

CHICHESTER. *Visible from both the sea and land, the Cathedral groups above the roofs of the city planned by Romans between the South Downs and the coast. The fabric has much Norman workmanship and later features. The spire was rebuilt after a collapse in 1861. Notable and unusual, the detached bell tower shown at the right is of fifteenth-century date.*

CHICHESTER. *The Cross and East Street. East, West, North and South Streets, meeting at this point, mark lines of the Roman town of Regnum and the existing walls indicate its boundaries. The Market Cross, built by Bishop Storey in the reign of Henry VIII, is a splendid work, not improved by the clocks given by Dame Farringdon in 1724.*

GRAFFHAM. *The village from the South Downs and Blackdown in the distance, beyond the valley of the River Rother. Charles II escaped through the wooded tracks of these southern hills after the battle of Worcester.*

OLD BOSHAM *at Quay Meadow, on an arm of Chichester Harbour. Bosham claims to be the scene of King Canute's encounter with the tide. The Bayeux tapestry depicts King Harold riding to Bosham whence he sailed prior to the Battle of Hastings.*

The prehistoric chalk ridgeway on the Berkshire Downs leading from the Thames to White Horse Hill, Marlborough Downs, and Salisbury Plain.

Wren tradition, Chichester

brings the thrill of crossing the actual ground where Taillefer the troubadour, singing his songs, led the French advance at that distant October dawn; where the offensive was ineffective against the stubborn English defence, which might have won the day—but for the one fatal error of a brilliant commander that caused a crown to be lost, a crown to be won, changed England's history, and permitted William to demonstrate to Harold that in war as in love the final miss is as good as a mile. Flushed with success and power, the victor feasted among the dead, then founded the abbey as an offering to the Almighty for what Cromwell would have called a "crowning mercy."

With my victory completed under the shade of the noble abbey gateway, I celebrated the event by taking tea in the Pilgrims' Rest, a timbered and hoary establishment pretty and interesting enough to make a new highbrow shudder (78). There I sounded my last post, and a reveille as well, to the little town of romance and hallowed memories. A finale led me past the abbey walls to the fields and the common adjoining the historic hills and the vale. An old man, gathering sticks for fuel, piped out, "How d'ye do." So I hailed the greeter, who appeared to be several centuries old, might have been the original Adam direct from *As You Like It*. In a wheezy voice he told me how his grandfather had said that his great-grandfather's great-great-grandfather remembered William the Conqueror's arrival from France for a very particular reason.

"So you be William of Normandy, be ye?" said the ancestor to the Conqueror.

"Ay," replied William, "I be come over from France."

"Pleased to see ye," said the ancestor. "What we want here, William, is shorter hours and higher pay than we got out of Harold."

"Don't know about high pay," remarked William. "But ye shall have short hours all right," and he up upped his hatchet and chopped off the ancestor's head.

91

The old Adam chuckled like anything. Apparently he thought the story funny. But I gave him half-a-crown, thinking this traditional item on an historical episode cheap at the price. Again, on my return to Warrior Square, a fellow campaigner in the billet, quite a stranger to me, evidently had discovered what I was up to. He presented himself and remarked, "If you want to know any more about the Battle of Hastings, ask me; I was there." Elsewhere at various points I often have noticed how vividly traditions survive in the neighbourhood of battlefields.

My advance from Hastings directed to Old Bosham to inspect the point of departure for Duke Harold's preliminary canter with Duke William, and incidentally to find one of the reputed spots on which King Canute squatted to prove that the Master of the tides is greater than earthly monarchs. But the church worked on the Bayeux Tapestry is nothing like the fine Roman, Saxon, and Norman structure now standing at the verge of Quay Meadow (89). Round about are the groups of houses, the creeks of Chichester Harbour, the delicate level greenery, all so often shown on the walls of the Royal Academy. The route from Old Bosham naturally leads to Chichester and, unfortunately for me at least, to the limits of the pages for this section of my book. Regretfully therefore, I can merely present my drawings of this fascinating city (86, 87, 88). It is not possible here to dwell on the Roman walls and the Roman lines of North, South, East, and West Streets; the inscribed Roman stone at the Georgian Council Chamber, a relic of the temple to Neptune and Minerva and a likely link with St. Paul, Pudens, and Claudia of the Bible; the Norman interior, the Romanesque panels, and the detached bell tower of the cathedral; Bishop Storey's stone cross by daylight and floodlit at night; retired clergy quarters between the gateways of Canon Lane; dozens of excellent Wren-ish and Georgian houses and doorways; and all the scenes of beauty and crowded interests stored in old Chichester.

3. ACROSS THE CHALK LANDS

BERKSHIRE, HAMPSHIRE, WILTSHIRE, DORSETSHIRE

The section of England included in this chapter appears on the map given below. It extends southward from the Thames to the coast, is bounded at the east by Surrey and Sussex, and terminates in the west by the irregular line made by the Chalk formation through Wiltshire and Dorset. The geology of this area clearly is not solely represented by chalk. But considered as a whole, chalk is the predominant characteristic. It has been an abiding influence in this country of smooth hills, ancient trackways, wide vales, plains, old forests, white and flint buildings, and clear streams famous for trout. Set in the chalk are this land's limbs, body, and soul. By traversing lonely ways, past earthworks and burial mounds of forgotten people who first made the tracks, it is possible to leave the Sinodun Hills in Berkshire, strike onward to the hub of England's first road system on Salisbury Plain, and reach the Dorset coast, yet all the way rarely or never leaving the chalk.

Changing from the general theme to the particular, a direct probe into the chalk may be accomplished by seeking—

THE VALE OF THE WHITE HORSE, BERKSHIRE DOWNS, AND KENNET COUNTRY

The Vale of the White Horse is King Alfred's vale, because he was born at Wantage. There the carved King stands, emblematic of the great builder and scholar. Nobly he faces the pleasant town below the Downs. *The Bear* nearby mounts guard on a post outside the hotel, and close at hand rises the interesting church containing a store of beauty. Within is a fine big brass commemorating Sir Ivo Fitzwarren, Dick Whittington's father-in-law. This vale of good crops and orchards naturally concerned other folk too. Richard Jefferies, for example, first saw the light and life of the fields at Coate, near Swindon. When the Vale reared Tom Hughes, that event brought the greatest book on boyhood that ever was penned. How Uffington and the Vale of the White Horse live on from generation to generation with *Tom Brown's School Days*! "I don't mean a flat country, but a vale; that is, a flat country bounded by hills." The memorable scenes of the book are there yet, still have power to charm with level fields, farms, and cottages, the schoolhouse, and "the old church with its grey wall and lancet windows." Away to the south the Roman road goes up and down. Pendragon's Hill, the White Horse, the camp, and the Downs, ever in view, tell of things both permanent and forgotten (108, 109).

And passing over other beings great and small who have known those ways ever since the waters smoothed out the Vale, villagers apparently of the stock of King Alfred's men or the Danes continue to inhabit this flat country bounded by hills. This, too, in spite of recent penetrations from afar by strangers bent on conquest and settlement in pleasant places. The marauders, armed with a smack of the towns, ideas on culture, tea parties, and suburban goings-on, here and there developed tactics for brightening the villages and uplifting the villagers. Yet in face of these signs of intrusive battle the older natives at least, ever loyal to "as it was in the beginning, is now, and ever shall be," managed to keep their hereditary balance, remained uncontaminated, and continued superior to urban influences offered for the betterment of their minds and souls. "Berkshire and slow" is an old saying that is supposed to describe them. But if they may be slow they also are sure. They have acute eyes on the main chance, are hard nuts to crack in a bargain. Sometimes they slyly touch their heads when meaning "touch wood," often remark "It's no use keeping a dog and barking yourself," and during hard wintry weather I have heard them call the state of the ground "hover" in true Anglo-Saxon fashion. Possibly they have never quite recovered from the weighty matter of King Alfred's presence among their forebears. The King, they may inform you, cut the White Horse to celebrate his victory over the Danes. It would be useless to explain that very likely this is a cock-and-bull story, or that nobody knows who cut the steed in the chalk. "Fiddlesticks," they would answer, "it's King Alfred's horse";

April in Berkshire. Apple blossom at SOTWELL,
near the Berkshire Downs

SOTWELL. *An old interior of typical Berkshire pattern.*

meanwhile laughing at antiquarian greybeards or myself vainly searching for Asser's "single thorn-tree" where the fight waxed fiercest, and trying to locate the Æscendun battlefield at King's Standing above Aston Upthorpe, or almost everywhere else on the heights between The Fair Mile and Ashdown Park near Wiltshire.

The churches in the Vale, though not especially remarkable as a series, are just the kind of buildings one would hope to find in this pastoral land of old settlement. Their walls and features, here and there dating from Saxon years, indicate centuries of service in the mission propagated by St. Birinus. Stonework, monuments, and records preserved open the book of village stories. Portraits of landed and rustic folk thus come to light again. Now and again the pictures are lively, depicting letting off with cudgels and fists to defeat chances of monotony in haunts far from the madding crowd; but more often they reveal an even tenor of human way along this sequestered vale of life.

Taken at random, the churches of the combined parishes of North and South Moreton are typical. The one at South Moreton shows building of various periods ending with the nineteenth century. The doorway at the west, most likely Saxon, faces an old castle mound and entrenchment. Under the church-yard wall the stream flows on to the mill, courses over the race by the silent wheel, and with music tumbles into the busy pool beyond. Church, mill, and setting, and the great yew tree as well, make a veritable haunt of peace, shy and secluded. At North Moreton the church stands boldly by the roadside. With old-fashioned mien it faces all who pass that way, as much as to say, "Here I am, and here I've been since 1265." The fifteenth-century tower of stone and flint rises high over the earlier nave and chancel. The Stapleton chantry chapel within, lofty, and completed in 1299, is brilliantly lit; its eastern window glows with the colours of fifteen scriptural scenes on medieval glass, and shows pike favoured by the fourteenth-century artist for the Miraculous Draught of Fishes from the Galilean Sea. This window is a treasure so rare that the parson cannot sleep o' nights for fear of what may happen to it while he is in bed! Football fans, content to keep within the touch-lines of the present, might seek the parish register in the vestry to read this historical note of how the game was played in May 1598: "Gunter's sonnes and ye Gregories fell together by ye years at footeball. Ould Gunter dreive his dagger and broke booth their heades, and they died booth within a fortnight after." The question arises—what became of Ould Gunter? Was he hanged? Or was he applauded for loyalty to his own side? History is silent. But I know that Gregories remain in Moreton to this day.

Churches such as these are spread throughout the Vale. Ever pleasing to see and often showing much of beauty, the buildings exactly reflect the spirit of an English countryside in which the life of past centuries is linked with the present. Among the noteworthy names are Drayton, for an alabaster reredos;

Sinodun Hills & Camp from Mackney

Stanford-in-the-Vale; Great Coxwell with its little church and great tithe barn; East Hagbourne, lovely throughout; Blewbury, "the cathedral of the Downs"; West Hendred, small, perfect, and unspoiled; Childrey for brasses; Uffington, cruciform in plan, Early English in style, and showing a bust of Tom Hughes in bronze.

But it is for villages that the Vale of the White Horse rivals anywhere in England. They are superb. Cottages, manor-houses, and farms cluster round churches and greens surrounded by gardens, orchards, many elm trees, and hedgerow fields of fine cultivation. Buildings of timber, plaster, chalk-stone, brickwork and tiles richly coloured, and thatched roofs as well, combine in variegated motives to yield pictures of unending delight. These combinations show the English village scene in very best mood. The garden and boundary walls of mud capped with thatching are notable and charming. Some villages— Blewbury is a good example—have such walls almost surrounding them, which make it quite confusing to find the ways in and out. Probably they are survivals of distant times when the villages were enclosed and thus in a manner fortified. Villagers firmly maintain that the Saxons built these walls, but not being an authority on mud I should say that these statements on age bear signs of imaginative invention. From the galaxy of villages it is only possible to indicate particular gems at Charney Bassett; Steventon, with the remarkable series of houses on the causeway; and in a line near the Downs, Aston Tirrold, Blewbury, East Hagbourne, East and West Hendred, Childrey and Sparsholt (106, 107). Almost every place in the Vale is full of interest and attraction. Many an old manor-house recalls a long possession by sturdy families, such as the Puseys at Pusey and the Fettiplaces at Childrey, who lived country lives, succeeded from father to son, kept clear of political intrigues and so, saving their heads, continued to prosper on their own acres for hundreds of years.

Up on the Downs scenes are changed. The richness of the Vale, visible from the heights, fades away into blue distances. But on the hills it is wide and lonely country, a land of solitude with few habitations and not many trees. Miles of springy turf, equally delightful for wanderers and the racehorses that train there, clothe the high surfaces and colour the contours curving down into combes. Gentium, sweet thyme, harebells, milkwort, and other treasures of Nature's bounty peep out from the long grass. Yet in spite of these delicate signs of life and splendid spectacles of horses in motion along the trainers' rides, these everlasting hills always appear immutable and tinged with antiquity. They seem so very old, whether by the face of the land or the things pertaining to it. That legend hovers around the stones of Wayland Smith's Cave and the Dragon Hill by the White Horse is not to be wondered at. Nor is it surprising to learn, as I once did, that strange voices sometimes are thought to be heard on the night winds over at Seven Barrows. The hills, too, carry the visible lines of great age. Many tumuli, earthworks, and camps send thoughts back to lost or but faintly known ages when Britons and Romans, Saxons and Danes knew these ridges, lived their little days of fame, and departed for ever leaving this well-worn stage ready for the tread of actors in new eras.

And crowning the heights is the old, old road, the trackway as ancient as any work of man in England, first blazed by primitive people and used ever since. To cover mile after mile along this track, breathe fine clear air, and meanwhile make nodding acquaintance with centuries of bygones, can send the blood tingling through any wayfarer's veins. After striking the road from King's Standing Hill above Moulsford, or reaching it from Streatley, where evidently the crossing was made over the Thames to connect with the Icknield Way on the Chilterns, the route lies clear ahead for a pilgrimage of hours or days (90). It passes the tumuli and camp at Lowbury Hill, reaches the White Horse, crosses into Wiltshire, directs over Marlborough Downs, and for hardy and

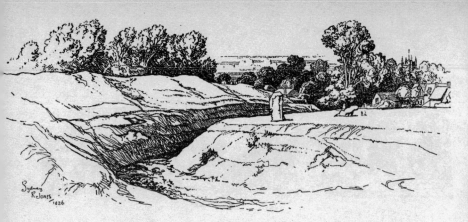

Earthworks and Stones, Avebury

brave toilers leads through Wans Dyke to Salisbury Plain and Stonehenge, ever on the chalk and splendid for views and fresh atmosphere. Almost everywhere the way bristles with points created by early mankind, who specialized in delving and piling up earth. Evidences of this form of laborious handiwork are visible at the Scutchamer Knob barrow of the West Saxon King Cwichelm, Letcombe Castle, White Horse Hill and camp, and over in Wiltshire, Liddington Castle, Barbury Castle, Avebury earthworks encircling the stones which are supposed to have made the exact number of 649 when first stuck up, the great mound of Silbury Hill, thrown there by nobody knows who to make the biggest thing of the kind in Europe—all these and other objects in dirt galore can be pondered on at close quarters. For those who like to swing the pendulum of time forward a bit, and think of house and home in terms other than dirt, more recent signs of man can be located. Near to the route lie such places as the Elizabethan Ginge Manor; Lockinge House,[1] rich in memories of Lord Wantage, V.C.; moated Compton Beauchamp, diversified with eighteenth-century grace and Tudor brickwork; Ashdown House, in John Webb's classic style; and the lovely gables and roofs of Avebury manor-house showing over clipped yews beyond the thatched churchyard wall (117). The trackway is pre-eminently a walker's or horseman's paradise. I therefore beseech adventurous souls with motor cars not to disturb its ancient peace.

Open and fresh, bleak and lonely, the high parts of these chalk hills offer all degrees of pleasure and hardship to those who live at the farms and cottages scattered few and far between. Winter brings trials. "I've had to go miles to get bread because the baker cannot drive through the snow," said the mother of a young family one day to me, thereby in a second summoning a stark contrast to my exhilaration brought by moving briskly over those same white slopes brilliant in sunlight. Shepherds' huts on wheels in isolated places suggest lonely days and nights spent by a fine breed of men who face all the vagaries

[1] Demolished in 1946, a victim of taxation.

of wind and weather during the cold lambing times. Look inside one of the huts and you will see straw for warmth, a lantern, and corked bottles for babies. Tales of lost human souls also are remembered—of those whose cries of "Man lost!" were unheard ere they departed to join the immortals in dark nights of snow and storm. Actually it is quite easy to lose the way on the Downs in the dark. This may mean, if nothing worse, spending a night out.

Such a chance I nearly experienced in crossing from East Ilsley during winter about forty years ago. All who have been to this pretty township will remember its past fame for great sheep sales. The high days when dealers and country people from near and far gathered in crowds at this spot in a cup of the Downs are yet recalled by the remarkable number of old-fashioned inns, some good houses, and sheep pens instead of buildings lining the hilly street. Over all rises the large fourteenth-century tower of the church, of course standing for honesty in bargaining. And in this prime region of horses and training East Ilsley's association with "Eclipse" cannot be forgotten. At Kate's Gore in the parish the very prince of racehorses was foaled at the stables of the Duke of Cumberland on the day of the eclipse of the sun in 1764. One wintry afternoon, engrossed with much to see and think about, I therefore stayed too long in East Ilsley before leaving to cross over the Downs on foot. The fading daylight quickly changed into one of the darkest nights imaginable. While ascending the hills a bitter and boisterous wind arose, bringing snow down in a blizzard. To locate direction was impossible; but luck or instinct carried me to the track signpost on the ridge. Then good fortune failed. Battling blindly on for half an hour only brought me to the exact place once more. A second attempt ended apparently nowhere at all. Evidently I was lost. To add to my discomfort, the snow and the wind if possible grew worse. Nasty ideas came to mind—of wreaths, funerals, and North Pole tragedies. What, I wondered, did ancient Britons and Romans do on such nights? and might not the snowy shade of King Cwichelm already be out for an airing from his earthwork? A more practical turn of thought suggested avoiding either uphill or downhill and keeping to the flattish top downland. That, surely, would lead somewhere. After struggling forward for a time comparable to an eternity, with spirits ebbing low through too much fresh air, wet garments, great appetite, and no food, the sudden joy of seeing a faint light moving ahead almost produced my collapse. Forgetting the correct formula of "Man lost!" I quickly yelled "Hoi!" A faint "Hoi!" answered back over the wind. Light and I advanced and met. A storm lantern illuminated a shepherd's face.

"Where be'st goain on a night like this?" asked the face in the snow.

"I don't know," I replied. "I am lost."

"Lucky I found 'ee."

A slow Berkshire narration proved me to be far out of my way. With good-shepherdly concern the samaritan at once offered to set the wanderer right.

And having done so, he then thought he might as well see me safely into Chilton. This accomplished, and arrived outside the *Horse and Jockey* (since rebuilt), we both agreed that a glass of something inside to keep out the cold might not do any harm. A blazing inn fire soon routed gloomy thoughts of untoward tragedies on the Downs. Yet of reward for what he had done the shepherd, with sturdy and genuine grace, would hear of no more than my thanks coupled, if it pleased me, with perhaps one more glass of something to keep out the cold until morning. When I turned into the blizzard again, then to continue on familiar roads, I carried away the picture of a rugged and kind face aglow in the firelight. But the kindliness born of true kindness of heart is a gift common enough among good shepherds, whose tender cares are their ewes and lambs.

The Downs slope southwards from the Berkshire and Wiltshire escarpments. Away from the lone heights the country of hills and combes, schemed richer with cultivation and woodlands, smoothes out into the valley of the River Kennet. The villages placed high or low are of usual old-English constitution. Most of them contain cottages with thatched and tiled roofs covering walls of timber and plaster, flint, and brickwork. These, with some newer buildings and houses for country people and parsons, are marshalled round churches generally ancient. The upper villages partake of the character of the Downs. Aldbourne, standing round a pond and a green in Wiltshire, and Aldworth and Chaddleworth in Berkshire are but three typical examples among many that well repay delving in. Aldworth also offers the unusual in a remarkable show of De la Beche monuments of hefty knights and ladies reclining or lying flat all over the church. Among the locals they are aptly known as "the Giants." Whom each figure represents is now uncertain, for, according to the diary of the Royalist Captain Symonds of 1644, Queen Elizabeth and the Earl of Leicester, after riding on a pillion from Ewelme in Oxfordshire, inspected the monuments, then pinched the parchment list of their names. The adjacent castle of this family of large frames and consequence in the Middle Ages vanished long ago.

Lambourn, the only real town in this chalk country for nearly 40 miles east and west, also claims affinity with the Downs through the activities of horsey gents who keep the venerable place bright, famous, and prosperous. The church, ever beneficent and here shedding the light over equestrianism, stable boys, and complications at starting-gates, confirms the town's ancient sporting proclivities by preserving hounds chasing the hare in carved stone hundreds of years old. The Lambourn stream, coming from the higher chalk, runs round the houses and sparkles "in the vale below," surely showing to the life Charles Kingsley's "Whitbury" in *Two Years Ago*. The stream joins village to village on its way to meet the Kennet, adding loveliness to a chain of pretty places as it winds beside the road. First there is Eastbury, notable for a great dovecote and manor-house turned farm. Beyond, at the manor-house of West Shefford, King Charles sheltered after the second battle of Newbury. Bridges and tall yews mark out Welford; the stream circles round Boxford and the mill-house; and the windings of water and story end in heroic vein at Donnington Castle and Shaw House, two vital Civil War landmarks. Particularly impressive are the ruins and fourteenth-century gatehouse at Donnington, ever glorious in memory of stalwart John Boys, who defied his king's enemies while towers and walls fell. The Lambourn flows to join its parent river. Surrounding slopes of chalk, woody and verdurous, extend down far and wide, making the border-lands of the Kennet vale.

The River Kennet, rising on the Wiltshire Downs to the north of Avebury and ending in the Thames at Reading, performs a course of 44 miles with charm and grace. It is one of England's delectable small rivers abounding in scenes that should, if anything could, change sinful man into something better and more soulful. The pools and eddies certainly delight fat trout and grayling that generally prefer to remain in clear waters instead of accepting fishermen's flies. These fish need a good deal of catching and I have heard unsuccessful anglers disturb the haunts of peace with dreadful expressions of defeat. Weighty ancestors, famed through centuries past, suffered for their own merits. Often they departed ignominiously inside epicures of note, and with no more bene-diction than Pepys offered in 1668, "very good troutes." The Kennet, too, introduces a slight excursion in geology in this chapter on chalk lands. After the river passes from Wiltshire into Berkshire the formation changes from Cre-taceous to Oligocene and Eocene, or, to use plain English, the higher chalk gives place to a lower country of clays and sands. Interpreted in terms of building, the clays and sands mean a prevalence of bricks and tiles. But here not common or garden bricks and tiles. The district is remarkable for the colouring and varied texture of its buildings. Walls, roofs, and features add bright and harmonious accents to landscapes, villages, and towns. Nowhere can be seen to better advantage an architectural style that largely developed through local products, the hidden treasures of clay and sand contained in the earth.

The Kennet landscape is choice, lovely, and wide in the vale. It does not pretend to be grand. But where opening out best it beckons its lovers to seclusion and pastoral quiet, to water meadows and feathery willows and lines of poplars gleaming out from full tints of elms. Cattle grazing move slowly over fresh green grass. There is the enchantment of wild flowers that spangle little stars of colour. They meet the river's banks, nodding to rushes swished by waters playing musically. Pebbles, the bed of the stream, and fishes facing the current or darting swiftly, show clearly through liquid transparency. Upward curves of rising ground and belts of woodland ever mark the confines of the vale to the north and south,

Substantial houses, some old and others newish and often surrounded by parklands, stand prettily within these scenes. Villages and churches as well add to the delights that abound in this vale. The borderlands yield splendid views. One of the many vantage points over the Kennet is at Hampstead Marshall church, standing on a bank at the borders of the deer park; in the park, and away from the river, gate piers alone remain to mark the great mansion of the Stuarts' favourite, Lord Craven, built in the seventeenth century but quickly consumed by fire. Other good viewpoints are at Kintbury (118), from the verges backed by old trees at Hungerford Park, and from Hungerford Down (110). The heights about Inkpen Beacon and Walbury Hill present remarkable panoramas; complete sections of the Kennet valley extend in vast compositions of Claudean or Turneresque magnificence.

No explorer in this valley can long forget that the Kennet and the famous Bath Road mean much the same thing, for river and highway from the Wiltshire chalk to Reading hug each other as lovers maybe are inclined to do, sometimes tightly, with prim interludes now and again at safe distances. And if the romantic appeal of the highway now has been somewhat pared off by tidying up, cutting away corners, and straightening tracks to suit new speeds and streamline efficiency, the road by the river, signs of old inns, towns, villages, and the parks and the places yet can stir chords in the recesses of memory. Times remote, distant, and recent, recalled by visible marks and associations, scintillate again by remembrances of the regular swirl of all sorts of somebodies and nobodies, from the chariot-wheel era to the advent of Rolls Royce, ever progressing along this route to and from the West for centuries and centuries. This is a highway of history. Its smooth and fast surface covers the tracks of time and period, tracks that served the great and the famous, wagons and coaches, masters of the ribbons, literary celebrities, society, highwaymen, peace, war, and especially Cavaliers and Roundheads concerned with Reading, Newbury, Hungerford, and Marlborough standing along the course.

River and road, after casually meeting under the shade of the great Silbury mound near to the green track of the Roman highway to Bath, make their ways more or less arm in arm to Marlborough. Certainly this town is famed for the College of abstemious youth incorporating the defunct Castle Inn, immortal for grand and bottle renown. The main street of amazing width, lined with gables, Georgian fronts, and columned arcades, ranks second to none (117). But the town sticks in my memory for reasons other than these. It served to embellish a few of those eventful hours in life that ever remain precious. On a summer's evening in a year not so long ago I entered a room with square window-panes overlooking this notable stage in the prime coaching days where horses were changed while travellers dispatched vast quantities cut from rounds of beef, choice hams, veal pies, and other landlordly offerings. For myself, a summer eve creature of a mechanical age, I sat down to a modest though excellent roast chicken, followed by raspberries and cream luscious and thick, with etceteras to round off the concoction. That fleeting excursion in the realm of mild epicurism alone merited a nitch in memory; it has since brought mental stimulus to moments of tragedy with ration cards.

Long before midnight, with the materials of fare comfortably accommodated to my interior, a pretty chambermaid's direction of "This is your room, sir," and my response of "Thank you. Tea at eight. Goodnight," led to settling down in sheets scented with lavender, etc., etc. Then, either soon or late, a most remarkable state of affairs captured my unconsciousness. People and objects seemed to stray about, all mixed up and glinting like the facets of a kaleidoscope. Romans in tunics and Georgians in wigs babbled of Aquæ Julis and Beau Nash; a king in charge of a parliament, evidently Henry III by his drooping eyelid, bridged a gap of a few hundred years by nodding to another king, Charles to the life obviously by Vandyke, surrounded by Cavaliers haranguing sulky and obstinate burghers; quite recognizable were Evelyn and Pepys, Wycherley and Congreve, Addison, Steele, Garrick, Mrs. Siddons, and through the crowd ever changing passed Gay adding last touches to *The Beggar's Opera*, the Duchess of Queensberry quizzing a white apron for future use, Fielding noting Ralph Allen of course for *Tom Jones*, Chesterfield polished and superior, Pitt hobbling with the gout, Johnson exploding with "No, Sir!" Reynolds in horn spectacles, Gainsborough instructing carrier Wiltshire on "The Blue Boy," Goldsmith working up notes on the city of fashion, Wesley fuming on "the headquarters of Satan" to the Countess of Huntingdon, Sheridan and Eliza Linley eloping, the Duchess of Devonshire smiling "How d'ye do" to Fanny Burney, and—Bang! Was it thunder or the end of the world? I awoke. A tap, tap on the door aroused my dull morning sense to just grasp the words, "It is eight o'clock. Your tea, sir." The perennial shades, once lively figures riding, posting, or coaching in and out, eating, making merry, grumbling, sleeping, and otherwise adding lustre and fame to Marlborough's wide street, faded to airy nothings in the sunlight of morning. But the town is a capital one for reminiscence, for stirring up its long past, for enjoying the present—and for exciting slumber after roast chicken and etceteras!

A slight tiff outside Marlborough causes the Bath Road and the Kennet to part company awhile. The big road haughtily rises for Hungerford through Savernake Forest, still a forest with beechwood glades stretching for miles to the south. Piqued, the river meanders away through pleasant meadows among chalk hills. Flirting with the original and winding Bath road for temporary suitor, it decks ancient Ramsbury with kingcups and watercress beds in sight of the big house built by John Webb, that architect's duet with his Ashdown Park some 10 miles away. The waters flow on. Soon they ripple past Littlecote Park and hall with never a shudder for Wild Darrell, once lord of the broad acres and manufacturer of an Elizabethan thriller. The house of many gables, fanciful

STEVENTON, *Berkshire, lying in the*
vale between the Downs and the Thames.

EAST HENDRED. *A village group below the Berkshire Downs.*

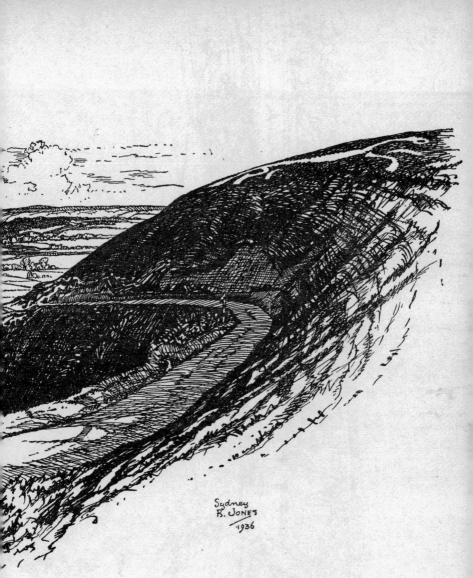

Sydney
R. Jones
1936

WHITE HORSE HILL *and the* VALE OF THE WHITE
HORSE. *The horse cut in the turf of the chalk hill is 374 feet
long and of unknown origin. The village of* UFFINGTON,
*the birthplace of Tom Hughes and figured in his "Tom
Brown's School Days," appears in the centre of the Vale.*

The KENNET VALLEY *from Hungerford Down.*

chimneys, and brick and stone mixtures of true English constitution, exactly hints at pretty romance of the past in a frame of peace, quiet, and beauty. But of course the place is sadly haunted as well. The picturesque outlines shroud secrets most foul and mysterious concerned with the story widely known for its highlights of a midwife, a masked lady in a four-poster, and a tall, ferocious man who crushed an unwanted baby to cinders on the Littlecote hearth. Rumour further embellished the tale by sending the tall man—Darrell of Littlecote to wit—on wild rides through the darkness chased by guilt until he broke his neck. Nor did the breakage finish him off. He continued riding the night for ever and ever in the shape of a ghostly spectre on a phantom horse, very terrifying indeed for natives returning home late from dark lanes, pubs, and evensong. As long as simple country folk had enlightenment enough to believe in ghoulish and wicked apparitions Wild Darrell haunted the country-side, though doubtless now he has been improved off the face of the earth. Clear of grim associations the Kennet jilts its suitor, the winding road. With smiles the river advances to the Bath Road and they meet again. The road full of speed, and the river full of fish, make it up near *The Bear* at Hungerford, a splendid old hostelry still, and celebrated as a meeting-place in 1688 for William of Orange and the King's Commissioners, then intent on settling the matter of the Throne just before James II bolted for France.

A long time ago the ancestors of Hungerford's trout knew of one John of Gaunt, and with fear and trembling. For when this son of Edward III granted a charter he really meant, among other things, that the prime trout could be caught and eaten by the human inhabitants settled round their waters. If the fish did not like the idea, the Hungerford people did. In token of benefits bestowed they ever afterwards honoured the memory of their John. To this day, therefore, they announce the festival of Hocktide with notes blown on John of Gaunt's horn. Then follow feasts, kisses for the girls, scrambles for pennies and oranges, swearing-in of officials, much business and all sorts of high jinks, completed by a banquet when the toast of "John of Gaunt" is drunk at midnight in silence. These goings-on, so ancient in origin and unique, are rare enough to call anyone to Hungerford at Hocktide. The festival begins a fortnight after Easter on a Monday, and ever since John of Gaunt's days the reigning Sovereign whenever passing through Hungerford has received a red rose, the payment of tribute due from the town for fishing and other rights. Thus King George VI, on the way from Marlborough to Windsor, March 12, 1948, accepted a red rose from the Constable, Mr. Roy Alexander.

In these motoring times of the highway by the river, *The Bear* "posting house," brick built outside and full of memories and oak within, witnesses more hurrying and scurrying along than ever it did in the great coaching era. Yet many hasteners to and fro quite fail to notice the real Hungerford stretching away up the hill to the common. The town is one of those nice places often to be met with in the middle of southern England: not too small nor too large, plentifully supplied with Georgian and earlier houses showing good brickwork and doorways, and spacious in a High Street of generous width, convenient for residents of at least four generations standing to park their cars and perambulate in comfort among shops of very old-established tradesmen. Hungerford has all the attributes both for living and making a living pleasantly. If the outward pattern has been changed here and there, the spirit of place abides in living continuance of old John of Gaunt's patronage. Bright colours of brickwork, white window-frames, shadows on trim doorways and under trees lining the street, help to radiate an atmosphere of warmth and friendliness. The town carries a neighbourly air; imparts a suggestion that the inhabitants have hobnobbed together long enough to take an interest in each other, even to the extent of nodding familiarities to next door or over the garden walls. Premises of shopkeepers, too, have an appearance of stability, deeply rooted. For example, the little square panes screening Mr. Nicol, ironmonger and saddler, are so bewitching in Regency fashion that anyone in a moment of admiration might be prompted to buy the complete contents within the window at a single deal. On the opposite side of the street, the nice frontage terminated by dormers in the roof quite clearly tells that Mr. Clifford and his ancestors never thought of changing quarters after they established themselves in the boot, shoe, and repairing business in 1700. To meet with such signs of fixedness can distil a gentle balm and sedative to this shifty, moving age. The fathers of Hungerford also continue to manage their own affairs in their own particular way without a mayor, council, or such common contrivances. They keep to the ancient of days. A High Constable, Port Reeve, Bailiff, and officials quaintly designated in the manner of hundreds of years ago send the twentieth century along in a flood of picturesque names and old-time ceremony. I only hope that bureaucracy, eager to sweep everybody and everything into a central pit, may never direct the axe on the good dwellers and town of Hungerford.

River and road continue through the valley, nearing the remarkable Norman church hidden away in peaceful seclusion at Avington. The big church tower and cottages of Kintbury group among trees on a knoll. The road then begins to strike away from the chalk country and gains Newbury at the collection of old posting inns at Speenhamland, with *The Chequers* deservedly prominent in the group. The river comes into the town, passes the church, and flows under the graceful stone arch and classic balustrades in Bridge Street.

Newbury never disappoints. Biggish, lively, busy, picturesque, and historical, it is a particularly good specimen of an English market town. Standing at the meeting of main roads from London, Bath, Winchester, and Oxford, it is well placed on the map. It satisfies all sorts of tastes. Here can be discovered townspeople proud of their town and tradesmen of two or three hundred years' standing, who perhaps frown on recent intruders squatting behind shop fronts

NEWBURY. *The late-Gothic church associated with John Smalwoode,
"Jack of Newbury."*

of standardized patterns highly coloured. Country people in for shopping enliven the streets with their tweeds and cars. Buses disgorging women with baskets from the neighbouring villages add further interest to effects. Other offerings and human attractions are lots of pretty girls, local characters in highways and byways, churches for the good, hotels for the comfortable, pubs for the temperate, cinemas for lovers (of films), antiquities for the antiquated, horse races for sportsmen, fishes for anglers, schools for youth, and an extraordinary number of homes for the aged. Those who like the rush of traffic may get heart's desire on the Bath Road, Northbrook Street, and around the Market Place. Contemplative souls can find nooks hidden away in seclusion. Variously sparkling and crusted, the town is a first-rate blend in the vintages of to-day, back a bit, and a long time ago.

Certainly Newbury does date back very far. When natives now talk of "the city," meaning one particular area, the words really recall the Roman site. Saxons settled later. The Normans built a castle now gone. The town was known as a borough with inhabitants called "burgesses" as early as 1187. King John busied himself with the great fair of St. Bartholomew in 1215. As a wool town it prospered and rose to first importance, being incorporated by charter in Queen Elizabeth's reign. The Civil War put the town into national history with the two battles of Newbury in 1643 and 1644, when Carnarvon, Sunderland, Falkland, and their gallant companions in a lost cause fell on the green lands of England between Shaw village and Speen. Shaw House, still magnificently Elizabethan as Dolman the clothier built it, calls to mind King Charles missed by a rebel's bullet on the morning of battle, and Donnington Castle ruins tell their own story of Sir John Boys and fateful days. When war's tragedies ended and the Restoration brought Charles II into the town, the coaches began to arrive. For more than one hundred and fifty years they jingled in and out carrying almost everybody of note. And after a lapse of time new sounds of motion filled the streets. The latest fliers of the road speeded with fast wheels to deposit our parents and ourselves into the thriving and bright town of Newbury.

The face of Newbury tells a good deal of the town's story. Buildings, houses, and inns carry the marks of circumstance and age. The big church is a monument to the woollen industry that helped to make England prosperous. It is also a monument to Jack of Newbury, one of the famous among those wool merchants who thrived, grew rich, and in thankfulness and devotion erected fanes to the glory of God in many parts of the land. Impressive outside and within and containing many treasures, the church is a notable example of architecture completed in Gothic style in 1532, just before the Reformation. And if Jack of Newbury and his son spared nothing on the building in Tudor times, their followers in recent years have been no less prodigal in their efforts and care for preservation and new beauty. The tower, shapely in weathered stone, stands well near the river; angle turrets and pinnacles mount sky-ward from panelled parapets and are reflected below in the waters (113). Quite near, and lying back at a corner of the Market Place, the Cloth Hall further upholds the old fame of wool. It keeps stout and firm the seven-teenth-century heritage of pointed gables, windows framed in oak, overhanging beams supported by brackets, and a wide doorway that leads into a capital museum filled with objects of local interest and relics of the Civil War battles. For old hospitals and almshouses Newbury holds its own with any town in which these charming buildings show to perfection. The collections bordering the Winchester road make a choice group, and each one of these abodes of long and good service stirs a gracious thought. Beams, gables, fine brickwork, and white walls carry architectural themes through the phases of Tudor, Renais-sance, and Victorian Gothic. Some of the foundations began early in medieval years and St. Bartholomew's Hospital, one of the most ancient but rebuilt in classic fashion round a forecourt approached by brick piers surmounted with elegant stone vases, is the very picture for the popular phrase "a harbour of refuge."

Interesting buildings rivet attention throughout the town. Along the river-side a mixture of Georgian and earlier houses border West Mill Street. Below the bridge is the early Waterside Chapel of 1697, glowing in the colours of local brickwork. Nearly everywhere along the main streets the quarters of towns-people of generations ago appear above new shop fronts or sandwiched between modern walls. Timbers wavy and carved, plaster surfaces screening more timbers, features bequeathed from Renaissance, Georgian, and Regency days, and sundry wrought accompaniments of a domestic past point to the years of old-time natives who worked and thrived on their business premises with wives, sons, and daughters around them ever keeping home sweet home in touch with occupations and the daily round. These evidences can make an observer look upward constantly. For so doing passers-by may quiz, with as much as to say, "What on earth are you looking at?" The answer would be, "Mostly brickwork." Newbury possesses Berkshire brick building at its best, which means as good as any in England. The period is largely late Renaissance and Georgian. For design and workmanship it is excellent. The colouring is marvellous. Northbrook Street alone presents a capital range of examples. No doubt it was to one of these domiciles that Mr. Pepys came on June 16, 1668— but not in search of brickwork! Then the practical worthy was concerned with food and entertainment. "There dined;" he noted, "and musick: a song of the old courtier of Queen Elizabeth's did please me mightily," followed by the reckoning of 8s. 7d., which prompted the parsimonious remark, "forced to change gold."

Of all the upper storeys in Newbury streets there is one I like best. It is not very conspicuous and stands at the corner of a narrow way of medieval pattern leading off Northbrook Street. Brackets curve outwards to support overhanging walls. The gable is full of close timbering and herringbone brickwork. Moulded beams wobble very much out of the straight and carved ornaments have the softness of long service. Continuing along the side of the narrow way are more timbers, panels of small bricks, and windows oddly placed. The general appearance suggests a once powerful man of strong limbs who has lived on to reach a robust old age, though with joints not quite so good as they used to be; which indeed is somewhere near the truth. The building denotes its Tudor origin and strength; it remains firm enough to serve generations to come (123).

Across the cobblestones and opposite stands a pub in and out of which customers come and go for and with pints and half-pints. Standing against the outer walls of this convenient viewpoint the old building can be well studied. At the same time it is possible to capture the years and a story of long ago, to delve mentally into this hiding-place and awaken the romantic personage of chapbook stories who in past times figured much as Dick Whittington did. For behind the timbering lived Jack of Newbury, alias John Winchcombe, the light of the town and of wide fame, hero of fanciful tales that stirred popular imagination, and by name at least still known to almost everyone.

John Smalwoode, probably born about 1470, was the son of a London draper thought to have descended from Simon de Winchcombe, a rich citizen of London and Sheriff in 1379. At an early age young John was apprenticed to a clothier in Newbury. Meaning to get on in the world, he put a shoulder to the wheel, made himself generally useful in the approved style of industrious apprentices, forged ahead, is believed to have courted his master's widow and completed the shrewd bargain before the altar of the Litten Chapel near St. Bartholomew's Hospital. Becoming a master man himself through this wisdom in matrimony, he rose to eminence in the manufacture of cloth. He employed hundreds of workers. From their industry and his own abilities he amassed heaps and heaps of money. His fellows acclaimed him the foremost man of the town. The fame of "Winchcombe kerseys," then the best woollen cloth made, spread about the country and abroad. Thus John's passage through the hard world appears to have been one triumphant progress. No wonder that Thomas Fuller rated this paragon "the most considerable clothier England ever held." In common with prosperous men of his time he did the gracious and customary thing by offering the rewards of benefits bestowed to the Giver of all good gifts. A grand parish church rose in place of an older one. To this day the carved bosses in St. Nicholas' Church, with the initials of J. S. on them, shine in remembrance of John Smalwoode, the eminent character truly known by historical facts and evidence.

But further deeds were associated with the name of Jack of Newbury. To the Tudor Crœsus was given the credit of entertaining Henry VIII and Catherine

AVEBURY *church and manor-house, Wiltshire.*

MARLBOROUGH. *The wide High Street on the famous Bath Road.*

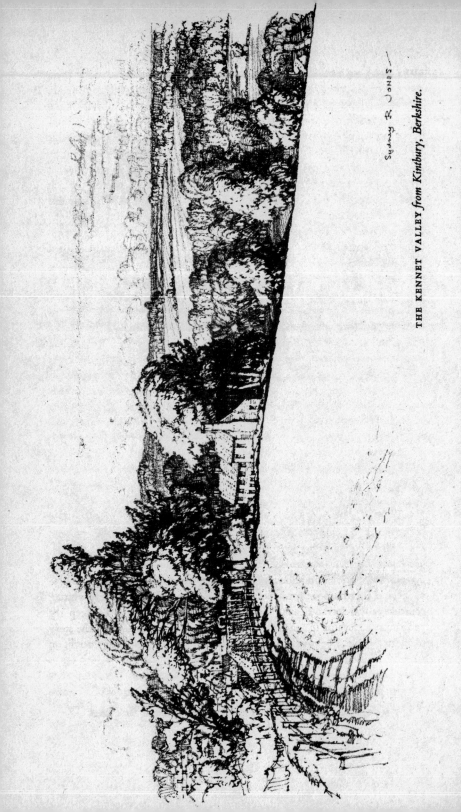

Sydney R. Jones

THE KENNET VALLEY *from Kintbury, Berkshire.*

of Aragon with all the magnificence commanded by wool. In practical effect this involved a lavish expenditure on cakes, ale, and other solids and liquids, as well as numerous pieces of broadcloth worth £100 apiece for the royal guests to put their feet on, and at a period when most people considered themselves lucky if able to kick about on green rushes. The King, ever remarkable for picking up abbeys, wives, and sundry valuables, demonstrated characteristic gratitude by stowing the broadcloths into his heavy luggage for future use, at the same time offering a knighthood of no cash value by way of payment, which stout John declined with thanks. The clothier also acquired a military halo. He was represented cutting a gallant figure in performing valiant tricks on the Scots at Floddon Field while leading 100 to 250 men (the exact number depended on the fancy of the story-teller), all splendidly equipped and mounted at his own expense. Finally, and according to hard fact rather than imaginativeness, the developed edition of the industrious apprentice certainly made a will on January 4, 1519. On February 15 following he left the stage of earthly triumph and departed to prosper elsewhere, fortified by the pious request, "Of yo charities pray for the soul of John Smalwoode, als Winchcombe." The record of the end of this remarkable man is visible for all to see on a brass in the church of St. Nicholas.

This shining catalogue of laborious days, crowned with the rewards bestowed by the gods on cute persons with an eye for the main chance, points a moral for ambitious young men, who should never marry for money, but where money is. Such, at least, was the opinion of scribes in the sixteenth century. In the events of the life of John Smalwoode they perceived material for a Dick Whittington type of story. Therefore, when the clothier had settled decently in his tomb he came out again, making a second appearance in book form. Through the printed word exploits quite thrilling developed from sober facts, and the late lamented emerged in all the glory of the legendary hero, "Jacke of Newberie." He returned somewhat like his old self, yet with a difference, and portrayed with Hollywood rather than Holbein brilliance. The pictures featured new lighting and effects for himself, Henry VIII, Catherine of Aragon, Cardinal Wolsey, broadcloths, knighthood episode, battle exploits, and ingenious inventions, amplified by close-ups lively and exciting with goings-on behind Northbrook Street between the home staff (female) and visiting courtiers, royal servants, and Will Somers, the King's jester. To keep the performance elevated in tone, a pretty thread of moral ran through the story to adorn the tale. The producers' efforts, first printed in black letter, caught on famously. Peddlers sold the chapbook throughout England. In various forms it appeared continuously for more than two hundred years in edition after edition. Although John Smalwoode died a century later than Sir Richard Whittington, the legendary Jack of Newbury appeared first, and afterwards rivalled Dick Whittington in popularity. If Newbury had been London or the town's woollen industry had not declined in the seventeenth century, Jack still might rival Dick on Boxing Night.

Sad to relate, many of the spicy bits worked into the Jack of Newbury legend are viewed with grave suspicion by sages who ponder over deeds and manuscripts by day and by night. It is argued that the choicest details for human consumption are not supported by contemporary evidence. King, queen, broadcloths, battle, maids, courtiers, serving men, and jester are summarily shot into the dustheap of doubt in company with Whittington's cat, milestone, and chimes of Bow Bells. Alas! for these unromantic times of proof, fact, and planned effects. But evidence is not everything. Nobody can stop anybody pushing the clock back a bit. The cobbled way and the Tudor gable off Northbrook Street at least remain solid and visible. So isn't it a pretty fancy to scan the old walls, imagine pranks with Will Somers behind them, glance up at the oriel window to picture Queen Catherine peeping out, looking at the blue sky overhead, then down to the pub opposite perhaps amused by worthy burgesses going in and out before and after refreshment, and to see Her Majesty just as she was before the fat King cashiered her to make way for Anne Boleyn?

The Bath Road, leading from Newbury Londonwards, makes a last duet with the Kennet before the inevitable parting at Reading. The historic tracks of the highway, now new and smooth for speed, resound with the purr of engines and the noise of a hurrying crowd sweeping along past petrol pumps and ribbon development, modern emblems that jostle old inns, houses, and relics of the measured years of horses and tuneful horns. The valley opens out wide to meet low uplands and distant woods. Churches and villages mark points where all sorts of people arrived, did all kinds of things, then departed after achieving their little deeds of fame. Over at Bucklebury Jack of Newbury's son built a fine house, visited later by Bolingbroke, Swift, and Gay; the Forsters planted the trees round Aldermaston manor-house; Padworth's gardens acquired the lawn like velvet; Arabella Fermor, bright with two locks in equal curls, welcomed Pope to the lovely home at Ufton Nervet when

" Belinda smiled, and all the world was gay."

A few miles from the Kennet, the Bath Road and Reading, the River Loddon winds between low banks to join the Thames. It threads through a field and hedgerow country pleasant with glimpses of winding waters, mills and mill-races, parks, groups of cottages, village greens, inns, and churches. Here and there scenes retain the homely and intimate character portrayed by Mary Russell Mitford's delicate prose. As long as *Our Village* is read and the sensitive and gifted author is remembered, the Loddon villages of Arborfield, Swallowfield, and Three Mile Cross will hold a place in literature, will suggest "the red cottage, the dwelling of the shoemaker, the house of the blacksmith, the village shop," and all those perfect and complete cameos set to words more than a hundred years ago. But lovers of the book should avoid the place of its source, Three Mile Cross. Though the house of the heroic life and the writing is there still, the surroundings of petrol pumps, garage rubbish, and ugly habitations, which have replaced "broad green borders and hedgerows," are the very antithesis of the Mitford tradition, a disgrace even for modern England. It is better to visit Swallowfield, and to think of Mary Mitford sleeping under the elm tree in the little churchyard surrounded by the treasured scenes of her last years on earth.

More to the east Berkshire stretches away to Maidenhead, Windsor, and the Surrey border, districts marking the outlying country of London. Therefore, turning southwards and to the hills, I invite my readers to explore the fair lands of Hampshire.

IN HAMPSHIRE

From the northern boundary of Hampshire the downlands lead up to the hills that trace a line from Wiltshire, across Hampshire, and into Surrey. In all directions evidences point to chalk country again. Many things tell of this, obvious by smooth and rounded contours, grassy mounds, wide areas of ancient turf spangled with myriads of tiny flowers, the nature of soil, woodlands, copses and undergrowth, spring shows of blackthorn, primroses, anemonies, bluebells, and the autumn glories of beech, fern, and gorse. The bright colours of the scenes, graduating to soft and delicate shades, have the translucent qualities peculiar to all regions where the light chalk underlies the soil. Unmistakable in its configuration and appearance, this chalk country slopes from the north downs across Hampshire, is parted by the clays and sandy areas bordering the coast and the New Forest, and across the Solent chalk again leads up to the downs on the Isle of Wight.

The escarpments of the hill region in north Hampshire are, in truth, very fine indeed. Mostly unwooded and without hedges, the green domes rise to impressive bigness at White Hill, Ladle Hill, and Beacon Hill in the direction of Kingsclere and Burghclere. In sweeps of wild and breezy uplands they continue over the county border to culminate in a little tongue of Berkshire at Walbury Beacon and Inkpen Hill, two eminences with nearly 1,000-feet elevations to mark almost the highest chalk in England. All the attractions of the high chalk belong to this line of downs, offering the joys and freedom of wide spaces, clear and bracing air, miles of springy turf, the open sky above, shy wild flowers below in the grass, with ever and always extensive panoramas that lead the eye beyond the foothills to the vales and far away. The big views visible at crowning points all along the ridge alone make these Hampshire heights memorable. They present true pictures of England's coloured counties. Beyond near fields, villages, and parklands, the Kennet valley traces a belt of rare luxuriance. Long distances over Berkshire, Wiltshire, and Buckinghamshire fade away to blue and purple horizons. The hills, too, carry many a sign of an antique tale. Earthworks, entrenchments, and tracks keep green the memories of unknown heroes, wandering tribes, early strife, and ancient man's mysterious performances. The Roman road, running from Silchester and mounting near White Hill, points straight as an arrow for Old Sarum. Seductive in decay, this remnant of conquest won and lost goes up and down, appropriately rising and declining over this county of Edward Gibbon's boyhood.

The downlands, continuing southwards, hold villages and hamlets rather sparsely placed. They cluster in their own particular combes, showing prettily against green banks. Tiled and thatched roofs, brickwork, and flint and white walls group around sturdy churches which often own Norman features, the proofs of long settlement. St. Mary Bourne and Hurstbourne Tarrant are two good and characteristic combinations of this kind of ensemble, both fresh and breezy places perched up beyond the noble trees and glades of Hurstbourne Priors park. Apart from all they offer to those who seek the delights of green hills and nature's shades, each village stands high in interest as well as elevation. The rare font of Tournai marble in St. Mary Bourne church is a wonderful creation, a worthy rival of the similar one in Winchester Cathedral. It is considered to be the biggest thing of the kind in England. That so small a place could make such large provision for babies eight hundred years ago must be a sad thought indeed for those who now deplore declining birthrates. In a beautiful setting Hurstbourne Tarrant introduces fame of another kind. William Cobbett loved this retreat. Tall and portly, and wearing "a scarlet broad-cloth waistcoat with the flaps of the pockets hanging down" in the style of a gentleman-farmer of the days of the Georges, the redoubtable Radical would ride in from the hills, enter the house with 1745 figured over the doorway tricked out in rubbed brickwork, and write descriptions of *Rural Rides* under the thatch. Later on, and in years remembered, Anna Lea Merrit passed in and out of the doorway. Under the same thatch she penned her observations on gardening, neighbours, homes, countryside, and intimate particulars of the quiet life, to delight readers of *A Hamlet in Old Hampshire*. In fact, the tracks of these two writers remind me of the peculiar rank belonging to Hampshire in the domain of books, and how this land of hills, valleys, and clear chalk streams seems to have been of the kind to inspire those who nobly enriched English literature. The catalogue of names and places in this connection is long and brilliant, one not easily to be matched elsewhere in such particulars as Charles Kingsley at Eversley, Jane Austen with *Pride and Prejudice* at Steventon and *Emma* finished at Chawton, John Keble's ministry at Hursley while the promise of *The Christian Year* was fulfilled, and Izaak Walton and Gilbert White perpetually shining in the

NEWBURY. The house of "Jack of Newbury", the famous clothier of the chapbook stories. Here, it was stated, he entertained Henry VIII and Catherine of Aragon.

SELBORNE, *from the Hanger. The hill, a feature in "The Natural History of Selborne," affords a good view over Gilbert White's village and home.*

crowd of the county's celebrities. Much more than the delights of scene can be gained by climbing the "zig-zag" at Selborne and viewing the village in the "sheltered vale, and running parallel to the Hanger," fragrant as ever with the spirit and charm of White's letters (124); while at Droxford, where Izaak fished and caught a wife, the joys of hillsides and flowing waters invite meditations on

> O the gallant Fisher's life,
> It is the best of any,

in *Piscator's* own "Hampshire, which I think exceeds all England for swift, shallow, clear, pleasant brooks, and store of Trouts."

The real and characteristic Hampshire extends from the northern barrier of chalk, stretching away in sweeps of rolling country to Winchester, the South Downs, and the coastal belt. Conspicuous hills here and there—Bury Hill (Upper Clatford), Danebury (Stockbridge), Tidbury Ring (Bullington), and Old Winchester Hill (Meon Stoke), to name but a few of them, carry the lines of earthworks and entrenchments belonging to far-off times. Through the valleys meander the streams, Meon, Itchen, and Test, lovely and fresh always, and beloved of fishermen long before and ever since Izaak Walton sported along them. Sparkling down from hilly birthplaces the clear waters reach the meadows,

> With here a blossom sailing,
> And here and there a lusty trout,
> And here and there a grayling.

Coursing and winding along, they swish past rushy banks, mills, and bridges, circle round village groups, greet quiet towns and King Alfred's city, ever singing and hurrying onward below smooth green slopes to the sea.

Over hill and dale go the old routes, ways that have been known and used throughout mankind's ages. The most ancient of them, the one trodden in due season by pilgrims journeying eastward from Winchester to the shrine at Canterbury, now serves modern needs. Yet by way of sentiment it preserves semblances of original form to show off ancestry. Those with an eye for country may still discover the tracks and yew trees round about Ovington (129). The Romans drove straight roads for communications with the galleys at Portus Magna (Porchester) and near landing-places. Other important ways over these Hampshire uplands served travellers of all degrees for time out of mind. The passage of years brought along an endless procession of people and vehicles; riders on horseback, strings of pack-horses heading for the coast, wagons rumbling slowly onward, coaches moving faster, flying machines speeding to the West through Abbots Ann and Middle Wallop or by Amport, with the accompaniments of highwaymen, footpads, and a perpetual throng that padded the hoof. Onward from the eleventh century crowds poured through Whitchurch and Andover to join more crowds bound for the great sheep sales, the bargainings, and the junketings of the October Weyhill Fair, always lively proceedings, the varied garb of which we gather from the descriptions by Will Langland, Cobbett, Thomas Hardy, and others who sought the famous institution during more than five hundred years. The royal road, coming down through Petersfield and skirting Butser Hill, ever and always bristled with the movements of kings and queens bound for or leaving Portsmouth; with the persons of naval gentlemen and sailors too, likewise Portsmouth minded, and possibly worried about ships, bulwarks, salty matters in general, or once, quite a long time ago, concerned with the first arrival of oranges in England, to be sent forward intact for the special devouring of Edward I's Queen. On sundry occasions royalty wisely tracked over the Hampshire chalk not very conspicuously, quite without the flourish of pomp and circumstance. Charles I, in flight to Place House, Titchfield, found a prison at Carisbrooke (132, 143). The Martyr's son, travelling dangerously after the battle of Worcester, reached Broad Halfpenny Down by devious ways in 1651, and, leaving the down ninety-nine years before Nyren made it the cradle of cricket, hastened on to the coal-boat at Brighton bound for Fécamp. Soon afterwards the Duke of Monmouth followed another direction. The fugitive from Sedgemoor proceeded from Ringwood to Tower Hill and the block.

Traverse it where you will, or even merely study the colouring of the map, this Hampshire is a particularly green county, both on and off the chalk lands. The extensive remains of forests, woods big and little, many luxuriant parks, and splendid trees among the fields and hedgerows show man's plantings and cultivation harmoniously combined with Nature's pristine forms in verdant landscapes. Scenes of pure, simple beauty, ever pleasing yet not too extravagantly schemed for human nature's daily fare, offer to worldly mortals just the type of environment for the "life more sweet than that of painted pomp." Certainly the two-legged species, always on the lookout for a good thing, never failed from earliest times to realize how agreeable this fair green country might be to abide in. Hampshire therefore carries a friendly air. The woody landscapes look sociable, dotted abundantly with old and new signs of hearth and home. The earlier touches of homeliness, in no wise connected with the later crop of villas, emphasize a long and constant settlement. They present a running commentary on domestic events, ways of life, and history, to be gleaned by pleasantly jogging along highways and byways and seeing many primitive earthworks, Romano-British Silchester, tessellated pavements at North Warnborough, Thruxton, and Abbots Ann, Saxon relics at Corhampton and Little Somborne, Norman monuments in parishes beyond reckoning, dwellings for people great and small in every developed style of architecture, numerous and remarkable parks and places, village homes, quiet towns of age and attraction, and Winchester itself a symbol of both the intimate and the national English story.

These things, with many more, tell how generation after generation favoured this green and wooded region.

And it is this generous green quality, pervading almost everywhere, that perhaps most of all still characterizes the Hampshire acres and colours the pictures. Trees in plenty, woods close together and many, and wide areas of old forest land also can send the mind wandering through the vistas of time to primeval scenes, dense and wild as they were thousands of years before clearing and planting happened. There lived the men who left their marks in the shaped flints garnered from the chalk, discovered at Barton Stacey, Froxfield, Liss, and scores of other places. Wood names, often pretty and suggestive, and the word "forest" in use, carry the twang of ancient custom, of things remembered. They localize old haunts of boars and wolves, harts and hinds, foresters, king after king on the hunt, queens shooting proverbial stags, and facts and fancies of a misty "Merrie England." Names tell of highwaymen's hiding-places. They label points where people got lost, as Pepys did in 1662, and direct to districts where the forest laws operated by cruelly dealing out death or the loss of both eyes to hapless stealers caught killing the hart or the boar. And nice quiet spots, aptly named, seem to have been favoured by countless village Robin Hoods and Maid Marions who early and late, both in time o' day and generation, slyly sought solitude in dappled shades under greenwood trees.

Over by Andover, Harewood Forest yet makes a pleasant green stretch, though when I was there in wartime a young Scot wandering about from an adjacent camp plainly told me of the dullness of trees compared with the beauties of Glasgow. Woolmer Forest, on the opposite side of the county, at least by name gives a reminder of royal favour and kingly hunting feats. Never wooded, it was for centuries a forest in the original meaning of the word: that is, a place for sport but not necessarily of trees. The Plantagenet Edward II spent far too much time in this royal playground, preferring the chase to affairs of State. In a more sedate reign Queen Anne reclined on a damp bank specially levelled to receive her comfortable person, and "with great complacency and satisfaction" reviewed about five hundred red deer on parade in the vale. Thus christening the spot Queen's Bank, she resumed her way on the Portsmouth Road. The end of Woolmer's deer is told in the well-known Letter VI by Gilbert White. The royal huntsmen, gorgeous in scarlet and gold, arrived with the stag-hounds. Horns sounded. Away went hounds and horses. The deer were rounded up for inglorious departure in carts to Windsor.

Southward from Woolmer the little Meon stream, springing to life near East Meon, winds down the valley enclosed by chalk hills. The slopes, rich in trees, are crowned with hanging woods, the "hangers" of Hampshire. The gracious lines of landscape sweeping upwards, patterns of colour, picturesque villages down from West Meon to Wickham, and always the windings of the stream in the meadows, make this region one of enchantment, a scenic prize of its own fair county. The green array continues over the hills to meet the considerable Forest of Bere, a splendid panoramic stretch to be seen particularly well, and most gloriously in autumn, from the height of Ports Down at the head of Portsmouth Harbour.

Narrow lanes, often hollow and with trees meeting overhead, wind up to remote tracks, paths, and almost untrodden ways where Nature reigns and "many a flower is born to blush unseen." Here are offered quiet and sweet content to anyone in search of these out-of-date desires. Actually the seeker unacquainted with the routes—round about Old Winchester Hill or on the opposite Meon heights, for example—quite likely may get lost and be reduced to the ignominy of searching for a good Samaritan to save the situation, always a trial to the spirit of the true and independent wayfarer. Such circumstances may introduce one of the breed of local natives, and in this fashion:

"Good morning. Am I right for so-and-so?"

"Ya."

"Straight on?"

"Na."

"Which way is it please?"

"Left"

"Any more turns to the right or left?"

"Borth."

After which terseness on left, right, left, the orator may have disappeared round the corner without waiting for, "Thank you. Good day."

My one experience of this economical style of speech happened because I ran off my section of Ordnance map while temporarily camped with Hampshire relatives. On repeating the monosyllabic passage to my cousin she bubbled up with excitement, for Margaret, though modern in the sense of fox-trot and Bradley, is also a dab on such matters as natives, Gothic, and earthworks.

"Why," she cried enthusiastically, "you have been talking to a Jute!"

"A what?" I queried.

"A Jute. You know what that is."

"The only Jute I've heard of comes from Dundee," I replied. "Sacking sort of stuff—in bulk, not mono."

"Don't be ridiculous," she returned disapprovingly. "This curious stock in the Meon valley is supposed to have descended from the Jutes. A whole lot of Jutish burial mounds were discovered at Droxford village, which you must have come through. And being a fisherman, I suppose you know all about Izaak Walton spooning with Anne Hawkins at the rectory there?"

"But these Jutes," I went on, keeping to the main question, "are all of them like the one I met?"

"That I cannot say," she said. "Everybody thinks them rather curious, both in looks and manner, quite different from us true-blue Hampshires."

THE PILGRIMS' WAY in Hampshire. The track between Ovington and Bishop's Sutton.

SYDNEY R. JONES

Sydney R. Jones

WINCHESTER. *The Cathedral rises over the city of King Alfred, the ancient capital of England. The buildings and towers of William of Wykeham's famous College show beyond the ruins of Wolvesey Palace at the left. Picturesque architecture abounds in streets and byways. High Street, seen at the right of the picture, mounts up from King Alfred's statue to the West Gate and Castle.*

TITCHFIELD. *Place House before restoration. This ruined home of the Earls of Southampton, made on the site of the abbey after the Reformation, recalls Shakespeare, The Sonnets, and the last hours of freedom of Charles I.*

WICKHAM. *Old houses in William of Wykeham's birthplace.*

So it seemed that perhaps I had chanced on a descendant of the marauders who plundered these parts quite early in A.D., who with customary campaigning technique made up to the local girls, produced the goods for succession, and thereby secured a continuance of peculiarities imported from the fatherland, including the mono-staccato in speech.

The New Forest, stretching from Southampton Water almost to Dorset, of course presents the climax in Hampshire forest scenery. The trees, glades, heaths, and wild open spaces still preserve the character of a forest, look like the real thing in this area of more than a hundred square miles, scarcely changed in boundaries for over six hundred years. Open-air joys without end are offered by miles of fern, gorse, and heather; under thick leafage where sunlight hardly penetrates; on plains and heaths where forest ponies roam; and at such heights as Pipers Wait and Bramble Hill, from which panoramas extend magnificently. The Forest's old lineage meets to-day with the oaks of Boldrewood and Knightwood, hundreds of yews at Sloden, beeches at Mark Ash and Ridley Wood, in thorn and holly everywhere. Ancestral and almost unchanged retreats serve squirrels, foxes, badgers, weasels, snakes, otters, and other quick and moving creatures. The magic of environment stirs substance of the bygone English tale, rouses the lively decorations of past huntings, exhilarating moments, and deeds good and bad done in the light or under dark shades. At any moment the forest time may swing back suddenly, sending the vivid hour into the realm of long ago, maybe at the sight of an earthwork or a barrow (there are many on Beaulieu Heath and Bratley Plain), on reaching a hamlet clearing centuries old; or with hearing "swainmote," "pannage," "estovers," and other words of the ancient forest laws still in use. This linking of the then and the now ever adds fascination to the loveliness seen in William the Conqueror's hunting ground.

In spite of the Forest's great favour with a populated, petrol age, it manages to keep this knack of signifying past event in present charm. I well recall one evening when we made the way through Cadnam for Canterton Glen and the Rufus Stone. It was the perfect evening hour. The late sunlight warmed foliage to broad masses of glowing colour and deepened the shadows. We left the car, walked forward, and reached the slope. Nobody was in sight. Birds singing vesper hymns and quick rustles in the undergrowth made by little moving things startled at our footsteps were the only sounds heard. We reached the bottom of the dip where the Stone is. It needed little from imagination to re-form the famous story—the hunting, the retainers, the horrid look of red-faced Rufus, the glancing arrow, the fall, the body thrown into a cart bound for Winchester, and whether it be true or not, Tyrrel hastening away towards the ford over the Avon below Ringwood. On the iron pillar we read the date, "the 2nd day of August, anno 1100." Soon the afterglow tinted the sky. The Forest, still, beautiful, and shrouding its secrets, settled down to sleep.

Favourable and friendly Hampshire is naturally a county of homes. Famous mansions in fine parks, houses, and cottages sustain the evidences of domestic life through times very old, oldish, and recent. Embattlements over the moat at Beaurepaire, Tudor outlines of The Vyne at Sherborne St. John, brick and stone at Bramshill, the dignity of numerous Queen Anne and Georgian fronts, Laverstoke's 1798 classicism, castellated Highclere in nineteenth-century pose, manor-houses at Linkenholt, West Tisted, East Meon, and elsewhere by the score peeping out from village trees—these, with many more emblems of home, convey a sequence in the development of the Englishman's castle, house-place, and hearth. They also mark connections with famous names: Stratfield Saye with Wellington, Embley Park with Florence Nightingale, Tichborne with the Tichbornes, and so on almost indefinitely. Of the wonderful parks, several have been said to be the most beautiful in southern England; Cobbett fancied Highclere, and Charles Kingsley loved Hurstbourne Priors best, gracious as ever to-day and rich with Sir Isaac Newton associations. Here and there ruined places jog memories. Beaulieu Abbey is a Cistercian dreamland. The stone walls and towers of Place House, Titchfield (132), now well cared for after years of neglect, stimulate fantasies that weave the threads of the past over the young Earl of Southampton, Shakespeare, the Sonnets,

> And beauty making beautiful old rime
> In praise of Ladies dead and lovely Knights.

The wreck of Old Basing is a shrine of artists, recalling Inigo Jones, Wenceslaus Hollar, Faithorne, and others who served under Robert Peake, England's first architectural publisher, in one of the most thrilling sieges of all wars. Nor can the recent be long out of mind in this district, where new houses continue to crowd in. Many of these efforts are nasty to look at, but some are nice. Homes of character have been contributed by a number of architects, including Marsh Court, Stockbridge, by Sir Edwin Lutyens, and good work round Petersfield by the Unsworths. The noble owner of Freefolk also has demonstrated that "Portal" houses can enhance and blend with their settings (137).

Hampshire is particularly distinguished by the quality of the smaller towns. Many of them are excellent examples of these units that add so much to the make-up of the English scene. Streets and byways wide and narrow, curious old churches and buildings, Georgian house-fronts galore, pleasant colour and fineness in brickwork, and trees lining pavements or making backgrounds, help to communicate an air of serenity to these country centres that appear to amble placidly in this hurrying, bustling age. The general look is just right for Jane Austen's homeland. Peeping through window-panes framed in light paint one even might expect to see pretty creatures drinking "tee" from cups without handles or juveniles making samplers! That, at least, is the idea Odiham brings to me; and through a window hereabout I once actually did see Mr. Campbell

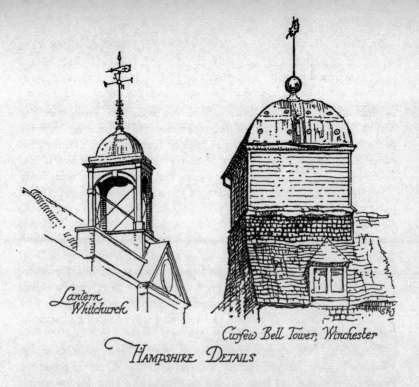

Lantern
Whitchurch

Curfew Bell Tower, Winchester

HAMPSHIRE DETAILS

Taylor painting one of those charming interiors in which he excels. This little town, one of the most attractive, has plenty of windows and doorways set in brickwork of old pattern, timbered houses as well, and castle ruins, almshouses, an inn appropriately dedicated to St. George, and a big old church with brasses and galleries inside it, all keeping alive past years. Or down by the coast there is Titchfield, where Charles I spent his last day of freedom—sleepy old Titchfield, which few people seem to find, dreaming away the hours among relics of bygone fame. Other good representatives of the choice collection are Whitchurch lying in a cup of the uplands, Alton once lived in by Edmund Spenser, Stockbridge with capital houses in the main street, Petersfield grouped round the square and "The Spain," William of Wykeham's Bishop's Waltham, Fareham at the head of its creek, Fordingbridge and Ringwood on the Avon where the river runs down off the chalk, and Lymington by the sea, of faded navy days and Southey's last home. And for treasures of domestic building and church splendour, what more could be desired than Romsey, ranged round the abbey as big as a cathedral, or Christchurch town, nestling under the walls of the priory in the green spot between the Avon and Stour rivers? (149).

The villages in pretty settings rather feature the towns, present the architectural family likeness of their larger neighbours in good brickwork, chimneys with moulded caps, tiled roofs, and timber construction. Substantial houses of big-wigs and middling village personages, variously shaped Tudorish, gabled,

135

classic, or Georgian, and set in well-favoured gardens, sometimes tempt strangers to break the first item and perhaps the second of the tenth Commandment. Homes of the smaller folk and cottagers, too, may arouse feelings of admiration, if not of envy, in those who appreciate these products of past humble life. In the eastern part of Hampshire, from the Berkshire border down to the Petersfield direction, the general character of the villages is similar to that common in the adjoining counties of Surrey and Sussex, seventeenth- and eighteenth-century refinements being a good deal mixed in traditional forms of earlier building. These combinations of features invite discoverers of good pictures to potter in almost every place, so I do no more than mention the neighbourhoods of Steep, Newton Valence, Selborne with the limes and butcher's shop old enough to have provided Gilbert White with rations, North and South Warnborough, Greywell, with a note of emphasis on Upton Grey, for years the home of Charles Holme, founder and first editor of *The Studio*, who cherished his village possession (137). More to the west, where the chalk uplands lead down to the coast, the common family likeness in villages persists. But here, at Wickham for instance, the discerning will trace less sophistication and stronger agricultural influences (132).

The rolling chalk country comprising so much of Hampshire shows off villages of a particular type, homely, indigenous to the soil, neither proud nor flaunting grand airs, yet none the less captivating. Looking demure against green backgrounds they can—as other sly things do—ever and again bewitch an enthusiast to stop a car, jump off a bicycle, or otherwise halt to look twice, or perhaps thrice, at really pretty pictures of the village graces of England, "how beautiful they stand," and so on. These country homes, with deep thatched roofs ending at eaves bulging out over white and timbered walls, make pictures from all sorts of likely and unexpected angles. Wattle-and-daub surfaces and the frequent glint of flintwork denote the local products of chalk country used by ancient forefathers. The bright and traditional effects delight onlookers, who come from near and far to see them. Others gaze sadly at these relics of age, and being short of mathematical straight lines, prefabrication, damp-courses, and modern conveniences, they continually incense authorities and windy wiseacres on housing reform, who would like to knock them down. Mercifully I was able to write these words in one of them, a survivor so far, and to write in remarkable comfort, too, beside an ample window much too small to comply with the by-laws, with a very low ceiling overhead ditto, though quite high enough for me! Some of the villages from dozens worth seeing are the four Wallops — Over, Middle, Nether, and Farleigh (mighty beings in Hampshire were the Wallop family), Amport and Monxton, Upper Clatford, Hursley, and Longparish—really long with about two miles of it.

Nor must Wherwell, called "Whorrell," be forgotten, the high-light of them all, famed in and out of its county (9). Wise friends often have told me

UPTON GREY *1906*. *Charles Holme's old cottages.*

FREEFOLK *1944*. *Lord Portal's new cottages.*

SOUTHAMPTON. *The George V graving dock in construction, November 1932. Early morning from the altars.*

that it is the prettiest village in Hampshire, though this is a rash claim to make for any village in any English county. Certainly Wherwell merits choice reputation, beautifully placed in the wide Test valley against high beech woods, the stream in the meadows for neighbour, and distant uplands visible over Winchester way. Cottages with white faces and coiffures of thatch invite down the hill to the temporal centre, marked by a decayed elm of enormous girth. Up the hill the children go, merrily bound for the school just over the crest. Other little faces and bits of Gothic stone show curiously on some of the house walls. These relate to the lost priory founded in Saxon years by Queen Elfrida after the convenient murder of her stepson, Edward the Martyr, at Corfe Castle in 978. Of course Henry VIII noted the priory at the Dissolution, hence the little faces aforementioned. But Wherwell bears more than the blazon of age and beauty. It keeps abreast of the times. Clad in white like an angel for purity (of beer), the pub sports the sign of "The 20th Century." Other visible evidences point to present sociability and friendliness. Even when I began sketching, a cat immediately offered welcome by purring round my legs and ignored all inducements to depart. Ladies passing by did not eye an artist capturing their preserves nearly so unfavourably as I have known them to do elsewhere. I noticed also that the immaculate cut of their slacks had the style of London west. Perhaps Wherwell has been discovered?

Of the coast, to which my rural meanderings with pen and pencil now lead me, little need be told. The watery outline that has influenced much of the Hampshire story for more than two thousand years is widely known, all the way from Hayling Island to Poole Bay. Therefore it is beyond my purpose to linger in these coastal scenes or to enlarge on such facts of common knowledge as are connected with Roman and Norman Porchester, Portsmouth and Southampton, Pilgrim Fathers, Nelson's *Victory*, Buckler's Hard building ships of New Forest oak for Trafalgar, Charles Stuart's prison of Hurst Castle on the mud flats, and arrivals and departures of a host of royal and famous personages who landed or embarked for good, indifferent, sinister, and aggressive purposes, some of them very seasick or about to be so. Nor need I dwell on the fresh brightness of the New Forest coastal belt, little craft on the Hamble River, Early English poise at Netley Abbey, Georgian charm at Lymington, impressions of Portsmouth Harbour from W. L. Wyllie's Tower House, the view of The Needles from Hengistbury Head, Osborne seen from Lee Point. It also would be futile to attempt one new word on the popularities of Southsea, Bournemouth, and smaller resorts, on the attractions of the piers, bands, and numerous contrivances for the relief and production of human boredom, or to dilate on secluded spots I used to know that now own villas, bungalows, and the curious erections of a new primitive civilization whose presence some people like and others do not.

I may just add that the Isle of Wight, continuously visible over the water except when blotted out by climatic vagaries, is delicious enough to compare with the original mentioned in Genesis ii. 8. It should be gained and explored by all who wish to sample the kind of haven they hope to reach on quitting this troubled world. This kingdom in miniature is concentrated essence of many good things, of downs, vales, woods, fertile lands, and chines, cliffs, and bays by the sea. It has a smiling eastern face featured with popular resorts for gregarious mankind. And there is the western half—my own choice—rare in rural beauty, solitudes, and wide open spaces leading to seaward distances. The inhabitants are genial and kind; and although I have been glared at for sketching where I ought not to have been, the offer of a glass of choice sherry also has come for doing just the same thing. Signs of the times, from Roman Brading to Victorian Osborne and yachts, touch and tumble down all the ages of history. Saxon and medieval churches, Carisbrooke Castle very wonderful (143), manor-houses tucked out of the way as at Kingston, Woolverton and Merstone, Yarmouth and Newport with quaint buildings and harbours, Calbourne, Shalfleet, Arreton, and Godshill (144) for villages and thatched roofs, St. Boniface Down rising to nearly 800 feet, and much else to allure, make this island "Paradise enow" in the living present, a veritable Garden of Eden for to-day.

But Hampshire, my recollections remind me, is keeping the English tale right up to date. Therefore, having dwelt mostly on old things, I will in conclusion touch on a new one, a mighty emblem of the twentieth century. It is the King George V Graving Dock, the wonder that has arisen beyond the medieval walls, gates, churches, and houses of old fame in the port used by Romans, King Alfred, Crusaders, soldiers of Crécy and Agincourt, and pioneers who sailed in *The Mayflower* to found a New England. This new triumph joins to-day with the past. It is a fresh manifestation of the far-flung enterprise that has made Southampton's name glorious for centuries.

I became quite friendly with this Dock because it was my job to picture the birth and rise to maturity during all the misbehaviours and excitements of its growing up. And in those two years of construction I saw the development of an idea born of the spirit of the times: a monument gradually reached a final stature truly significant of this era of big conceptions, huge organization, and massed effort. The creation represented the daring feats and achievements of Civil Engineering, now one of the most potent forces in the world.

This dry dock, commenced in 1931, had been planned the largest ever contemplated, a giant cradle for giant ships, notably the *Queen Mary* then building. The construction was to cover the vast area of more than double the length of the near Gothic monument at Winchester and almost twice that cathedral nave's width. In two years the Dock had to be finished. Under a summer sun the conquest of earth and water began. Battalions of machines and an army of men pressed forward the attack. Without ceasing by day or night, in daylight and arc-light the work proceeded. Steam navvies shifted mountains of earth. Upward, down, and around swung dozens of cranes. Engines puffed about everywhere, bumping lines of wagons along, and in almost no time new railway tracks appeared on excavated ground. Giant machines pounded and throbbed, washing gravel and mixing cement delivered daily in trainloads from Kent. Electric pumps, never stopping, kept the constant menace of water at bay. The noise of it all in most elevated moments sounded like a barrage in modern war, or might have issued from a gang of cyclops settling their differences with monstrous implements. With slow yet irresistible haste raw materials were turned to their many uses. Order developed from apparent chaos with precision and regularity almost uncanny. The massive concrete walls rose higher and higher from the wide and deep trenches. Fleeting days and nights brought the dock floor to completion. The caisson chamber became an instrument to hold back the tides, and chambers for pumps and constructions to serve all kinds of purposes took shape and place while the growing months of this marvellous Dock sped along. For behind this wonder of work, ever watchful and guiding it, were the engineers and contractors, wizards whose jugglings with natural forces and materials would have been traced to the black arts and witches' cauldrons in the good old days. Their details of organization, calculations, and blue-prints, of water pumped out, mud and earth removed, concrete put in, granite dressed, iron fixed, machinery used, and railway tracks laid, ran to data and figures far too bewildering for the grasp of ordinary mortals liable to headaches and worse at the mere sight of logarithms, cross-sections, magnetos, and cog-wheels.

During these happenings at Southampton I sought and noted impressions amid all the noise, dirt, and flying dust; stood in water, on high draughty places, in the sun and the rain, at dawn and sunset, sometimes splashed with concrete dripped from huge buckets swung by derricks, or just missed by trains shooting by. But always the immensity of the work as a whole dominated the mind. It dwarfed the details, and seemed to reduce the human multitudes to no more than swarms of busy ants. Grand effects developed with the concentrations of energy, movement, and massed bulk on the big scale. Under the ground there was the mystery of cloisters and crypts in great caverns arched and vaulted. When sunlight lit the bright dock walls or dawn and evening shades lowered tones to silhouettes, this enormous work for commerce might have been a castle in the air, a temple, or a cathedral in the making for the glory of a Rameses, a Cæsar, or Christendom. But no; history had never known such a feat as this. It represented the twentieth century, animated, enterprising, furnishing its own monument in the mood of the times (138).

At last the promised days came. The long, tall walls ended at the final height. Floated in from the sea, the caisson rested in its chamber, ready for opening or closing the Dock. Pumps and machinery were in position. Momentous tests revealed neither fault not weakness. All things were perfect. The work was finished.

On a cloudless day in July 1933, a new throng assembled at the Dock. Thousands and thousands of people, bright summer frocks, decorated stands, and coloured banners, made a gay and animated spectacle round this great effort in concrete. At the expected moment the Royal yacht slowly approached from the sea, with the Royal Standard on the main mast. The prow broke the red, white, and blue ribbon across the dock entrance. Cheer upon cheer rang out, and hands, flags, and handkerchiefs waved on every side. King George V and Queen Mary landed. The vast assembly stood in silence while the band of the Royal Air Force played the National Anthem. Then the crowds cheered again. The Royal visitors passed to the dais, the King declared the Dock's name, the Queen poured Empire wine into the water bedecked with flowers, and in a grand moment thousands of voices sang "All people that on earth do dwell." Following the tremendous finale of "God save our gracious King" and cheering and cheering resounding, the King George V Graving Dock, named and christened, was ready to serve.

For me, at least, the completion of the Dock brought certain regrets. My crawlings in mud and water, sunlit days on concrete blocks, hairbreadth escapes from sudden accidents, chances of pencils and rubbers blowing away or drowning, and perpetual offers of the cups of tea beloved of all true engineers—these things were no more. The impressive moments, the romantic scenes of construction, and all those marvels of creation exhibited by Civil Engineering vanished for ever with the work finished. Neatly smoothed and furbished, the Dock looked no more than a gigantic bath, a huge tub ready for a Polyphemus to wash in! My only reminder of this lost magnificence of modern work in progress is a gracious note of appreciation from His Majesty for my small connection with the great Dock at Southampton.

WINCHESTER AND SALISBURY

The two cathedral cities of Winchester and Salisbury, each neighboured by downs and watered by clear streams, adorn the chalk country.

Winchester! How the lights and shades of the English tale seem to vibrate again at the thought of the name! This capital of Hampshire is truly a landmark of history and to-day, set in the vale where the rounded chalk hills curve down to the Itchen river. Patterned with old years, rich in a heritage dating far back to remote antiquity, occupying the site of the most important British settlement in southern England, a lost Roman centre, once the seat of Saxon kings, the cradle of moving events for centuries after the Conqueror built his palace there, and glorious with the longest cathedral in the land, the city stands as an emblem, an epitome, of the ideals and circumstances that made England and its people.

No English city is more interesting than Winchester. Its crowded past recalls the country's capital before London gained first place. It held the Saxon shrine

CARISBROOKE CASTLE. *The outer entrance
and fourteenth-century barbican leading to
the prison of Charles I, and the ruins of
the notable shell-keep on a Norman mound.*

GODSHILL, one of the pretty villages on the Isle of Wight, with thatched cottages grouped round the fifteenth-century church.

of St. Swithin. Here scribes penned the *Anglo-Saxon Chronicle*. Pilgrims thronged the streets, streets along which on a day in 1100 a cart carried the hated body of Rufus, dead with an arrow in the breast, for burial without prayer or hope in the cathedral—a profanity, so the legend runs, followed by the collapse of Bishop Walkelin's central tower. At Winchester treaties were made. Plantagenet kings sat at court in the great hall of the castle amidst medieval pageantry and colour. William of Wykham's acts at the cathedral and the college contrasted with the deeds of Cromwell's men who smashed wonderful treasures untold. Above all reigns the memory of King Alfred, king Great in name and deed, whose dust rests in this vale in a grave unknown.

And no city excels Winchester for beauty. Thriving and busy, it presents sights to delight the eye and impel the fancy. The great cathedral, goal of pilgrims ancient and modern, of course ranks first. It merits setting out from the uttermost ends of the earth in order to enter the interior, stand in front of the central west door, and look eastward and upward at the longest nave in Europe. Thus is viewed an expression of exalted stateliness, a triumphant rendering of thought and harmony in stonework unparalleled. Immense Norman piers, clothed in a later grace of crowded shafts and mouldings, mark out bay after bay to the far distance. Arches succeeding arches lead up to the pattern and enrichment of spandrel, triforium, and clerestory. Slender shafts sweep high to foliated capitals, and the vault, crowning the grandeur with curves of fretted ribs and carved bosses, extends unbroken and majestically from west to east. Perfect balance, true scale, aerial grace, rhythm and poise, the tints of stone, bright harmonies and deep shades cast by light glinting down, and the spirited craftwork everywhere, perfectly unite in this sublime achievement of cathedral building. This temple of high purpose is a shrine of the men who created it with loving care and devotion. And it is the great monument of William of Wykeham.

When William was born in 1324 at Wickham, a village some miles to the south of Winchester, his parents could never have dreamed of the eminence which destiny held in store for their son. For Sibill and John Long occupied a lowly station in this world's concerns, though it proved to be one of those obscure nesting-places so often selected by genius for hatching its offspring. Evidently William developed into the bright boy of the village, for his youthful promise attracted notice. Men of consequence provided the means for his education at the prior's school in Winchester. This kind act gave the boy his chance in life. He improved the shining hours of school days, then served a period of employment at Winchester Castle, and entered the royal service at about twenty-three years of age. Progressing rapidly, he subsequently became the great man of the land now remembered as the confidant of Edward III and Richard II, Chancellor of England, Bishop of Winchester, founder of Winchester College and of New College, Oxford. The prosperity, courtly influence, and wealth that he commanded moved his contemporary, Froissart, to declare "he reigned in England." He lived near his first home in a stately palace, largely built by himself, at Bishop's Waltham, where former splendour and scenes can still be imagined among ruins. But the man of fame never forgot the patrons who first encouraged his talents. To his last day on earth, in the year 1404, he kept green the memory of the benefactors that helped the village boy William to become the illustrious William of Wykeham.

This remarkable man, accomplished, rich, favoured by kings, and living within the conditions of medieval England, had ample opportunities to forward his purposes and heart's desires. That he aimed high is told by the records of his life, his many works and foundations, and pre-eminently by the grand interior that shows so nobly from the western end of Winchester Cathedral. These evidences point to a beneficent nature, lofty ideals, refined taste, and great enthusiasm for building. Good fortune attended his years. He lived and served through the reigns of Edward III and Richard II, two of England's most artistic monarchs. It was the age of Chaucer, pageantry, chivalry, and holy zeal, even though shadowed by the Black Death. The social background was favourable. Hand work and individual effort characterized the period. Men and women, from the highest to the lowly, practised domestic crafts and accomplishments. Things of use, fashioned and constructed beautifully, as is obvious to this day, increased in number for the purposes of the daily round. Artistry, previously the claim of the few, began to pulse through the veins of the nation; rising from traditions planted in the past, it was generally and normally expressed, became an impulse that painted the country's story bright for more than two hundred years.

In the sphere of building great leaders strode the land. Employers and men of distinction, including kings, nobles, William of Wykeham, and Chaucer, possessed good abilities to direct schemes which they controlled. Yet more important were the talented and skilled master-craftsmen, inspired thinkers of their age. Ably qualified, they guided the bodies of workers engaged on building operations. The golden autumn of the Gothic time thus developed from a combination of the many working in harmony for common ends. Then the crafts were strong and vital. Patrons, masters, and tradesmen happened to act in unison for the creation of loveliness. All was not honey of course. Then, as now, the ambient air whiffled over pay and hours. Working times, which extended from sunrise to sunset in summer and winter, did not suit everyone. Skilled masons sometimes grumbled over their pay of 7d. a day. Fines and chastisement descended for slacking, lack of discipline and absenteeism (not so politely named in the 1300's). But the heritage of the fourteenth century tells its own tale of striving and high endeavour. Triumphant building developed afresh as a glorious phase of Gothic art rose in splendour, inspired by such geniuses as Henry Yevele and William Wynford, the master-masons of Canterbury and Winchester naves, and Hugh Herland, the master-carpenter of Westminster Hall roof. This glitter of accomplishment shone in a brilliant act, one that sprang from antique mists to sparkle in new maturity. A hundred years later destiny's stage management prepared to ring down the curtain on the artistic lights and shades of the Middle Ages.

Favoured by time, circumstance, and his own endowments of taste and enthusiasm, William of Wykeham had the further advantage of professional knowledge gained during years of experience as clerk and surveyor of royal works at Windsor Castle and many other places. Enthroned at Winchester in July 1368 and appointed Chancellor of England in the September following, he rose to the pinnacle of his career. With renewed keenness he soon turned to fresh schemes of building. And though he was forced to resign the Great Seal in 1371, the consequent relief from statesmanship enabled him to pursue with vigour the founding of colleges and improvements at the cathedral. His predecessor, Bishop Edington, had devised projects for Winchester, but little actual progress had been made. From these beginnings the new bishop developed a large and magnificent conception, one that dictated almost recasting the old fabric. The type of building that awaited this transformation is still shown by the north and south transepts, massive and strong with arches, masonry, and features all in the Norman manner. On such a basis William of Wykeham and his fraternity began their work. The lower series of round arches between the nave piers were removed and single pointed arches were built to sweep up to the triforium in each bay; the immense and closely spaced Norman piers—they yet remain—blossomed anew with outer casings delicately wrought in Caen stone; high, slender shafts mounted to the clerestory; and over all, in place of wooden ceilings, the wonderful vault of stone curved into rich and intricate patterns. Ten years of endeavour advanced with precision and order accomplished the change. The Norman nave had become the lofty rendering of Perpendicular architecture, a masterpiece of English art.

In other particulars this sacred building, massive outside, of extreme length, and capped by an unimpressive tower, is a veritable treasure-house within. Medieval craftsmanship constantly impels admiration. The Romanesque font, early choir stalls, the famous iron grille of pilgrim days, and Cardinal Beaufort's stone reredos are but a few of the notable features. And the range of chantries and tombs in and adjoining the twelfth-century retro-choir give cause for wonder that human hands could reach to such achievement. Screens and canopies, panelling, tracery, pattern, and the overflowing riches of the lost golden age perpetuate the names of Beaufort, Waynfleete, Fox, and other men who worthily carried forward the traditions of the master.

In the fifth bay of the nave, and beneath his own stone vault, is the tomb of the master himself, William of Wykeham. The effigy rests in the chantry of lofty perpendicular lines and carved canopies and pinnacles, a fit framework

Figures thought to represent William of Wykeham's Master Mason, Master Carpenter, and Clerk of the Works: in the Wykeham Chantry, Winchester.

to guard this symbol of immortality. The fine figure tells of the work of its own fine period. It lies at full length in bishop's robes, angels support the head, and three curious little men sit in a row at the feet. The repose of the figure, features calm and noble, hands uplifted, and the dignity of stone around, prompt the thought that here this benefactor of mankind, forgetful of calumny suffered and encircled by the fruits of his exalted mind, sleeps well and serene after life's full journey. Near to him, not dead but living, his motto for his college and the world stands out clear and true, "Manners makyth man."

I like to muse on those three little men seated in a row at the feet of William of Wykeham's monument. They have funny faces and tonsures crown their heads. With hands together all appear to be at prayer. Maybe they represent the three monks who were to say masses three times a day for the bishop's soul. Tradition also labels them as William of Wykeham's clerk of works, master-mason, and master-carpenter. The truth, of course, nobody knows, for the very learned are querulous folk. Face to face with these faces, even though they be funny, I deliberately prefer to cast all doubts aside and to see in them the very likenesses of three in the company of men that in the golden age did not depend on the pay-packet for a higher standard of living, but worked for the good of mankind and to the glory of God without thought of name or fame, yet for ever known by their deeds. Then, in looking along and upward at the nave, the little human images seem to unite with the nobleness visible and arching away to join earth to heaven. I illustrate the three little men. The nave I have not attempted. The majesty of it is beyond the scope of representation. It is a treasure to be seen, meditated on, and retained in the mind. All who do not know this wonder in stone and value the highest in human effort should hie to Winchester before the last trump sounds, which may be very soon—who knows?

Outside in the close the cathedral homes group choicely, neighboured by gardens, lawns, lime trees, and the site of the cloisters now gone. Houses of all sorts of dates present a prime collection of stone, timbering and brickwork,

CHRISTCHURCH. *The rare town with the Priory, famous for Norman work and a splendid interior, occupies the green spot between the River Stour and the Hampshire Avon.*

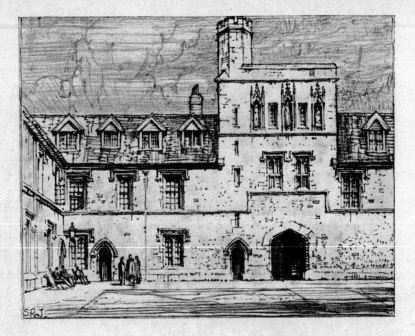

WINCHESTER. *Medieval masonry in Chamber Court of William of Wykeham's renowned College. The West Gate leading to High Street, and near to the Castle known to many Kings of England.*

arches, gables, cornices, and chaste doorways. They speak volumes, not only of building but of a sequence of domestic and human episodes concerned with the doings of ecclesiastics variously powerful, active, contemplative, learned, or dull, and wives and families who surely doted on such callers as Izaak Walton, Jane Austen, and Anthony Trollope while unhurried years passed along from century to century. Now and again the usual serene atmosphere quivered to the stir of big events. On a summer's day Philip of Spain entered one of the doorways, finding handy quarters for his marriage with Mary Tudor in the cathedral on the morrow. Nearly a hundred years later heavy treads resounded past the houses and through the close. Cromwell's men appeared, eager to destroy shrines, statues, and old painted glass. Few sacred buildings suffered more terribly than Winchester Cathedral in the Civil War.

More treasures of this wonderful city extend on every side beyond the gates of the close. Near to the ruins of Wolvesey Palace and the Wren buildings, the walls of William of Wykeham's college, ranging from the fourteenth to the twentieth centuries, symbolize the spirit of permanent things and of a founder's message that has spread to the ends of the earth (150). Riverwards, again, the Hospital of St. Cross nestles in the meadows. Here, since 1133, has been upheld the pious cause of charity in care for the aged; and for eight centuries past way-farers have received free bread and beer, both in times when it was needed and even now when it isn't. But St. Cross never failed in its trust, nor in beauty, for the group of Cardinal Beaufort's quadrangle and hall facing the late Norman church hardly could be surpassed.

At a distance from this tranquillity, and in the opposite direction, the colour of Winchester's coat changes. The narrow ways north of the cathedral close, lined with jumbles of buildings bearing the shapes and bumps of long service, lead to High Street, where the centuries seem to part. The busy world of to-day opens out. Movement and noise hustle away quiet, old theology, and antiquity. People crowd on the narrow pavements, under The Pentice, round up-to-date shops, and traffic pours up and down the highway. This thoroughfare of city business for untold ages certainly is very much alive in maturity. Beyond it extend the newer areas complete with railway station, gasworks, petrol pumps, houses with all conveniences yet not worth looking at, and the other adorn-ments born of this graceless era. But almost everywhere throughout the city lots of curious things can be discovered. Hemmed in amongst the old and the new are ancient churches, bits of the medieval walls, narrow winding passages, dwellings Georgian and earlier, and unexpected reminders of spacious days to make wandering exciting.

High Street alone can be quite a thriller. You may come to it through the West Gate just by the castle, a narrow-arched gateway sturdy with stone and flintwork that has been on guard for six hundred years (150). It presents a windowless face of fierce mien to the ancient route for Old Sarum, and is

Hospital of St. Cross. Oriel and Ambulatory for "Men to walke togither twaine and twaine, To keep them drye when it happed to rayne."

featured with arrow-slits, grooves for a portcullis, and machicolations suggesting teeth firmly set, all devised for putting the wind up evil intruders by promising a welcome of arrows, missiles, boiling oil, and molten lead. Retired from a long spell of such behaviour, the gate looks squat, a trifle worn, and even ruminating, like an old fellow who has got beyond work. The narrow archway does not do for twentieth-century traffic. As I write the relic is about to be pensioned off, pushed onto the dole by providing an outer road to prevent speed merchants either knocking the gate down or being knocked down by the antique guardian. Even so, this warrior of the past may still have a future. When the age of science and machinery has worked its own destruction, the human survivors, if any, may decide that bows, arrows, boiling oil, and molten lead advance civilization much better than petrol, T.N.T., and split atoms. Then the machicolations and arrow-slits will come into their own again.

Mild excitements await those who appreciate the notable old thoroughfares in England all the way down this High Street from the gate to the pretty bridge over the river at The Wiers. The antiquated gables, timbering, dormers, bow windows, plastering, and Georgian brick fronts display the features, moods, and fashions of house and home favoured by citizens in both comfortable and lean years of long ago. Passing and noting these mellow structures observers may often prefer to look upwards and keep the soul high, thereby pretending not to notice the lower breed of the up-to-date in shop fronts, rebuilding, and showy evidences of certain gentlemen of commerce who invade many towns by a process of multiplication.

Quite near to the West Gate the sport of seeking in High Street is at once rewarded by finding the butcher's shop, Regency all over, two tiers of corpulent bow window at the side, and new joints of meat looking so appetizing in the old setting that they might be just waiting for young bucks returning, rather worn, from a fling with the Prince Regent at Brighton. Picturesque upper storeys next usher in the eighteenth century. The time of year protrudes deliciously with a pair of portly bow windows owned by quite a gem of a shop. Is that the original *Humphrey Clinker* or *The Vicar of Wakefield*, hardly dry from the printer, on view through the little square panes? No. But it is, in fact, *The Hampshire Chronicle*, which has been appearing pretty well as long as the windows have bulged. On again, and the years flit back to the early 1700's with the appearance of Queen Anne. Perched up in a niche she looks well, robust, and dignified, and if unkind critics have credited the royal lady with "little talent and less learning," surely this mother of nineteen children might be considered a champion paragon, be perpetuated with a medal for something by political vote-catchers masculine and feminine who deplore declining birthrates in our already overcrowded island. And in case present hours may be forgotten during a backward progression down High Street, the Queen presides over a huge old bracket, richly carved, and supporting a clock that ever goes forward to warn backsliders. High over the Queen's head is the curfew tower, an attractive erection of 1713 whose bell still commands the citizens to "coeverfu" and go to bed at a time when they really wake up for the evening. On other occasions the bell rings according to ancient custom and then the city fathers with exemplary obedience hasten to meet at the modern guildhall.

Following Queen Anne's presentment of a sedate decade the High Street centuries oscillate alarmingly. To light on the site of the Conqueror's palace under an archway causes a breathless slip back almost to the 1066 event. With little chance for pause after this long jump, the house of God Begot opposite spins time back again to the Saxons, for the hoary timbering and gables are mere juvenile successors of the original foundation. Cardinal Beaufort's city cross, rising slenderly between the Saxon and Norman relics, helps to steady the flow of the years by an urge forward into the 1400's with the aid of detached shafts, pinnacles, and a carved figure of William of Wykeham standing in a pretty square of walls and gables quite medieval in character. Even though much of the cross and all but one of the figures are modern, it is almost possible to hear from the steps used for proclamations the voices of long-defunct criers who loudly bawled "Oyez! Oyez" in the cause of Oyer and Terminer. Adjacent, the round classic columns which support The Pentice accelerate the advance of the ages, telling of sweet lavender days dight with quilted hoods, gowns of brocade, embroidered waistcoats and periwigs. Yet up above this still delightful covered way the gables frown down ominously with Tudor suggestiveness, threatening to push the years back again. Beyond this overhanging shelter the highway opens out wide, and lines of buildings and houses continue to dip into the past while leading on to the fresh to-day. In a final extensive sweep High Street's symbols of the march of time bring all the years together. Central in the broad way is the parking place for your Rolls or your bus. At one side the Guildhall, grown large for present service, flaunts the Gothic of the nine-teenth century above lawns and gardens where a queen founded the abbey ten centuries ago. Opposite stands the chapel of St. John's Hospital, ancient, lowly, and grey. Wall frontages and roofs carry the marks of many periods. And com-manding all, set firmly on a block of everlasting granite, Hamo Thornycroft's new statue of old King Alfred, founder of the Kingdom and the Nation, holds high the sword in honour of "Winchester and the English name!"

It's a wonderful street to wander down, this route of old pilgrims. At the end of it you can stand on the bridge by the mill where the steep hill begins to rise, and the stream of the centuries flows on down the vale, and think what a full image of English life and times this High Street represents. I place it in the first rank of the streets in England. And then you can turn up Magdalen Hill, follow the footway on the right, ascend the left-hand steps to the top, and on the height be enraptured with the panorama of city, beauty, and history, a precious jewel sparkling in a green setting. It is a steep climb, but the reward is a vision (130–131).

And having previously stated that all good beings in this bad age should see Winchester before they die, I deliver this parting message: The City Abounds In Tea Shops. I dare not recommend places for luncheon or dinner, because my efforts in this direction have been rewarded sometimes with unkind remarks on the roast beef and apple tart of old England. It is impossible to gauge the requirements of other people's stomachs. But tea in Winchester can be enjoyed in all sorts of nooks, crannies, and surroundings that may quite bewilder any-one who cannot help mixing China and Indian with the shades of time and period. The cup that cheers can be sipped on Saxon foundations, where William the Conqueror gnawed bones before table-forks were invented, under great beams black in "ye olde" manner, and in atmospheres varying from Queen Anne-ish and Georgian to the elegant, the simple, or the up-to-date multiple style. In fact, anyone possessing the necessary wardrobe could quick change quite correctly for tea all down the ages of Winchester.

$$*\qquad*\qquad*\qquad*\qquad*$$

In many ways Salisbury resembles its friendly rival Winchester. Each county capital combines the recent with the far-away, tells of high noon and afterglow, and carries the suggestion of young to-day and the very old party playing coquette.

The spire of world renown, of course, is Salisbury. Much else the city has, but the cathedral spire poised triumphantly is pre-eminent. Go to Salisbury

SALISBURY. *The Poultry
Cross, a fine specimen of 1330
work. Below, St. Anne's Gate
leading to the close. The
walls contain stonework brought
from the Norman cathedral
of Old Sarum in 1331.*

SALISBURY *from the old mill and river meadows. The Cathedral spire, built in the fourteenth century to a height of 404 feet, is one of the loftiest in Europe. This lovely feature, a favourite subject with John Constable, adds glory to a notable city and is visible over miles of surrounding country.*

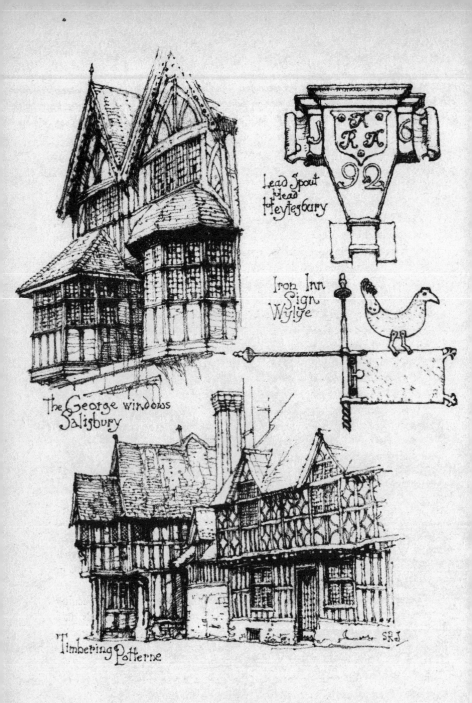

Lead Spout Head Heytesbury

Iron Inn Sign Wylye

The George windows Salisbury

Timbering Potterne

SRJ

WILTSHIRE DETAILS

however you will, whether by the Roman route from Silchester, down from the Plain, through any of the five near river valleys, over wide meadows, along the good roads that converge like a spider's web, or even arrive by train—from whichever direction you approach the city, there in all its glory the incomparable spire is seen pointing 404 feet upwards and shedding lustre over level and fair prospects. This treasure of Salisbury and Winchester's cathedral nave, twin beauties of adjoining counties, unite in signifying man's highest inspiration and endeavour.

This spire, too, beckons a beholder to seek the water meadows, counselling, "Look long at the scenes immortalized by John Constable." They are there yet, not greatly changed since the artist saw and painted them—ever delightful to watch under the big open skies as the sun and the shade bring endless variations of effect and atmosphere to these lovely compositions of cathedral, verdure, and running waters. Salisbury people are proud of their master and of his and their views. All the inhabitants, from the bishop to the police, know these scenes and the pictures, and a thoughtful local authority has provided seats for contemplative souls to contemplate from. If by seeming chance a constable is asked merely for the direction to the meadows, as it might be for the way to the moon in order to cloak the enquirer's art proclivities, as likely as not the reply will be, "You are looking for Constable's pictures? Go straight ahead" . . . and so on! Such, at least, was my first experience in unfledged youth while vainly affecting studied artlessness to smother any suspicion of being "arty." Everyone that does not know Salisbury from the meadows should get to the cathedral close to-morrow if possible, and to save contacts with the police, I direct them through the gateway into High Street, along the first turning on the left past the stone archway of Church House and Crane Bridge, proceed to the wooden bridge, cross the stream, and follow the path through the meadows. A picture worthy of Constable's brush appears at every few yards. Perhaps the best of all is the last one at West Harnham. The foreground is dappled with sparkling waters, rushes, and foliage; bright chequered stone and flint, bricks and tiles, give wonderful colour to the Tudor mill. Over the river, flat meadows stretch away to delicate and soft greenery of trees. High above the rare spire points in a grand majestic sweep to the heavens (156–157).

Long before John Constable or the spire were thought of, a series of peculiar events happened in the neighbourhood. People with inquisitive minds may notice that the streets in the central, or oldest, part of Salisbury are set out with order and precision quite worthy to be called "town planning" even in these enlightened days when magnanimous bureaucracy is ever devising schemes for the welfare of the common man, and themselves. And strange though it may seem, this antique interpretation of a subject now so very much in the air came about through the influence of draught. It is generally known that before Salisbury was invented the city resided at Old Sarum, a high, bleak spot much favoured by pre-historics and Romans on account of the view. Later dwellers, however, grown soft in the process of civilization, did not appreciate this elevated site bountifully supplied with currents of fresh air from the north that bounded at full gallop for Old Sarum after sweeping like racehorses over the clear miles of the Plain. Those of my readers who know Salisbury Plain well, and particularly in winter, will be fully aware how efficient this fine open space can be for emphasizing the discomforts of wind, cold air, rain, sleet, and similar abominations sent from above for the questionable good of man's body and the probable loss of his soul. When Thomas Ingoldsby warbled, "Oh, Salisbury Plain is bleak and bare," he exactly expressed the sentiments of the Old Sarumites, living about the year 1200. The natives all sneezed in unison. Many developed "rheumatics" the old scribes wrote. Influenza germs blew in, a pretty pickle with neither Boots' Cash Chemists or Armstrong's Mixture then in the place. The clerks in the cathedral could "hardly hear one another sing" because of the constant noise made by the wind, and for the same reason the congregation could not follow the Mass. Other complications brought more unpleasantness. There was a medieval housing problem, caused by the town growing too large for its site. Overcrowding and conflicts for power upset general harmony. Church and town at loggerheads with the castle supporters provoked rows. And always that horrid wind blew, positively wedded to the direction of the North Pole.

It is not surprising to glean from contemporary records that miserable humanity packed on this mound felt truly sorry for themselves, and decided to do something about it. At that moment in the early 1200's good Bishop Poore, the man of many parts and great qualifications, reigned at the cathedral which had been founded in 1075. He acted promptly, got permission from Pope Honorius III in 1219 to depart lock, stock, and barrel, and evolved a gigantic pantechnicon operation for removing things human, spiritual, and temporal from Old Sarum. But whither could his furniture vans go? Tradition kindly answers. The bishop conjured up a vision, the common dodge for solving difficulties in olden times. He then shot an arrow into the air, chased it, and sprinted almost two miles to find the arrow sitting just where Salisbury Cathedral now stands. The destination for the furniture vans had been clearly indicated.

These preliminaries completed, means for depositing the contents of Old Sarum demanded consideration. Bishop Poore and his stout fellows therefore put their heads together. Of course they were not so clever as we are now—had never heard of commissions and committees skilled in producing white, blue, and other coloured papers, and knew but little of axial lines, cross-sections, centres, and all our paraphernalia of angles, sines, tangents, and levels for planting communities in lines and curves on the ground like rows of onions and geraniums. But the simple churchmen did their best. Without talking overmuch or waiting for experts, they set about doing what is an easy and plain thing to do, viz. they made a plan for their town, workmanlike, practical, and suitable for the needs of the period. They fixed the position for the cathedral, arranged for a spacious close of half a square mile, which remains one of the prides of England, and schemed the town in convenient arrangements of rect-angular "places" and "tenements" to make the "chequers and squares" that serve and delight to this day. Nor was that all. The plan, these wise men knew, would be quite in vain without seemly buildings on it, so with right good will they determined to have them, after securing a charter for New Sarum from Henry III about the year 1220. From these beginnings, framed with skill and care, the design developed while the years rolled on. The fane and the city grew up in medieval splendour and prospered. The cathedral with its spire, trans-lated from thought to actuality, shed benediction over churches, hospitals, fair houses and buildings gathered round the gates of the close in the smiling and sheltered vale. And in remembrance of the early home, draughty though it had been, the close was walled with Norman stones from Old Sarum, given by Edward III in 1331 and in part still standing at St. Anne's Gate (155). Thus Old Sarum and its belongings became Salisbury; and there it is now, rare and beautiful, in spite of the knocks delivered by modern spoilers.

Old Sarum faded, but its fame spent long a-dying. Centuries after the wind and the weather had swept away the town and little more than earthworks and a tree marked the site, the mound continued to send two members to Parlia-ment. When the Reform Acts brought this notorious rotten borough to an end, just over a hundred years ago, the tree under which elections were held also went rotten and expired.

Everything that might be written on Salisbury Cathedral has already appeared in print. Therefore I give the following summary only in case some of my readers should happen to lend this book to others less informed than them-selves. The work is a remarkable and complete example of Early English architecture in local Chilmark stone and Purbeck marble. It was commenced by Bishop Poore in 1220; a temporary high altar in the lady chapel and the whole site were consecrated in 1225 before an enormous audience; and in 1258 the consecration of the main building took place with great pomp under the eye of Henry III. The upper tower, very beautifully erected early in the fourteenth century, gained more beauty with the spire in 1335. Due largely to extraordinary craftsmanship on the part of the masons, the interior looks as if it had been completed the day before yesterday. It is enriched with much splendid carving in figures and tombs. The cloister and chapter house outside, dating from 1263, again show the acme in masoncraft and remain perfect.

Long after the men of the old faith had departed from their shrine, Wyatt the architect visited the cathedral in the eighteenth century. His idea was restoration. Capable though he could be at manipulating classic columns and pediments, he demonstrated his badness at Gothic art by carrying out alterations and destruction worthy of Cromwell's worst bouts of fanaticism. Scott followed in the 1860's, doing his best and worst with pots of varnish, paint, encaustic tiles, and other diabolical products of the period. Yet with all these shocks suffered, it now seems no less than a miracle that most of the exterior did not woo restoring gentlemen. Thus jilted, the cathedral managed to retain peculiar outer grace, and to keep intact the tower and spire, the wonder unique, a permanent joy for the million, an inspiration for artists, the "blonde beauty" of Henry James, Dickens, Hardy, and other literary celebrities, the highest effort of the kind in England both in elevation and sublimity.

Nevertheless the spire and tower of Salisbury shared the lot of its neighbour, Winchester Cathedral, in passing through exciting moments and bad days. Winchester's foundations, laid on tree-trunks in a swamp, gradually sunk, an alarming condition only recently remedied. At Salisbury the height and consequent weight of the tower and spire threatened complete disaster to the cathedral when the marvel in stone, completed in 1335, showed signs of falling down a hundred years later. Fifteenth-century masons saved it by building flying buttresses and the great stone girders, now to be seen spanning the transepts at the crossing. Danger threatened again about 1640, for then the spire had settled rather more than two feet out of the perpendicular. Sir Christopher Wren subsequently applied iron braces, strengthened the structure, and on completing a commendable job complained that the spire was much too high! Through these and other efforts the spire continued upstanding, and although more than two feet awry, it is now thought to be safe.

Far below the spire's top point, the green lawns of the spacious close extend to the surrounding buildings and houses, a wonderful collection just suitable for this noble expanse. There stands the Palace commenced by Bishop Poore and with a fifteenth-century hall. There, too, are the Tudor Church House, the Deanery, and homes for the quiet life, secure from the bangs and noise and horns of the outer world under the protection of medieval and beautiful gateways. These lovely places, preaching sermons in stone, plaster, and bricks, show off all the fashions of time arrayed in battlements, arched openings, chequered stones and flint, mullions, gables, bay windows, and the finery of Renaissance and eighteenth-century detail. Withal an adorable spot, tranquil, framed in gardens and trees, hardly to be matched in the realm.

Salisbury's streets and by-ways carry themselves in the way expected of a medieval city grown up. New things jostle old ones collected during more than seven hundred years' growth. Curious features made many an age ago shoulder, overhang, or jut out with great-great-grandfatherly benignity against modern erections. People and motorists ever move along, thread in and out the arches of the fine gateways, or make rings with cars round the Poultry Cross. Up and down, wherever you go, this or that is bound to recall past years.

MIDDLE WOODFORD, on the River Avon between Salisbury Plain and Old Sarum.

The *Bear* Hotel

DEVIZES. *Sign of the famous coaching inn, and* KNOOK *manor-house, in 1908, on the River Wylye at the border of Salisbury Plain.*

SRS

Bygone centuries revive. They stir afresh with visits of kings, queens, nobles, and statesmen, pageantry and gallant steeds, coaches rattling in and out; times of Parliamentary meetings, strife, beheadings, junketing, cakes and ale, marketing, trade; and the sequence of events big and little that happened while folks great and small came, stopped, and went on, sometimes to delight and sometimes to affright the townspeople and ecclesiastical gentlemen who permanently squatted at this important point on the great road to the West. Here and there delightful peeps of town buildings show over the winding streams, as noted by Evelyn and Pepys. Ever and again the rare spire is discovered from unexpected angles, pointing up beyond coloured roofs. Old and new, stone and timber and brick, and the signs of Georgian, Elizabethan, and Middle Ages mixed with recent constructions of medium or abominable appearance, set the variegated background for the current of day-to-day life that flows busily through this ancient city packed with architectural treasures.

Certainly the streets have these treasures in plenty. The gates of High Street and St. Anne, both very beautiful, have been mentioned already. The Poultry Cross, of the fourteenth century, is lovely too (155). Within a radius of the Cross, that is in High Street, Silver Street, the Market Square, and St. John's Street, many black-and-white walls and gables still hold their original places. The bright and bizarre effects of their timbers and plaster panels are almost startling, particularly when the sun shines. A trio of churches includes St. Thomas of Canterbury, as old as the city itself and surrounded by picturesque groups of tile-hung gables. Capital domestic buildings and homes are strongly represented, notably at the Hospital of St. Nicholas near Harnham Bridge, and by the College of Matrons and Mompesson House, two prizes in a choice group of later Renaissance work.

Of course, Salisbury's streets provide nice tea-shops for its nice inhabitants, visitors, and for my nice readers, who really must hasten to this city to share the excitements I always have found there. And standing at the junction of highways from the east, west, north, and south, this venerable seat never failed to specialize on refreshments in general. Therefore it always offered, and still does, a collection of pubs galore for hungry and thirsty souls, which is just as it should be in a centre where farmers congregate, land-lovers meet, and soldiers on pass chase the girls. These harbours of refuge, gay with cheerful signs and names, shed a fine flavour of antiquity over the streets. Archways and long yards agitate thoughts on defunct cavalcades of horsemen, rumbling wagons, and on the coaching days when the "Quicksilver," the "Eclipse," and many another champion of the road, down from London or up from Exeter with Charles Ward, Moody, and a galaxy of celebrities at the ribbons, bounded in and out while the music of horns and tally ho! tingled the air of an adventurous and unrationed past.

There, in High Street, stands *The Old George*, or rather did until badly damaged by a recent fire. It weathered centuries with the same timbers, gables, and two fat oriel windows that bulged out over the heads of the populace on the pavement below (158). Keeping the spark of life running mellow through the aged woodwork and plaster, most likely it mused in the still of the night, chuckled perhaps, on all the sorts and conditions of folk that had pushed through the doorway—Pepys, for instance, who asked for a lodging in 1668, lay "in a silk bed," and paid "the reckoning, which was so exorbitant that I was mad." From "the George Inne," it will be remembered, this father of the British Navy set out for the Plain, got lost, and only escaped a night out by finding another shelter and a bed, "good, but lousy: which made us merry." Stout fellow! Merriment in the face of elusive foe clearly denotes unusual philosophy. *The White Hart* in St. John Street swings the years on to the end of the eighteenth century. Trim with chaste columns and complete with a sleek and symbolic animal perched on the pediment, it blossomed out in Ionic pretension to replace a more humble ancestor. The two big lamp-brackets still presiding right and left of the entrance once shed a glow over lesser twinkling lights of the flying machines arrived for changing horses ere departing again into the nights of the coaching years at their zenith. In an earlier and more gruesome style the chronicles of Salisbury's inn episodes disclose that the Duke of Buckingham's headless remains were discovered beneath the kitchen floor of *The Saracen's Head*, a reminder of Richard III's peculiar fancy for murder. Shakespeare delicately indicated this mishap without exhibiting the axe—for further particulars see *Richard III*, Act 5, Scene 1, presenting the unlucky gentleman on All Saints' Day, 1483, meditating on his doubtful chance of shining in celestial society. Other hotels and inns, either thriving in new fame, standing as relics of glory departed, or even abandoned by mine hosts, carry the stamp of old years. They reveal quaint courtyards, black winding staircases, and other leavings of bustling times that faded long before the motoring age came, to create fresh stories at the inns of Salisbury for future historians to unearth and ponder on.

In 1945 I visited Salisbury just before the German defeat in World War No. 2. The cathedral close was adorned with huge tanks full of water. In the north porch I encountered a fire engine sort of thing anchored there in readiness for emergencies. Creeping round this vermilion article, I opened the cathedral door and peeped inside. Arch upon arch shone bright and fresh in the midday light. But near to me on the paved floor a heap of sand covered the recumbent effigy of the Crusader William Longespée, Earl of Salisbury. This did not look nice, so I went outside again. There rose the matchless spire, emblem of faith beyond matter and earth. Three bombers, flying low, cut noisily past it with mathematical precision, the angular shapes of the machines marking dark silhouettes against billowy clouds and the azure. The form, movement, and drone of the aeroplanes contrasted vividly with the delicate grace of the spire, static and seemingly set for ever. This combination of old and new signs gave a queer impression, even made me think, "What a rotten state of affairs after all Bishop Poore and his like did and tried to do for the good of the world. Why! the spire might be knocked down to-morrow." Without pondering on regrets or disgust, I decided to depart, went to the railway station, and left the city. Standing hemmed in by sailors and soldiers in the corridor of the train, with a kit-bag sitting on my toes and the end of a rifle projected into my back, I made up my mind to try to forget that visit to Salisbury and only retain memories of the placid city in piping times of peace set in the meadows loved by John Constable. As the train shot through Whitchurch I sent a thought down to old Winchester in gratitude for happy hours spent at the shrine of William of Wykeham in past times that certainly were "the good old days."

FROM SALISBURY PLAIN TO DORSETSHIRE

The chalk continues through Salisbury Plain to the Dorset coast of the English Channel at Swyre Head, Lulworth, Worbarrow Bay, and Swanage Bay.

Salisbury Plain, previously introduced in my note on fresh air, is too well known and celebrated to call for many words from me. Yet everybody perhaps is not acquainted with its little village of Imber, tucked miles away from anywhere, and remembered at Devizes for the north chapel in St. John's Church presented by a native. Imber used to be one of the most remote and shy pretty spots in southern England. Now it may be no more. The military arrived in the war years and treated it disgracefully. But the general habits of the airy Plain certainly are known to most people. It is dear to the British Army and cursed by other ranks for a shortage of pubs. The diversity of heights, downs, and heaths make it anything but plain. It has ancient fame as a kind of Piccadilly Circus in our earliest road system. It is renowned for being the headquarters of pre-historic offerings to baffle the learned and the wise. Searchers find and sometimes sit in damp holes and pits, clamber up the earthen castles and camps, and meditate on stones mysteriously disposed in the circles and other formations favoured by earlier residents, who maybe owned long beards and not many clothes, though of the exact coiffure and sartorial fashion no man living can tell. And of course there is Stonehenge. Secretive, the concentric circles and mighty sarsen stones have refused to confess either origin, goodness, or sin to any of the antiquaries who have tried in vain since the ninth century to connect them with rites of the sun, moon, stars, Stone and Bronze Ages, Druids, Romans, Danes, Boadicea, Merlin, and nearly everybody and all else in the heavens, on earth, and in the bowels thereof. Inquisitive prying from aeroplanes now has made enigmas even more puzzling, for what on the earth can be meant by another circle apparently set out by unknown beings who performed in woodwork at a rival Woodhenge? Very perplexing indeed. Still, these things are there, and to see Stonehenge against the sunset—that is, on the approach from Amesbury in the evening—is an experience not to be forgotten. The stones loom up ominously, vast, mysterious, and keeping their secrets. Earlier risers than myself also tell of their peculiar and eerie grandeur at dawn. This aspect has been powerfully expressed in words, and nowhere better than in Chapter 58 of *Tess of the D'Urbervilles*, devoted to the meeting of Tess, Angel Clare, and the police in appropriate surroundings after the bloodthirsty business at Sandbourne (Bournemouth).

Alluring though Salisbury Plain may be for those with a fancy for fresh air, forgotten ancestors, the pleasantries of war, and getting lost in the dark, this expanse of mystery is surrounded with borderlands full of varied attractions when the weather is nice and the daylight is broad. Landscapes rich in foliage stretch away to far distances; good specimens of them are seen when passing under wooded hills through the pretty villages of Great Cheverell, Earlstoke, and Edington. Here and there timbered walls and gables introduce black and white amongst the colour of brick and stone, notably at Potterne (158). Parklands surround mansions and noble gardens, with Bowood, Longleat, Wilton, and Amesbury ranking famous in the number. Churches, manor-houses, and cottages lie snugly embowered in the greenery of roads and lanes, and near to clear waters rippling down the valleys of the Bourne, the Avon (163), and the Wylye (164). The country of these Wiltshire rivers is the best region in England for observing flint combined with stone, chalk, and brick in old buildings. Homes and thatched garden walls, chequered with squared stones and flint-work, shine and glint in the villages and byways. These materials show delightfully up the River Bourne from Winterbourne Earls, along the River Avon from Stratford-sub-Castle, and in the direction of Wylye on the River Wylye.

WYLYE, WILTSHIRE.

FOVANT, *one of the villages in the Nadder Valley*
below Boxbury Hill and White Sheet Hill, haunts of
W. H. Hudson. MELBURY HILL *(below) from Compton*
Abbas at the border of Thomas Hardy's Blackmore Vale.

SHAFTESBURY. *Cottages on Gold Hill, the abbey wall, and the view south. This town of a great past has preserved little of former grandeur, but it commands wonderful prospects from a hill-top elevation of more than 700 feet.*

On the borders of the Plain also are several country towns, teeming with pictures and stories. It is heartbreaking to lack space for dwelling on each one of them when I think of cheerful Calne, the home of prime bacon, noted for the tenth-century legend of the miraculous escape of St. Dunstan in a collapse of floor-joists ingeniously arranged by himself for supernatural effect; and with thoughts, too, on Devizes; Warminster's High Street; Heytesbury; Wilton, the parent of Wiltshire, remembered for a bishopric, its great house and English carpets; and Amesbury, of royal and abbey days, the place of Gay's epicurean decline under the Queensbury roof, and the scene of events at the old gabled *George*, the "Blue Dragon" of *Martin Chuzzlewit*. Alas, shortage of paper means lingering in but one of these fascinating quarters.

Devizes shall be the choice, a characteristic specimen in the above collection, and a market town bright enough for any but most dismal souls. Standing on a bit of a bump for fresh airiness, it caters for all sorts of tastes, being very antique, middle-aged, and quite up to date with movies, stores, and nearly all the modernisms. The Thursday market-days and Saturdays are brisk and lively. Human entertainment is provided by the crowds gathered in from the country-side. They look merry and healthy, and with Wiltshire appetites sometimes gobble up all the food, for more than once in rationed years I have been sent tea-less away. Those on the lookout for objects other than people or food will find the town generous in its offerings. Certainly the castle with the large Norman keep has gone, once one of the strongest in England and famed over Europe, but a capital assortment of signs of the past keep old times in touch with the new. There are two fine churches with two fine towers, Norman at St. John's, Perpendicular at St. Mary's. The early masonry at St. John's is no less remarkable than the richly wrought splendour of the south chapel, built in the fifteenth century by a Beauchamp of Warwick. St. Mary's Perpendicular grace continues from the tower to the nave, and the interior charms with beautiful and delicate proportions beneath a notable timber roof.

Devizes carries itself remarkably well on the secular and home front with a mixture of timbering, plaster, stone, brickwork, and tiles, to show the sort of thing the townspeople made of home sweet home for many generations past. Under the timbers and storeys overhanging the narrow way of St. John's Alley time's clock points to Tudor hours. Other patterns of home carry the years a decade or two forward. But the big display belongs to the late seventeenth and eighteenth centuries. Dozens of houses hint to the reigns of William and Mary, Queen Anne, and the Georges. Chaste doorways, square window-panes set in wooden sashes, and trim brick fronts nicely finished off with cornices, stone mouldings, or quoins have the fragrance of sweet lavender days. The Post Office, where people now crowd in for stamps and pensions, is but one of many delightful reminders of that ribboned and coquettish age, and forecourts here and there, quite stately with pillars, urns, and wrought-iron gates, as are seen at Brownston House, add dignified qualities to these quality streets. Such architectural trifles, dating back a bit, are exactly right in this town of prominence on the famous road once travelled by the celebrated company that posted and coached to classic Bath. Nor is it surprising to discover a snuff factory of more than two hundred years' repute still in action at this point, for Messrs. Anstie have been delivering the goods ever since wigs, sneezing, Gay's *Wife of Bath*, and Sheridan's *Rivals* were the fashion.

Moving about on the busy days, threading among Hebes in skirts and slacks, girls from the land, and masculine figures browned and hearty, anyone able to move an eye off the splendid Wiltshire humanity for a moment may notice the peculiar names of the thoroughfares and quaint narrow ways. Some of the designations imply antiquity. For instance, The Brittox, The Little Brittox, Monday Market Street, and others are both curious and suggestive. The Market Place of course is, as in most English towns, the proud and central point of activities. Here it has the usual corn exchange, picturesque outlines all round, and an open space wide enough to give ample elbow-room on the most august of occasions. In the centre stands the emblem that has given Devizes a fame for truthfulness hardly equalled by George Washington or the Babylonians according to Herodotus. A solemn reason for this virtue can be read on a tablet at the market cross, placed there for the public weal by the Mayor and Corporation. The account tells of Ruth Pierce of Potterne and her attempt in 1753 to swindle her neighbours by falsehood for a quarter of a sack of wheat, followed by a swift and tragic retribution, "She instantly fell down and expired." With this statement of fact and warning before them, the inhabitants it is needless to add have read, marked, and digested the words with profit ever since. That is one of the reasons why the town is so pure for shopping. No statements heard can be doubted, nothing is hidden under counters, and it is unnecessary to examine change.

Opposite the market cross stands *The Bear* hotel, a great bear among many bears in this mid-western country. This bear, carved in relief over the entrance, has been gnawing the product of the vine for many years, yet with no visible result (164). Doubtless he is still at it. But although engaged in this wise, he perpetually guards day and night, summer and winter, an edifice of most comfortable appearance, one half of it presenting a traditional plaster frontage, with the other half moulded in an Adam-y elegance of classic refinements, bay windows, and sundry chastities. The building of course demanded two porches, so one stands for tradition and for the Bear to perform on, and a second one, delicate and curly with ironwork, serves for R. Adam. Far from frightening anyone away, the Bear oozes a kind of welcome from his fluffy coat and ruminating eyes. Therefore, after outside observation, few better things can be done than to go inside. And for a number of reasons. One concerns the meal that surely will be found, whatever sinister activities controllers of rations may be up to. There is also a bar, with the Lawrence room behind it, and great old beams, lowish ceilings, a staircase winding up to unsuspected hiding-holes for all you know, and peeps into the long yard that once was alive with horses, coachmen, and ostlers; everything withal seeming tinged with allusion and memories to make the crowds almost come to life again who made their stages here, consumed prodigious fare, emptied bottles galore, and played the inevitable games of cards before departing on their ways in the summer suns and wintry blasts of the old Bath Road in its heydays.

Fancies roam again on passing from the ancient quarters of the house to the eating department. A few paces from the timber framing transport you to another realm. Ceilings are high. Details and fittings insinuate politeness and refinement. A staircase of superior grace, rising from floor to floor, might well lead to an upper heaven, a paradise specially reserved for ladies to garb and deck themselves as muses attended by cherubim and seraphim. Amidst all this classic purity you forget your own tweeds, and perhaps recalling

> In teacup time of hood and hoop
> And when the patch was worn,

quite expect to find Miss Burney and Mrs. Thrale absorbed in a game of cards; which indeed they were at this same *Bear Inn* during the month of April 1780. Then the old story in the *Diary* comes to mind. You almost share in the tap, tap on the door that enabled these bright and brilliant ladies to first place the youthful Thomas Lawrence on the pages of fame before he got himself into fame with his pictures. Faded figures again flit into their earthly niches. There goes Lawrence senior, lawyer turned innkeeper, with Mrs. Lawrence behind him, not quite at home in the business, and the two daughters, handsome and bewitching, their souls wrapt in music. And along come Fanny Burney and Mrs. Thrale, the card-playing forsaken, agog with excitement at finding "a most lovely boy of ten years of age, who seems to be not merely the wonder of their family, but of the times," and already adept at taking portraits or reciting Milton, just as the guests fancied. Benignant with old port, madeira, brown ale, roast beef, and feather beds, lively with distinguished company, and a home of good books, poetry, paintings, and music, *The Bear* thus fostered one of the most meteoric careers in English art. Sir Thomas Lawrence certainly achieved a remarkable record. This is it—born 1769; patronized by beautiful women and men of rank in his studio at Bath at the age of twelve; awarded the silver pallet of the Society of Arts for work of his thirteenth year; a popular idol on arrival in London; elected Associate of the Royal Academy in 1791; Painter to King George III, 1792; Royal Academician, 1795; knighted 1815; and on the death of Benjamin West, unanimously chosen President of the Royal Academy. What a store of other memories and secrets the old Bear must have gathered while perched over the doorway engaged with the product of the vine for many a year, and on the watch for arrivals and departures at Devizes!

From Salisbury Plain and its environs the chalk country continues southward. Beyond the Wylye valley the uplands mount to the long, green miles of Great Ridge and Grovely Woods. Here the Roman track points to Salisbury. The chalk slopes lead onward, down to the Nadder valley, then rise again to the impressive line of heights topped by Boxbury Hill and White Sheet Hill. Farther to the south the borders of the ancient and royal hunting ground of Cranborne Chase are marked by Win Green's 911 feet and the high entrenchment of Winkelbury.

A grand country, this, all the way from Salisbury Plain to Cranborne Chase. Views from ridges and top points show magnificently. The uplands are open and lonely, just as W. H. Hudson found them when he made his wonderful observations for *Afoot in England* on the Easter Sunday spent at White Sheet Hill. For those who still use their feet, the miles can spin out along prehistoric trackways, good for both mind and appetite. Camps, barrows, and relics, rarely out of view, swing thoughts back to Romans and Britons. If too much of the antique palls, an antidote is presented by the army badges cut in the chalk above Fovant, an effort of heroes competing with King Alfred and White Horses during the 1914–1918 war, and one calculated to befog antiquaries three thousand years hence. And concerning things olden, the name of General Pitt Rivers shines for his classic work in revealing secrets of this district. Much now can be learned by visiting the capital museum at Farnham provided by the archæologist, a grand old man as I remember him, one of the old type with flowing beard, and abounding in kindness. I last saw him at the Larmer Tree, the point where Wiltshire and Dorset meet, and thought to be a rendezvous for royal huntsmen when stationed at the very old and interesting hunting-lodge known as King John's House at Tollard Royal.

In this Wiltshire country adjoining Dorset and Hampshire the villages, noble seats, and parks are mostly in the vales, though a number are high placed. The Nadder valley, plentifully wooded, shelters a line of cosy and thatched villages. From Burcombe they continue through Compton Chamberlain and Dinton to the park surrounding Wardour Castle, a classic house with notable interiors. The medieval gateway and great barn of the Abbess of Shaftesbury at Tisbury lie on a tongue of stone country; but adjacent, and meeting the chalk, the deep woods of Fonthill rise to screen the relics of the short-lived building experiment inaugurated by Lord Mayor Beckford's son William the eccentric dilettante and author of the famous oriental romance *Vathek*, who laid out more than a quarter of a million pounds for little permanent effect. More lasting architectural fame belongs to the two villages east and west of Fonthill. Chilmark gave the stone for Salisbury Cathedral. At East Knoyle a tablet records: "In a house near this spot was born Sir Christopher Wren." The two neighbouring towns of Hindon and Mere, both small, with long pasts, and situated up on the old Exeter Road, also do not lack architectural interest. But their great days

SHAPWICK, *the relic of a preaching cross (now the war memorial) and a thatched inn and* STURMINSTER MARSHALL *with thatched cottages and an interesting church.*

IN THOMAS HARDY'S WESSEX

BERE REGIS. *The stone and flint tower of the church which contains a hammer-beam roof and the memorials figured in "Tess of the D'Urbervilles." BLANDFORD. Hardy's "Shottsford." The Georgian market-place with church, town hall and houses, a notable group chiefly due to the builder-architect family of Bastard after the town was burned in 1731.*

belonged to the coaching era, when some of the fastest flying machines passed that way. The *Ship Inn* and other buildings at Mere uphold the former glory, while Hindon, once a pocket borough contested and lost by Lord Beaconsfield, pursues a sweet maturity without even hinting at political complications. With a gracious wide street shaded by trees, it just charms all who go that way.

The Ebble stream in the next vale over the hills from the River Nadder touches another chain of attractive villages. All down from Alvediston under Winkelbury camp, through Broad Chalk, and to the *Fox and Goose* at Coombe Bissett, the outstanding subject is thatching. Houses, cottages, big barns, and boundary walls show thatched roofs to heart's content, with here and there grey church towers upstanding above them.

Melbury Down and Hill (169), breezy and open places, lead from Cranborne Chase to Shaftesbury, "one of the quaintest and queerest spots in England," according to Thomas Hardy, and from which the novelist sent Sue on the eloping expedition via Bimport in *Jude the Obscure*. This town of splendid name and elevation, and remarkably pleasant to be in, promises more through fame than it actually shows. Modern pilgrims in the bright and hilly streets will not find much to recall an exceptionally grand past, for many notable possessions were cut off in their prime or age by various scoundrels and vandals. Few towns of my acquaintance which once were magnificent have lost more than this one, or can bring more bitter tears to the drooping eye for things that have passed away. Nor do I forget that many years ago I almost passed away myself through sleeping in a damp bed there, and only just missed keeping alive a tradition of destruction. Shaston, to use the old name printed on the milestones, certainly is an ancient of ancients, though perhaps not quite equal to the birthday date of 1000 B.C. presented by Holinshed. But in a very long life it collected many trappings and accessories, gathered lively and deathly incidents of history as well. King Alfred, for instance, founded a nunnery, with his daughter as first abbess. Canute expired at Shaston. With pomp and splendour the body of Edward the Martyr arrived from Wareham after the murder at Corfe Castle in 978. The remains equipped the shrine of St. Edward, made it second to none in the land, and attracted vast wealth from countless pilgrims of fame, fortune, and indigence. The hillside town developed walls and gates. It had a ring of fair churches and three mints. Even to-day natives tell that Gold Hill is full of treasure. The Benedictine abbey crowned the height with beauty, as recent excavations have proved. Little remains to tell of all this grandeur. St. Peter's in decay, last survivor of more than a dozen old churches, has an embattled tower, a fifteenth-century parapet, and fan tracery in the western porch. Inside this ichabod the Jacobean alms-box, meekly imploring "Remember the poore," may move charitable folk to deposit a little something, in view of the town's past losses and the present financial plight of this pilgrim's church. Of a domestic past no more than a number of stone houses and cottages have weathered the centuries. Old Grove Place in Bimport, one of the best of them and panelled within, is favoured for the Hardy house in *Jude the Obscure*, though now liable to be obscured itself by cinema fans bound for the adjacent horror absurdly named "Savoy." The particular and picturesque view within the town is from the top of Gold Hill behind the Town Hall, a combination of cottages, abbey walls, steep cobbled way, and a notable distant prospect (170). Another good scene is Thursday market-day with streets full of country people and smiling healthy faces congregated in this thriving agricultural centre. If Shaftesbury to-day may appear lean in relics of weighty years, its situation makes amends for deficiencies. The position is wonderful. Perched over 700 feet high on a hill, the lie of the site is certainly dramatic. Long views are commanded from every compass point. Perhaps the one most productive of human breathlessness is from Castle Hill: the tremendous expanse includes the whole of the Blackmore Vale and extends to and beyond the distant chalk ridge marked by Bulbarrow, Nettlecombe Tout, and Bubb Down.

Seven miles or so across the vale from Shaftesbury lead to Marnhull. This quiet village with an interesting church lies among the meadows encircled by the remarkable windings which the upper Stour makes after bubbling down from the lovely source at Stourhead. And Marnhull, being the "Marlott" home of Tess of the D'Urbervilles near to the "Stour" in the "Vale of Blackmoor" of course means that Shaftesbury directs right into the heart of Thomas Hardy's Wessex. Beyond the chalk ridge to the south of the Vale are Dorchester, the hills and deep valleys round Maiden Newton and Beaminster, meadows, bridges, and old villages in the Frome valley, Blandford on the Stour, and the wide heaths extending between Wimborne and Wareham. This Hardy country has fine church towers in plenty. Many good country houses, parklands, and woods are to be seen. The villages and hamlets generally look sequestered and often stand in remote spots. Cottages and houses with cob walls, lightly coloured, form bright groups in lanes and round greens. Thatching here, there, and everywhere, one of the glories of Dorset, rises steeply over the farmhouses, big barns, and the village homes in this land of broad fields, sunny slopes, and woody dells far from the madding crowd.

These Dorset homelands sometimes suggest the sombre lights conveyed by the Wessex novels or they hint at the fresh gaiety enshrined in *Under the Greenwood Tree*. The Hardy place-names, or the originals of them, crop up constantly. During my early meanders through these parts the Hardy spirit of place could be more easily captured than nowadays, for then a new heaven and a new earth had not been promised through the medium of drain-pipes, water supplies, council cottages, and free paper money to be picked up on Tom Tiddler's ground. In those years of golden sovereigns it must be admitted that some of the villages appeared rather forlorn and poor, were just sleepy, old-world spots such as I remember at Shapwick ranged round the ancient cross

(175), Sturminster Marshall under the big church-tower (175), Winterborne Kingston, the Puddle villages, and elsewhere. In them lived the last relics of Thomas Hardy's gallery of humanity, men and women who used to tell of bygone customs and ways, recollected wages at seven shillings a week, and related amusing stories. No doubt these good souls departed long since, and carried to the unknown their picturesque and distinctive figures, their quaint clothes and whiskers, and their speech, which the Dorset poet, William Barnes, set to rhyme:

> The primrwose in the sheäde do blow,
> The cowslip in the zun,
> The thyme upon the down do grow,
> The clote where streams do run.

But at least the attractiveness of the villages and countryside in this precious piece of England has remained. Literary pilgrims for many a long year to come also will seek out the originals of Thomas Hardy's pictures, finding the local habitations of "Hambledon Hill," the "Froom" river, Cerne Abbas for "Abbot's Cernel," Puddletown for "Weatherbury," Dorchester with the amphitheatre and great earthwork of Maiden Castle for "Casterbridge," old, old Wareham in its ramparts for "Anglebury," and the other quarters that have gained fame through the novelist's words.

The towns and villages of the Hardy country, delightful as they are to wander in, contain plenty of interesting buildings. Cranborne, for example, remembered as "Chaseborough," surely has the loveliest gem of the county in the manor-house formed round a medieval hunting lodge by Robert Cecil early in the seventeenth century. At Milton Abbas, adjoining "Middleton Abbey," chestnut trees and high woods make exquisite surroundings for the model village built in the eighteenth century by Viscount Milton. Where could be found a better main street of Georgian completeness than at Blandford, the original of "Shottsford" (176)? It was created by the builder-architect family of Bastard after a great fire in 1731. Woolbridge manor-house, the best known Hardy landmark and the "Wellbridge" of Tess's honeymoon, stands prettily by the bridge over the Frome, and few explorers in this neighbourhood could think of missing Bere Regis, "Kingsbere-sub-Greenhill . . . a little one-eyed, blinking sort o' place," yet once of royal favour, and graced with a church, rich in a notable interior, tombs, and tower of stone and flint, to mark the source of all the Durbeyfield family troubles (176). But the varied interests of this lovely tract of Dorset can be only lightly indicated here. They are almost inexhaustible.

The River Stour winds down through Wessex. It ends by meeting the mouth of the Hampshire Avon at Christchurch Priory, where the beautiful stonework of Norman times and the Middle Ages, rising over reflections in the water, adds peculiar grace to the scene at the confluence (149). Many of my readers will know that the course of the Stour throughout is artists' country. It has been a sketching ground for years. But to all in search of England these tranquil lands of vale, stream, and wide pastures offer company enough for anyone. Sometimes my footsteps and sketch-books have travelled that way. Yet one experience developed not only from sketching, scenery, and solitude. It was in part due to Frederick Alfred . . . now gone, rest his soul.

Frederick, a family connection of an older generation than myself, once took me in hand in my sprouting years. With characteristic good nature he proffered my first introduction to the Stour, for the improvement of my practices and to benefit by his precepts. He flirted with mistress Art himself, belonged to the tribe then called Bohemians, and like good King Wenceslaus had a beard. His buoyant nature cherished many enthusiasms. These, never constant, darted here and there, veered round and circled as do swallows in summer. He belonged to the race of beings that can do many things easily and tolerably well while never shining notably at anything in particular. His turbulent hours therefore turned in quick succession to a multitude of occupations which furnished results not quite faultless, not quite perfect, and never quite as they should have been. As a child of the established church his devotions were rather scanty for those distant days when provision for the Sabbath had a recognized place in life. To him, however, even religious tastes needed the spice of variety. So, remarkable to state, he preached on occasions, not quite eloquently, but with great success, to congregations of nonconformist persuasion who adored him alarmingly, perhaps because of his bachelorhood and good looks when perched in chapel pulpits after he had cleaned and dressed himself up.

One Sunday F. directed me to accompany him for my artistic improvement. "The better the day the better the deed," he said, no doubt remembering an absence of preaching engagements. "We will go up the river towards Wimborne." From that proposal I hoped to see the town of Saxon kings with the splendid minster towers, the medieval clock and chained library, the bright main street, and three notable pubs. But that was not to be; only afterwards did I glean the joys of Hardy's "Warborne." We set out, weighted with easels, stools, and all the tackle needed for producing art masterpieces. The season was at the end of August. Blue sky and light cloud overhead, foliage mellow in colour, corn turning golden, lush meadows, and the river waters when we reached them, all attuned to the mood of quiet and apparent serenity that unmistakably denoted the one day in seven. It was truly a day of days, one to enchant and to offer a picture at every turn. F. at once located a subject he wanted me to do and I didn't. Ordering me to work, and how, he then settled down to do just what he fancied. We duly produced two masterpieces which an unenlightened public ever after failed to esteem. On completing these works the afternoon began to wane. Our inspiration likewise declined. After scant

CORFE CASTLE *ruins on the Norman mound occupy a remarkable site. After Edward the Martyr was murdered at Corfe in 978 the later stronghold became a royal residence, a prison for Edward II and Richard II, and dark deeds happened in the dungeons. Heroically defended for the King by Lady Bankes in the Civil War, the castle fell through treachery.*

BATH, unique among English cities. The view from Beechen Cliff before the German raids, showing the sixteenth-century Abbey with the Roman Bath adjacent, the South Parade at the right and the lie of the classic city in Nature's amphitheatre below Lansdown and Solsbury Hill.

LACOCK, *the Wiltshire village famed for lovely dwellings of stone and timbering adjoining the Abbey founded in 1232. Village and abbey are now owned by the National Trust.*

WESTWOOD, *a fifteenth-century stone manor-house on the Wiltshire–Somerset border, now protected by the National Trust.*

rations snatched during the day we felt the pangs of hunger, for the maxim that "An army marches on its stomach" embodies an idea applicable to persons who advance with pencil and brush over paper or canvas. Quite naturally, therefore, our thoughts on art were eclipsed by delicate speculations on food. Though I do not recollect that we deliberated on the flavour of cow-heel, as Sancho did in a like situation, we certainly did wonder what might be preparing even then at the place previously arranged for stoking up. Buoyed with anticipation we quickly packed our belongings and departed.

The paraphernalia we carried made evident our Sunday pursuits. Thus burdened, we turned into a path through cornfields, plodded along, and soon reached a collection of pretty cottages. The cottars, not looking quite themselves in garments commonly worn after the conclusion of the rites of the weekly hot joint, gossiped round open doorways in the warmth of early evening. Though obviously not in church, they thought we ought to have been. That much was said when we appeared. One dame, an outsize edition of Mrs. Joe Gargery, led the attack with boldly commenting on our evil ways of "making pictures of a Sunday." The leader's sentiments were supported by the company, which had increased with fresh arrivals in search of relaxation from weekday toil.

To me the atmosphere of that lovely evening seemed to grow tense. The situation did not accord with the poet's notion:

> Sweet was the sound, when oft, at evening's close,
> Up yonder hill the village murmer rose.

Young and green, I concentrated on counter-attack. Then I glanced at Frederick. One look only steadied my bloodthirsty intentions. He was quite unmoved. For a second or two he looked away dreamily over the golden harvest of the cornfields. Next, quickly and suddenly, he turned on his accusers, fixed a glare on the second Mrs. Gargery and commenced to preach! Evidently he had garnered from the cornfields the second chapter of the Gospel of St. Mark. This unexpected manœuvre caught the Pharisees by surprise. They blinked. Under a battery of words on the sins of condemnation uneasy movements in facial expression suggested dumplings on the boil. But when the preacher warmed to the Bible story, with St. Mark for the text, he carried his hearers from interest to enthusiasm while they listened intently, standing loosely at attention in sight of the corn. In a final effort the discourse ended with telling effect—rather suddenly I thought and perhaps not quite in the style of a bishop. Showered with applause and goodwill we left our late enemies repentant. I began to understand the success in the pulpits.

F. said we must hurry along. It occurred to me that the quick end to the preaching quite likely had been influenced by the equivalent of cow-heel. Late arrivals signify spoiled meals. Nevertheless, in talking of the recent event F.

seemed much pleased with himself after victory in counter-attack. We arrived for supper later than arranged. The cow-heel appeared in the form of prime local salmon, so of course was delicious. These happenings occurred in the 1890's. Times have changed since then. Now anybody can sketch, or do anything else for that matter, in the valley of the Stour at any time, Sundays included, and nobody bothers two hoots.

The Stour duly ends near Hengistbury Head, the splendid viewpoint and camping ground favoured alike by the tribes of the Iron, British, and present ages. The other notable river in Hardy's south Wessex, the Frome, flows into the sinuous channels of Poole Harbour after winding past Roman and Saxon Wareham. The long belt of chalk, extending across England from the Norfolk seaboard, terminates in a geological mix-up of clays, sands, and oolitic stone on the Isle of Purbeck, which isn't an island. But whatever it is and is not, Purbeck carries Corfe Castle, or all that remains of the stronghold, a pathetic ruin decorating one of the most wonderful sites in the country (181). Here at last we arrive at the source of Edward the Martyr's murder, aforementioned in these pages, the romantic scene of Queen Elfrida's expression of mother love in 978. If Edward had favoured teetotalism the course of history might have been different. Now everybody knows that the offer of a nice drink ended unpleasantly and caused Elfrida's son Ethelred to reign in Edward's stead. Two consequences of the wicked lady's misdeed towards her stepson we have met at Shaftesbury and Wherwell, though the gorgeous shrine and the priory, created to appease heaven, are even more extinct than Corfe Castle. Another lady performed with distinction at the later castle on this Norman mound. The defence by Lady Bankes, her maids, and a few men is a famous and gallant story of the Civil War. Welcomed with boiling water, red-hot cinders, and stones, the Parliamentary commander, unlike King Edward, temporarily turned teetotaller in order to stimulate his courage! When the castle fell through treachery after holding out for three years, the Roundheads scurvily acknowledged heroic deeds by blowing up the place with gunpowder. Those with an eye for demolitions may still trace the holes for galleries and mines of destruction. Thus splendour had its fall. No wonder this ruin, one of the grandest in the land, kindles sparks of romance.

Finally, at Purbeck, the chalk ends in sight of the sea. Nine Barrow Down leads to Studland and to Swanage, Thomas Hardy's "Knollsea, lying snug between two headlands as between a finger and a thumb." On the opposite side of this imaginary island the great prehistoric camp of Worbarrow, partly eroded by the waves, almost joins a tongue of stone country. So good-bye to Chalk Land.

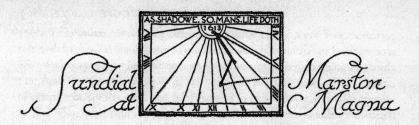

Sundial at Marston Magna

AS. SHADOWE. SO. MANS. LIFE DOTH
1613
IX X XI XII

4. STONE COUNTRY

WILTSHIRE, SOMERSET, DORSETSHIRE

Years ago I came by chance on this message of dubious cheer, "As Shadowe So Mans Life Doth goe." The words were carved on a stone sundial, dated 1613, set in a wall of the old manor-house at Marston Magna in Somerset. Through a sunny day the shadow from the gnomon moved across the dial, marking the hours. In the evening it reached the figure VI and neared the little word "goe." Soon the shadow faded. Then it went the way of earlier shadows that had crept across the dial ever since King James reigned; shadows that year by year told the time on bright days without stopping or being wound up, and counted serene hours for all who looked and perhaps read the dumb carved homily, the sundial's sermon in stone, consigning all humanity, sooner or later, to the eternal shades. With the sunlight gone and the dial's hours ended, the unlit maxim remained to point the moral. Yet I knew the shadow would reappear with the sun to count out a new day. What need had the sundial for moralizing? For itself, a creature of on days and off days, nothing had changed since the year 1613. If nice and fine, work would begin again shortly before VII o'clock in the morning and terminate soon after VI p.m., for this particular sundial, evidently a trade unionist, did not favour starting labour too early or finishing it very late. As for the gloomy warning of the maxim, it could afford to ignore that and point such wisdom to those intimately concerned with going. A sundial ever has reckoned on a to-morrow and always will while the sun continues to shine.

The shadow and the message on the sundial did not cause me to meditate on my decease. On the contrary, with two feet on the firm earth and no thought of wings in heaven or central heating elsewhere, I sketched this quaint conceit fixed by a kind somebody to face the sun when clocks were scarce just ten years after Queen Elizabeth died. The mason who placed it there, and neatly finished "Mans Life Doth goe," probably never reckoned, before going himself, that his handiwork would remain to show the shadows still going after more than three hundred years. And having spent days in Wiltshire, Somerset, and Dorset, with the bravery of stone for company, my mood dwelt more on the permanence of work, and especially stonework, than on the frailty of men that accomplished it. For much goodness belongs to good stone. It is one of the finest among building materials, one of the most durable, and very responsive to the human touch. Near and far, in many lands, it presents some of mankind's highest efforts. It gives reality to bygone tales and hints at forgotten times. In the country that is the subject of the following pages the native stone tells of endeavour, continuance, history, and of much else concerning matters great and small. It imparts lessons, meaning volumes.

The area now in mind, and including parts of Wiltshire, Somerset, and Dorset, is shown by the map below. The principal geological basis of this district is stone. The long structure of oolite and lias, making a belt across England from Yorkshire to the southern sea, covers north-west Wiltshire, runs down Somerset, and continues through western Dorset to the coast. Uneven in limits, this belt in the south stretches in places to a width of about 30 miles and is bordered by the greensand and chalk country summarized in my previous chapter. Stone also extends across Somerset with the limestone and sandstone rocks of the Mendip Hills, which figure on the landscape almost to Weston-super-Mare. The chief differences from the stone formations are recognized in the Recent deposits of the low lands that mark flat stretches of country largely subdivided by dykes and drains known as "rhines." These levels face the Severn estuary and the Bristol Channel from Clevedon to Bridgwater, and extend

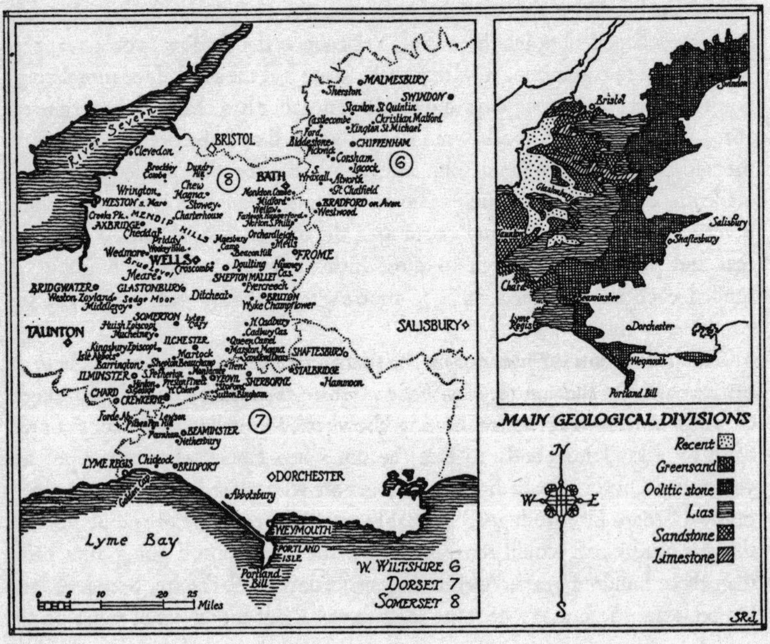

MAIN GEOLOGICAL DIVISIONS

Recent
Greensand
Oolitic stone
Lias
Sandstone
Limestone

W. WILTSHIRE 6
DORSET 7
SOMERSET 8

BRADFORD-ON-AVON. *Town Bridge, with ancient chapel on it, serves the lovely stone town built up the slopes of the green Avon valley. The famous Saxon Church near the waterside is beyond the left of this view.*

MALMESBURY, once one of the sights of England when the rich and powerful Abbey arose in completeness with a central spire higher than Salisbury's. This foundation, patronized by Saxon kings, began before the coming of St. Augustine. Now a place of seclusion and great charm, the medley of churches, ruins, relics, and stone roofs adorning an eminence almost encircled by the upper Bristol Avon.

inland on each side of the low Polden Hills through Brue Level, Sedge Moor, and the course of the River Parret.

This geological framework embraces a piece of England abounding in scenic harmonics and contrasts. Combes in Wiltshire and round Bath are deep and wooded. Watered by sparkling streams, they enclose choice homesteads and villages. The high tableland of the Mendip Hills is broken by gorges which, as at Cheddar, present spectacular magnificence in rocky shapes. The Mendip bastions of immemorial age, with the hills and abrupt tors in the Wells and Glastonbury direction, overlook the low and wide expanses of reclaimed marshes and dyke lands. Past the Somerset plain hills again lead beyond Yeovil, Crewkerne, and Chard into Dorset. From north to south there are fine pastoral tracts where dairy farmers flourish and produce famous cheeses, and the rich soil of the flat districts is so productive of Income Tax that local agriculturalists rarely love the Chancellor of the Exchequer. Considered as a whole this area might be ranked almost second to Milton's earthly Paradise. It offers a profusion of trees, natural luxuriance, smiling pastures, wide panoramas, and orchards that promise cider. Secluded lanes everywhere are particularly seductive. Spangled with wild flowers, and in spring bright with primroses, they thread among meadows and lead between deep banks up and down hills. Notable and lovely are many of the place-names. They ring musically, carry the tang of old medievalism, are in tune with the history, traditions, and tales that developed in this home of warm-hearted people. In fact, these names, with the peculiarities of scene, sentinels such as Malmesbury's mound, Glastonbury Tor, Cadbury Castle, Hamdon Hill, and the Fosse Way of unknown antiquity bisecting the country from above Malmesbury to Ilchester and Chard, are all just of the right kind for this stronghold of truth, legend, and myth, the breeding place of stories of Joseph of Arimathea, King Arthur, silver horseshoes, knights, and King Alfred burning cakes.

The generous supply of good stone which nature gave to this tract of country lay ready to serve a kindly people, who learned to use it sympathetically and with great skill. Quarries at Doulting (the source for Wells cathedral and Glastonbury), Ham Hill, Portland, and elsewhere, established their great reputations, others in local places supplied local needs, and the fame of the masons, especially of Somerset, spread far and wide. Nature's gift of stone, worked by man, came to represent life and times in the flow of centuries. It expressed in visible form much of the story of aspiration, hearth and home of generations for whom stone in a measure was part and parcel of existence. As the harvest of stone accumulated over hill and vale, the light of the sun and the shades of time played on churches, splendid towers, manor-houses, villages, hamlets, and towns mellow and charming, set out point by point legend, romance, history, tradition and beauty. Arches and walls, mullions, chiselled devices, and innumerable features intricate or simple and all of stone decorated the landscapes and gathered meanings. They told, and still tell, of dwellers in castles and mansions, churchmen in cloistered seclusion, squires and their ladies proud of ancestral gables and walled gardens, parsons and villagers in country parishes, beaus and flirts in surroundings of Restoration and Georgian elegance, and the stock of yeomen, craftsmen, tradespeople, and workaday folk who lived domestic days and nights within thick walls lit by windows deeply set.

Architecturally the medieval spirit held fast in this home of old ways and quaint lore. Gothic work advanced to great excellence in ecclesiastical and domestic building and persisted with remarkable tenacity in parts little affected by the changes of time. The wave of classicalism that made Bath new and wonderful spread to the towns, manor-houses, and some of the villages. But whether Gothic or Renaissance canons were followed, the men who laid and carved the native stone by methods long known brought to their work something of imagination and poetry, a measure of their inheritance and themselves. Signs of graciousness in life, and reminders of the storied past, ancient custom and usage, abound in this geological division. Hills, vales, and lowlands and the gifts of the earth and artistry at every turn offer sermons in stone.

NORTH-WEST WILTSHIRE

The top piece of this southern section of the stone belt belongs to Wiltshire. It is well wooded, undulating in parts, has delicious combes and rich, green meadows, and is bisected by the pretty windings of the upper Bristol Avon. The combinations show true and characteristic English scenes. Those who like peace and quiet will not seek in vain. Often the signposts have patriarchal dignity, not in their make but from the place-names they carry. Who could not feel the challenge to romance and old ancestry on reading Christian Malford, Kington St. Michael, Stanton St. Quintin, Lydiard Tregooze, and other fascinating names by the score, or fail to rise to their promise of leading to saints in the flesh, tilting knights, and miraculous doings in progress? But euphony sometimes ends in discord. The owners of these titles sounding sweet may disappoint, for hereabout modern man and local councils have contrived of late, and with much success, to add ugliness to loveliness. More scars on the landscape are proposed, though as yet the grace of authority still permits stone walls and stone roofs of churches, cottages, and houses to blend lightly and harmoniously with luxuriant natural backgrounds. Villages of brown and mossy stone present subjects for present pleasure and the inward eye of memory. Well represented by Biddestone and Sherston, they reach a climax at Castle Combe and Lacock (10, 184). Both are exquisite and justly famous. Castle Combe, particularly, might be a creation of fantasy, a vision of stone embowered in wooded slopes and gathered round the market cross, church, and manor-house.

Great Chalfield Manor-house

The renderings in stone of churches and towers throughout the neighbourhood are generally interesting, often notable, and tombstones in quiet churchyards here and there, as at Kington St. Michael, admirably carved and lettered, exhibit last traces of the traditional skill and invention that distinguished the grand days of masoncraft.

The homely and domestic past is typified in this district by signs of more than common goodness. Substantial houses bear the medieval or Tudor stamp of old families and squires. Sometimes a gatehouse or a moat impels admiration, both for picturesqueness and for ancestral foresight in keeping the vulgar at a distance before policemen were invented and we all became equal. Numerous other houses, trim, sometimes almost stately, and eked out with mouldings and classic embellishments, send thoughts to a past local society that flocked in Georgian years to be polished up at Bath. Almost all the villages have at least one of these houses of the early, middle, or later periods, with fronts gabled or square and windows of mullions or sashes. The older ones include such prizes as Great Chalfield, guarded by a moat; South Wraxall, very tempting, dating onward from the fifteenth century, and owning a gatehouse; the home of the Gascelyn and Hungerford families at Sheldons, near Chippenham; a fine neighbour at Ford, now a farmhouse; and the long lines of Lower Westwood manor-house, which show prettily from the churchyard for anyone to see (184). Examples of the later periods crop up continually — behind gate piers at Atworth, a shell porch at Pickwick Manor, and so on. The country towns continue this story of stone with streets and byways schemed in the prevalent bright tone. Chippenham, for example, retains its character and is best seen round about the church, the fifteenth-century guildhall, and the *Angel* hotel, next to which King Alfred had a hunting lodge in days of long ago. Corsham is remarkably good for streets of early and late houses, cobbled ways, the Court,

CORSHAM, *Wiltshire*

and a wonderful range of almshouses with lines of dormers and carved armorial bearings capped by a stone-tiled roof. Bradford-on-Avon, again, is full of delight, both in situation and buildings. From the bridge, the church, and the celebrated Saxon chapel, the town piles up the steep hillside in terraces (189). And there is Malmesbury, ever appealing. Redolent with the ancient of days, it demands more than a casual halt.

Malmesbury reaches the heights in name, fame, and natural elevation. It stands rather out of the beaten track and has a railway station of suitable smallness for the single line that almost debouches into the road. I mention this railway matter because of its importance to Malmesbury's present, past, and soul. Line and station are of the kind provided for the purpose of preserving sections of rural England and keeping some of our choicest small towns pure and undefiled from invasions by crowds, vandals, cigarette ends, and the scattered leavings of untidy humanity. Distinguished by buildings, rolling stock, coal dumps, and appurtenances all conveniently small, and with funny engines, services meagre, and nothing doing on Sundays, these assets of transport organization have been known to move grateful hearts and prompt voices to sing,

> My heart leaps up when I behold
> A single railway line;
> For then I know the wood and wold
> Are almost wholly mine.

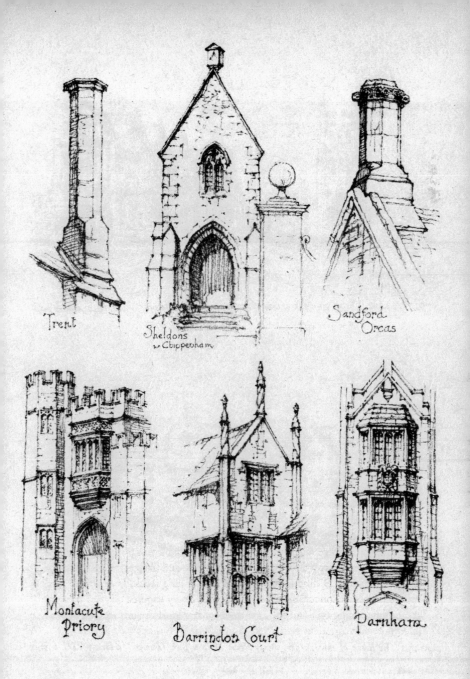

Trent

Sheldons
or Chippenham

Sandford
Orcas

Montacute
Priory

Barrington Court

Parnham

STONE DETAILS IN WILTSHIRE, SOMERSET, AND DORSET

DITCHEAT. *The seventeenth-century home of the Hopton family adjoining the churchyard.*

MELLS. *The home of the Horner family since "Little Jack Horner" in Henry VIII's reign.*

SOMERSET MANOR-HOUSES

The example that ends at Malmesbury upholds the species. It serves the town adequately, not very often, and is unobtrusive. That its fascinating goal has weathered recent times pretty well is largely to the credit of this inconvenient, admirable, and single line. And though good roads from the north, south, east, and west direct to this point in Wiltshire, it is no less than a sin to gain it by means other than the railway, even if so doing means parking a car at Swindon or Chippenham. For the benedictions of the single line approach ought not to be missed. They exactly prepare for adventure in the unknown. The getting to Little Somerford junction, waiting about for something to come in, the arrival of the something, finding an empty compartment pining for company, the start off round the curve of the solo track, the carriage window making a frame for fleeting and tranquil pictures of green, green meadows, willows, and the limpid Avon—all these diversions deliberately and without hurry lead expectation onward. In its own good time the engine fusses noisily. Darkness follows. The train has shot into the tunnel. It quickly comes out again, and lo! you are deposited in wonderland, feeling as Alice must have done when she bumped out of the end of the rabbit-hole. You skin your eyes in amazement, forget to give up the ticket, omit to confirm that the 6.30 p.m. is the last and only hope for returning to the twentieth century. The only thing that matters is a vision of old England: the desecrated abbey, stone walls, and gables pile up high on a bluff over trees. Foliage embowers the mill. The stream meanders under a footbridge (190). Once I espied an antique figure garbed like an ancient Briton tending swine, a van Ostade foreground touch to a subject worthy of Ruisdael. This introduction to Malmesbury, due reward for a pilgrimage of miles, can account for any lapses at the railway station! To all true adventurers I therefore repeat my advice: do not miss this train on the single line.

Up the pathways and steps lead to the town perched on a hill almost encircled by Avon streams crossed by six bridges. Steep streets, walls mostly of stone, stone roofs coloured by weather and lichen, ancient features, ups, downs, bridges, and running waters keep the searcher wondering what next may come into view. The groupings made by this hillside collection are big and fine, and the one visible from the Avon at Daniel's Well, topped by the abbey and solitary church spire, rivals the remarkable scene from the railway station. The town's centre, at the ways and squares round the abbey, is marked by a Tudor cross, arched and reminiscent of the older one at Salisbury, yet itself old enough to have known great days when

> Bishop and abbot and prior were there;
> Many a monk, and many a friar,
> Many a knight, and many a squire.

Long-established shops and nice houses of course line the streets, the number of pubs per acre indicates liquid cash in ample supply, and the long yards seen from the archways of *The King's Arms*, *The George*, and elsewhere, recall horsey days and smart turn-outs. The name "Athelstan" figures a good deal; this evidently is in gratitude for great benefits bestowed by the golden-haired grandson of King Alfred, though it is unlikely that all the cakes, very light luncheons, and printed items attributed to the name have any real connection with this Saxon king. The cinema of low height and purpose, iniquitously dumped almost on the top of the churchyard ancestors, should not be noticed. More exciting for study is the cunning device of a large mirror placed at the dangerous churchyard bend, for it shows through the looking-glass who goes in and out of this wonderland; it safely guides to the hallowed place of faded glory that long ago was the crown, and is still the pride, of this charming town of old wool fame.

How the Benedictine abbey of Malmesbury once appeared can only be imagined from buildings carefully preserved and ruins. In its prime the sight presented must have been one of the grandest in England. Standing loftily on the eminence, more than three times longer than at present, adorned with a big western tower and a central spire sweeping upward twenty feet higher than Salisbury's top point, and surrounded by monastic quarters, fancy alone can piece together the wonderful scene shattered and gone. Founded before the coming of St. Augustine, the abbey rose to fame under royal and noble patronage. There King Athelstan was buried. King Edgar's interest brought the town a charter in 972. New magnificence developed in the twelfth century with the grandeur of strong Norman masonry. A great man, William of Malmesbury, the Anglo-Norman chronicler, then busied himself in the library, moulding the course of English literature in lively and flowing narrative. While he penned delicate word-pictures for us to know something of the England he knew, he saw the pristine brilliance of the masonry we see, and noted "erected at vast cost, and with surpassing beauty." Century by century fresh loveliness came to the temple. The continual measures of prayer and praise rose, fell, and echoed round pillars, arches, and the high stone vault. Clouds gathered. The storm of the Dissolution broke. The monks departed and their noble offering to the Giver of all good shared the fate of glittering jewels throughout the land. William Stumpe arrived. This wealthy cloth merchant enriched Henry VIII with £1,500 and the abbey was his. To the sound of looms instead of plain-song the south chapel and transept became a cloth factory. The clothier, to his credit, presented the abbey nave to the town for a parish church. Thus it remains, nobly cherished and supported. For the rest, most of this splendid foundation has faded away as surely as its Saxon abbot St. Aldhelm, scholar, poet, bishop, the ninety-sixth predecessor of the present Bishop of Salisbury.

Of this abbey church of St. Peter and St. Paul, enough remains to show the impressive character of the magnificent creation built by Bishop Roger of

Sarum and his followers. The keynote of the once vast interior that developed from the middle Norman period is presented by massive columns five feet in diameter, scolloped capitals, zig-zag and billet mouldings, early pointed arches, round arches in the triforium, the Decorated clerestory, and the fine groined vault of the ceiling. In this wealth of bright loveliness, now lovingly cared for, particular things call for examination. There are the eastern stone screen bearing the arms of Henry VII; the curious stone projection over the south aisle thought to have been an organ chamber; and the south porch, a masterpiece of composition and style ablaze with Romanesque enrichment and bas-reliefs, the like of which cannot be found elsewhere. Among the ruins outside the flanking tower of the west front denotes perfection in late Norman craftsmanship, and broken masonry alone marks the loss of one of the highest spires in Europe.

Turning from the misty past to the sixth year of the dynasty of Rations, my memory tells me that I revisited Malmesbury on the ninth day of June 1945, an important date to sportsmen and all English-speaking people who "put a little bit on" at least once a year. Sketching was my purpose, and also to verify William of Malmesbury's words at the actual place where most likely his shade walks as softly and slowly as the ghost in *Hamlet* when midnight strikes and cocks are sound at roost. On that sporting day radiant sunlight also happened to brighten the halo of another literary celebrity. I arrived correctly by the single line, was enthralled again with the view, commenced to sketch it, and obedient to the call of midday time and internal warnings, ascended the steps in search of something to eat. Anticipation suggested fare for which Wiltshire is famous. Expectation rose with the remembrance of Mr. Harris's epicurean announcement of the porker's purgatory at Calne, read a few hours earlier at Chippenham station. Quiet and charming as ever and with not many people about, the sunny streets might have changed hardly at all since King Charles limited his visit to one bed and one breakfast in 1643. But lunch in 1945 was coy and elusive. "Very sorry, no rations," and sad wagging of heads always answered my request under the sign of *The Bell*, *The King's Arms*, and other empty indications of provender in this old place where so much else had perished. Ministries apparently knew not of Malmesbury's existence, a relic lost in a pigeonhole since the Reformation without hope of coupons or points for jam. Hungry, I returned down the steps without fuel for inspiration.

Renewed hope, and thoughts of tea long before teatime prompted another ascent to the ruins, past the cinema queue (small), and to the square round the market cross. Here a certain liveliness prevailed in place of the normal calm. Something must have happened. Cars and people were about. Even the aged natives, usually rooted to seats under the arched cross stood up. A young man, strong and browned, at once greeted me with warm familiarity. He exclaimed excitedly, "DANT'S won, and I've got a double!"

"Hurrah," I rejoined, for he was so pleased with himself, so voluble and friendly, his infectious joy made it impossible not to rejoice with him for having found something that might have been lost—by a short head at the winning-post. This bright event foretold a general rise in sporting chances. The chit for Malmesbury must have been traced to the pigeonhole. The rations had arrived. I quickly sought and found the cheapest tea within living memory, viz. lots of toast, cakes, pot of tea, jug of milk, unlimited sugar, price sevenpence. Without requesting financial details of this transaction, I presented my benefactor with a complete shilling and ignored the change; a magnanimous act inspired by the knowledge that I too had accumulated capital by placing one shilling on the Derby winner.

Refreshed and eager, I hastened towards the sketching point. Halfway down the steps a pretty A.T.S. girl, sitting on the seat there, smilingly remarked and apparently to me, "Dante's won!" We exchanged pleasant glances. I really wondered if her beaming face did not indicate winning a treble. But the sights of Malmesbury are so wonderful, there is no telling what they may offer on Derby day or any other time.

All too soon the 6.30 p.m. train fussed in readiness to start. It was unnecessary to fight a struggling crowd to get into it. Sole monarch of a compartment, the carriage window framed for me a good last look of the ruined abbey, grey Tudor gables over trees, the stream rippling below, an elegy soft in the glow of early evening. Then off! A smoke-screen rose from the engine. Darkness and the tunnel followed—and Malmesbury receded into the land of dreams, bygones, shrines, and beauty. May it remain there undisturbed by ministries, planners, spoilers, and hard knocks from babes yet unborn, even if this means a shortage of rations from officialism.

FROM BATH TO WELLS

As the crow flies, Bath is less than 20 miles from Malmesbury. Yet what a contrast that short distance brings! The sweet old town of lost years is exchanged for one teeming with the movements of humanity, cars, buses, and all the liveliness of the present progressing against a background bright with evidences of days before yesterdays and long ago. In spite of so much continually going forward and the accumulation of modern effects to keep the old place right up to date, the past never seems to be far away. It is always just round the corner, reminiscent of Ralph Allen, Beau Nash, and the Woods, who created the classic city; Bishop King, who fathered the splendid late Gothic church; John de Villula and the succession of churchmen at the great and lost Norman monastery; Romans, who bathed; and the host of figures and celebrities who came to this favoured spot for the good of their health, wealth, or pleasure onward from that legendary period when Bladud, in league with the Devil and father of King Lear, magically heated the water that brought fame to Aquæ

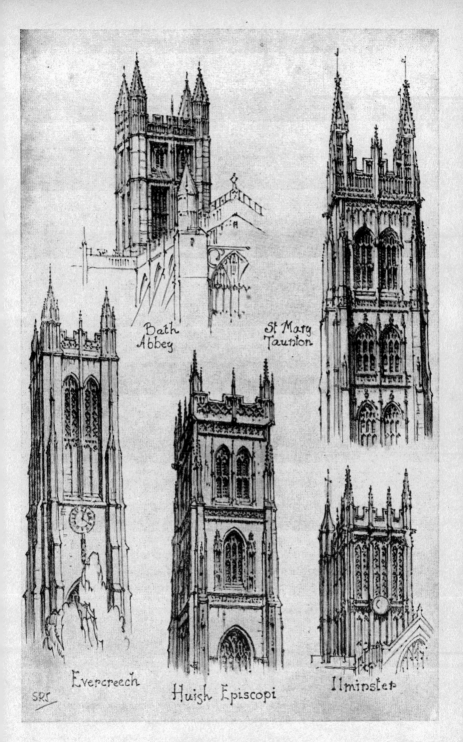

Bath
Abbey

St Mary
Taunton

Evercreech

Huish Episcopi

Ilminster

SRS

SOMERSET TOWERS.

EIGHTEENTH-CENTURY BATH. *The house of Thomas Linley, the singing-master, in Pierrepont Place; from 1767 to 1771 the home of beautiful Elizabeth Anne Linley, subject of Gainsborough's pictures and with whom Richard Brinsley Sheridan eloped.*

Sulis, lustre to eighteenth-century Bath, and has shed a warmth of popularity right down to this present moment.

Particularly in Bath, you cannot move forward without going backward. The traffic lights, now green, now red, change and wink merely as the current versions of those other lights that have shone brilliantly, mellow, or dim in this same vale since Ptolemy knew of it nearly two thousand years ago. You thread between the colonnades to the King's and Queen's Baths and, meditating on the 83-feet span of water contained in Roman lead brought from the Mendips, quite easily picture early bathers, visitors from the Legions at Caerleon, Chester, York, and from Cirencester, who left their names on inscriptions. The band plays in the gay, crowded gardens by the river, but there, just beyond, you see the splendid sixteenth-century tower and abbey traceries, successors of Minerva's Temple and the Norman fane, rising graciously over the moving traffic (201). In but a moment you change the bustle of the streets for the seclusion of narrow ways, attracted here and there by new goods displayed behind little panes of old shop fronts, or intrigued by moulded stone doorways leading to grave staircases fitted with forests of turned balusters that once knew the swish of silks when sedan chairs were the fashion. Down a narrow passage you quiz the front of the first house Ralph Allen built for himself. In Lilliput Alley behind it the sight of Sally Lunn's name arouses delicate speculations on teatime, though not to be forgotten are the Bath buns and Dr. Oliver's eighteenth-century invention, for such delicacies, like Banbury and Shrewsbury cakes, all discerning people know are only the real things in their name-places. Or you may dive between columns and merry urchins into Pierrepont Place to find the Linley House (202)—oh! to think that pillared doorway framed beautiful Eliza and Richard Brinsley Sheridan's love! Turning into Old Orchard Street, itself sadly faded as its own painted sign, you meet the relic of the Theatre Royal. Its 1750 walls are neither theatre nor royal any longer, yet still they are vivid in promptings, for Sarah Siddons, the Kembles, Elliston "joyousest of once embodied spirits," and their company painted in fame, all wafted long since from the magic boards to prank in eternal green-rooms impervious to mortal eye. Out in the spaciousness of parades, squares, terraces, and streets giving vistas of stately stone houses you join with the short-skirted and trousered throngs, yet ever conscious that the same ways used to know the tread of red heels and shoes gay in embroidered patterns and jewelled buckles. Perhaps in the Royal Crescent or North Parade you observe the generous width of the stone pavement, ample for moving along without jostling passers-by, yet also just the thing for the elegant promenade *à la mode* of a Mrs. Malaprop to take the air while keeping a guardian eye on Lydia Languish attended by Captain Absolute. You come to the pleasant view at the end of South Parade, the river below, and green slopes stretching up towards Prior Park, and glancing sideways at the windows of Amelia House, remember how Fanny Burney looked out to "meadows, hills, Prior Park, the soft-flowing Avon." And in The Circus, Gay Street, Queen Square, past the Assembly Rooms, over Pulteney Bridge into Pulteney Street, here, there, and everywhere you meet the name tablets admirably placed by a thoughtful civic authority to locate the quarters of those figures who came to and fro to polish up their health, abilities, pleasure, or scandal, and thereby sent along a host of illustrious past names to mingle with the city's new and memorable record. You gain the elevated surroundings, as at Beechen Cliff (182–183), and view panoramic scenes sparkling in nature's amphitheatre of slopes and verdure, seeing towers, spires, and formal lay-outs spread below like fantasies of dreamland. Howsoever you look at the city, from the heights, at ground level, in full daytime, when evening steals over it or the night lights twinkle, this creation in stonework is ever appealing. As a grandam of past and perennial beauty, it presents a face of charm and attraction that neither age nor new times have eclipsed.

Yes, Bath is still Bath, unique of its kind in England. It remains so, too, in spite of the German raids of 1942 which spread ruin far and wide when the city became a burning mass and flames shot up high into the night from towers and church steeples. Yet after that ordeal, marked by gaunt patches levelled to the ground, the Assembly Rooms merely a shell, the Royal Crescent and Queen Square damaged, St. James's and other churches gutted inside, and other effects of war beyond reckoning, it is remarkable to see so much remaining intact, and to find how the actualness and spirit of place have survived. With a fine general aspect continuing, it should be possible to make good a great deal of the loss and, under capable and sympathetic treatment, to restore the delicate beauty of past years.

More terror, perhaps, is to be feared from raiders in our midst. Already Lord Methuen and Mr. E. M. Hick have given warning in *The Times* of further possible destruction under the guise of rehabilitation. If the plan is proceeded with it will involve the elimination of features of historical, architectural, and social importance in sweeping away Georgian streets, buildings of notable character, and, among various places of interest, St. James's church, where Queen Anne worshipped and Mrs. Thrale married Mr. Piozzi, the houses of John Palmer and of William Herschel (Lady Huntington's organist at the Octagon Chapel who discovered the planet Uranus), and the lodgings of Sheridan and W. H. Hudson. It is to be hoped that those in charge of the city's present welfare will accept their responsibilities for the heritage of the past and realize their duty to future generations.

But the delicate beauty of Bath seems almost too precious for our bustling times, might be improved out of existence any day or blown to shreds by our mechanical contrivances and drills. When in the city it always occurs to me that a place so rare ought to be kept under a glass case or protected somehow, only to be viewed on production of identity cards certifying the holders' correctness of mind, manners, clothes, and deportment, and merely presented through spy-holes to the impure and defiled of this age. People, including myself, appear so odd bumping about amongst columns, pilasters, and the elegant adornments of classicalism. Our clothes are wrong. Our hair is not right. Figures look skimpy and streamlined, lack the fullness and colour given by the departed satins and brocades. Certainly the ladies' faces are painted, but where are the patches and high wigs? The noise and pace of the streets never suggest the appropriate and once familiar slow promenade, "Egad!" and "Oh, gemini," lavender cries, and the tap-tap of hoofs. So much seems square-pegged in round holes. The sweep of the Royal Crescent is too severe for us to-day, The Circus too perfectly round, Gay Street not gay enough, and Pulteney Street too magnificently straight for our quick and shifty ways. How residents manage to live up to their backgrounds I never discovered; perhaps, and wisely, they do not try to do so. Now and again, possibly, some of them pant, as fishes out of water do, for on casually meeting a native aged seventy-two, the occupier of a house built by John Wood, he apologized for his soft hat and lounge suit and for his deficiencies in habiliments downward from a periwig. "We don't fit the houses and streets at all," he added. "The only times the place becomes itself are when the costume balls are held in the Assembly Rooms. Quite wonderful then. Everybody dressed up, the lights, the music, and the old dances. I almost fancy this street and my house alive with ghosts. But I do not expect to see those nights again now the Assembly Rooms are in ruins."

And of ghosts, Bath of course may stir up flights as numerous and notable as any English town can command. They flit over the pages of history and haunt the intimate chapters of the country's domestic story. Their earthly names, doings, capers, and local habitations are common knowledge through many and excellent books devoted to every aspect of Bath's historical, social, and architectural fame. The face of the city tells much of its memorable past. It is beyond my design to dwell on the wonderful Roman relics and finds, how the Roman baths were discovered in 1755, the decline and decay of the Norman cathedral, the medieval borough with markets, fairs, and a woollen industry, the abbey that rose over the ruins onward from the year 1500. Evelyn told of the "streets narrow, uneven and unpleasant" in 1654. Pepys observed "the walls of the City, which are good, and the battlements whole" in 1688, when he also eyed "very fine ladies" in the Cross Bath, bathed himself, was "carried away wrapped in a sheet, and in a chair home" to bed, but disturbed by a notion, "methinks it cannot be clean to go so many bodies together in the same water." I need not particularize on the later phases that developed after Queen Anne's visit in 1702, Bath's rise to the pinnacle of fame, and the city's rebirth in fresh grace and splendour guided by the trio of notables, Ralph Allen the Cornishman, who grew to be rich and universally beloved, John Wood, the architect from Yorkshire who, with his son John, created the stateliness visible to-day, and Richard Nash, the Welshman and adventurer who ruled as a king, ended almost as a pauper, and was buried with pomp at the abbey. The attendant comings and goings of the great and the famous, of hosts of somebodies and nobodies, old and young, well and gouty, beautiful, plain, clever, witty, and dull, who sought health and fortune, pleasure, gaiety, devotion, vice, and all that life offered in the jewel set within the sweet Somerset hills—the gallery of past figures, their quarters and surroundings, and all the colours of the brightest years of the fair city of the waters are too well known for me to attempt to paint them again.

We can explore Bath in its several dressings, staged on enduring Roman foundations, and ever feel grateful for its old heart of fascinating ways about the abbey, the classic beauty of two centuries ago, and its cheerful and bright to-day. If Walter Savage Landor considered the city excelled only by Florence, there is no need to disagree with him. And those interested in their country's and Bath's past will never forget the name-tablets which endow walls with so many great names. They beckon everywhere: to Gainsborough's house in The Circus and fourteen years of wonderful accomplishment; to No. 2 Alfred Street, inhabited by Thomas Lawrence, a little boy in his teens who drew portraits of beauties and beaux at half a guinea a time; at every turn out come the shades of Burke and Clive and Nelson, Chesterfield and Lytton, Goldsmith and Wordsworth, Dickens, Carlyle, and throngs of notable and notorious souls that polished Bath's stones with lasting fame. We leave them, perpetual monarchs of the squares, the terraces, and the streets, bid them goodbye on our eve of departure. Finding the hotels packed, as they usually are, my readers with me may do as old-time visitors did—seek a lodging for ourselves and our cars as others used to do for themselves and their chaises. Passing between the pilasters of a stone doorway, we may cross a flagged hall, ascend a wide staircase positively winking and impish with the shine of turned balusters, and enter a panelled room under a delicate plaster ceiling to find good luck offers a meal and the modern apology for old madeira as the summer day fades into night. Perchance, away from the sounds of the motors, we may fancifully hear faint music not of this world echoing a tune of Bath's old years,

> Let the toast pass,—
> Drink to the lass,
> I'll warrant she'll prove an excuse for the glass.

The Fosse Way runs out of Bath where the South Gate used to be, directs over the Avon up Holloway, and continues through the heart of Somerset. This great and ancient route from the Exe in the south-west to the Humber in the north-east, transformed by the Romans into a highway, and a continuous trace in history since earliest record, represents a good deal more than an

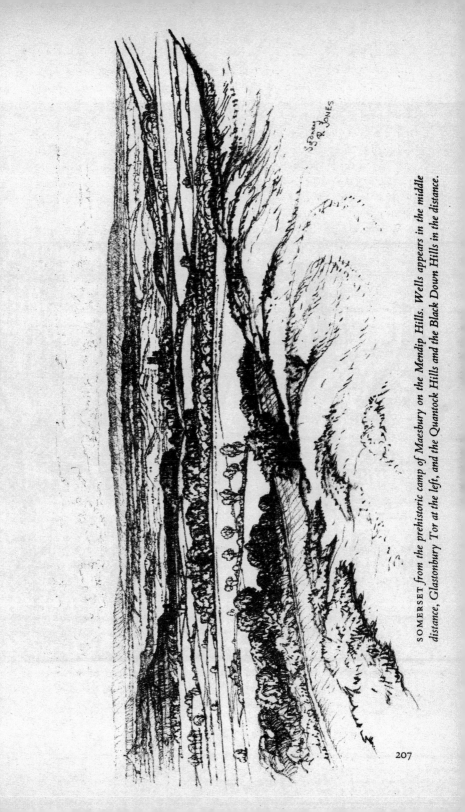

SOMERSET from the prehistoric camp of Maesbury on the Mendip Hills. Wells appears in the middle distance, Glastonbury Tor at the left, and the Quantock Hills and the Black Down Hills in the distance.

207

Sydney R
JONES Wells

WELLS. *View at the market-place near the conduit. This homeland of old faith and dreams is an incomparable survival of the Middle Ages in England. It fascinates with gateways, domestic buildings, clerical homes, and a moated palace, which group round the Cathedral's central pile of 1321, the perpendicular towers, and a wealth of medieval art and early Gothic sculpture.*

George Inn

Abbot's Kitchen

Tribunal

LIGHTS OF GLASTONBURY

archæological line on the Somerset map. It promises much to twentieth-century travellers—speed for the fast, a collection of gradients, and something to see and think about for inquisitive and contemplative souls. The old, old road leads to country beautiful to look at and hospitable to be in. It introduces kind people and soft sounds in speech, weathered stones of homes and churches, the romance of legends and traditions. The road points the way to rocky gorges, caves for damp English-Arabian nights, to haunts once ruled by the hyena, the ichthyo-saurus, and other beasts with unpronounceable names, to high spots command-ing expanses that Moses might have envied, to earthworks of forgotten men where solitude, quivering long grass, and nodding harebells reign. And the Fosse Way presents turnings for Wells, the medieval treasure that can fade the hard light of modern materialism with its own glow and spell. For Wells remains a prize reminder of the lost golden age.

Between Bath and the Mendip Hills enchanted valleys lie to the left and right of the Fosse Way, steep valleys closely wooded, with streams coursing down and clusters of stone cottages and farms shining out. These delicious scenes continue from the Avon vale to Monkton Combe, Midford, Wellow, all the way to Stowey, Chew Magna, and to Brockley Combe, delightful now as it was to Coleridge in May 1795:

> With many a pause, and oft-reverted eye,
> I climb the Combe's ascent; sweet songsters near
> Warble in shade their wild-wood melody.

Overtopping all is Dundry Hill, a height of almost 800 feet for grand views over miles of English counties, the Severn estuary, and Wales. Churches and towers, as seen at Wrington, Chew Magna, and elsewhere, give foretastes of greater glories awaiting beyond the Mendip barrier. Sutton Court, a picture of battlements, Tudor and Elizabethan walls, is but one sample of the flavour of the choice country houses. Towns in this tract are few, marked in the west by Weston-super-Mare, beloved of the multitude, and by Frome in the east, an old wool town full of hills and singularly empty in signs of its more than one thousand years' age. But Frome, with good Bishop Ken's grave in it, makes amends for itself by urging one out into the surrounding country. Nearby are Orchardleigh and an island church; the *George Inn* at Norton St. Philip, medieval in front and courtyard to remind of wool merchants, strolling players, and a shot through a window at the Duke of Monmouth in June 1685; a ruined castle and tombs of the mighty Hungerfords in the old parklands of Farleigh Hungerford; the adorable village, church, and manor-house at Mells, the plum which "little Jack Horner" pulled out of King Harry's Dissolution pie (196); and Sir John de la Mere's four round towers, dating from 1373, rising over the castle moat at Nunney. These, with the neighbour villages, hills, valleys, streams, the trees and the fields, charm and charm again through the summer days.

The Fosse Way leads on and up to the Mendip plateau. This stretch of table-land, the top of the mass of limestone and sandstone extending westward to the sea, reaches to a height of over 1,000 feet at Black Down. Far down below are subterranean streams and curious caverns, the popular Cheddar Caves, and Wookey Hole, which seems to have been the earliest eating-house in England judging by the relics left there by Flint Age men, the hyena, bison, elephant, and other departed natives. Above ground, clefts in the bare hills expose rocky shapes piled up in startling and majestic effects hundreds of feet high, mag-nificently shown at Cheddar Gorge and at Barrington ravine, the birthplace of Toplady's "Rock of Ages" during a thunderstorm. The mention of weather reminds me from experience that Mendip top is a most unholy spot to be caught in during a downpour, even without accompaniments of thunder and lightning. At any time it is bleak, lonely, and silent, though good for the lungs. Mystery and solitude reign over the prehistoric camps, barrows, trackways, and about the route used by the Romans for transporting lead from the mines at Charterhouse and Priddy. To-day it is unlikely to meet Romans responsible for stamping "Vespasian" or "Britannicus" on the pigs of lead found at Priddy, to see a hippopotamus or a lion corresponding to the bones discovered in caves, or to chance on Palæolithic hunters, who shaped flints while in possession of these ageless heights when Britain joined the Continent. But it is still possible to do what no doubt the previous residents did—stand on the southern Mendip

NORTON ST. PHILIP, SOMERSET.

escarpments and admire the views, with the advantage of observing the work accomplished by nature and the ages of man since the early days. Prospects are splendid all the way from Beacon Hill to Crook's Peak (207). Stretching far away from the east to the west immense panoramas set out our own true England in coloured harmonies of hill and plain, woods, trees, villages, and the patchwork of fields. Ever and again, gracing the foot of the slopes, Wells is seen shining in its hallowed acres of beauty and dreams.

You may first glimpse Wells on the high roads leading from Bath or Bristol. Or one may descend the Fosse Way to Shepton Mallet's notable church and market cross, diverge for Croscombe, with a church full of carved woodwork too good to be missed, and so continue to the wonderful look down at Wells from the south-east. And having gleaned promise from the hills, rewards beyond expectation await. The crowning masonry of the cathedral's central tower, completed in 1321, rises above western Perpendicular towers. From the east and north the great church groups wonderfully. The western front, created by Bishop Jocelin (1206-1242), remains unsurpassed as a grand display of religious presentation in figure sculpture, though decayed, restored, and shorn of the original brilliance of gold, silver, and colours. A daring conception of nave, transepts, and choir, shows Early English art of the earliest and best, born almost before its time. The exquisite Lady chapel and octagonal chapter house; the cloister of Bishop Beckyngton (1443-1464); chantry chapels and complete windows of old glass; flying buttresses, pierced parapets, and quaint figures carved on capitals rich in the artistry of the famous West Country masons; Jack Blandiver, born about 1390, still kicking the time on the astronomical clock; the fifteenth-century bridge and range of domestic buildings in Vicars' Close; reflections of the bishop's palace in the moat; the town's fine church, inns, homes, almshouses, and the market place showing Beckyngton's gateways, old houses, and the conduit (208-209)—these and hosts of other sights yield more than enough to see and dwell on for ages. A hundred explorations or the visit of a lifetime could never exhaust all that Wells offers to the eye, the mind, and the heart. Whether you arrive by mechanical contrivances of petrol or even on the steel frame of a bicycle, if you are conscious of buses parking, trippers about, sightseers enraptured or looking bored, young men in training for parsons, shoppers laden with bags, countrymen bunched at corners, imps sucking ice-cream cornets as I have just witnessed, and notice lots of other mundane things— no distraction of the moment can dispel the magic of this homeland of old faith in Somerset. After all the tumblings of time, Wells breathes the medieval spirit. With beauty it charms and endears. In twentieth-century England it tarries, our incomparable town of the Middle Ages.

THROUGH SOMERSET TO THE
DORSET COAST

Many points on the Mendips give the wide views mentioned in my previous note. Maesbury Camp is one of them, hardly to be bettered and a favourite of mine. So if you please we will ascend the broken path up this hill, just as I did on a hot July morning for the purpose of making the drawing illustrated on page 207. As we stand on the earthen ramparts at the top, a fresh breeze sings through the gorse and thin grass. To the south the wide world spreads out. Miles upon miles of pure English landscape glisten in the fresh light, and we look into the very heart of Somerset aglow with luscious greens and shades, bright hill points, and vales of hedgerow and fields shining joyously in panoramas of present glory.

Yet without invoking gymnastics of fancy, all the centuries seem to meet and extend in bird's-eye perspective at this height, now so quiet and still. The tumbled mounds on which we stand were thrown up ages before the Romans found them when they carried their route onward to the spoils of lead at Charterhouse. Two miles away runs the old Fosse Way. Down below we see the towers of Wells. Far and wide, fading in distances to the Quantock and Black Down Hills and the Dorset heights beyond Crewkerne, the vast plain sets out an enchanted land. Grand expanses, beautiful with undulations, levels, and curious conical shapes, hold secrets of romance. The broad sweeps give local habitations to legends, stories, and deeds. To stand and look from the earthworks is to see pages of the English epic opened, and by sight and hint to trace much that has marked the years since the distant times of the first makers of Maesbury Camp. The Tor of Glastonbury and the sacred acres round it mean Avalon, isle of departed spirits, the end of Joseph of Arimathea's pilgrimage, the Holy Grail and the Thorn, and perhaps the earliest outpost of the Christian faith. On its own hill a dozen miles from the Tor is Cadbury Castle, on which of course we may pick out with a mental telescope brave figures of King Arthur and the Knights of Camelot. Under the far blue haze are Somerton, Muchelney, South Petherton, and a chain of lovely places that knew the tread of King Ine, conqueror of Somerset, wise maker of the earliest known code of West Saxon laws, the man of many palaces, and patron of Glastonbury, Wells, and shrines now gone. There are the Polden Hills—we think of lonely Sedgemoor behind them, where King Alfred hid, may have burned cakes, and certainly prepared to smash the Danes in 878 and gain the peace made at Wedmore lying out beyond Wells; and we recall, too, that later fight in those marshes which brought Monmouth's downfall near Weston Zoyland in the last battle fought on English soil in 1685. Onward from point to point thought follows thought, continuing to track old legends and true happenings to their sources.

Wherever the eye may lead over these wide expanses, here brilliant in sunlight and there softened by shadows from passing clouds, we look into a very home

SHERBORNE. *The Conduit in Cheap Street with the Abbey Church beyond which contains magnificent fan-vaulting. The ancient and famous School, Tudor and later buildings, Norman castle ruins, are among the attractions of this stone town, once the seat of a bishopric.* SANDFORD ORCAS, *a choice manor-house of Ham Hill stone with a gate-house and gables of sixteenth-century character. It stands in a hilly Dorset parish almost surrounded by Somerset.*

HAMMOON. *The thatched Tudor manor-house with an Eliza-bethan porch and classic archway. It is remotely situated near the Dorset Stour and the name is derived from the powerful family of de Mohun who held the manor at the time of Domesday.*

of medievalism, a stronghold of faith and traditions. Names alone pulse with meaning. Down below and far away might be a map freshly set out and illuminated with words by a monk of the Middle Ages. Scores of places, some of them visible from this height and others lost in trees and filmy belts of colour, proclaim long heritage by their names, titles of enchanting sounds and full of present promise, past associations, and harmony. Wyke Champflower, Queen Camel, Middlezoy and other "zoys" in the marshes, Huish Episcopi and Kingsbury Episcopi, Shepton Beauchamp, White Lackington, and Hinton St. George (221) in King Ine's country, Preston Plucknett (221), Sutton Bingham, and more and more names are delicious enough to urge any explorer onward in happy expectation.

Further, at Maesbury Camp we know that miles in sight overlie the stone beds of oolite and lias which cover eastern Somerset and stretch through Dorset to Portland Bill. This means beauty on beauty piled with lovely stone in churches, halls, and homes. Near and far stand the famous towers, of a magnificence not to be excelled in all England, and waiting to be seen in stately procession when we descend to country ways and pass east to west from Shepton Mallet, Evercreech, and Bruton to Taunton, or go south from St. John's, Glastonbury, through Weston Zoyland, Huish Episcopi, Isle Abbots, Ilminster, Crewkerne, and to Sherborne, where the stone belt continues along the north Dorset border. Villages and old towns, too numerous to mention, show these emblems reared by men who worked in faith and with skill. The towers, generally at the west and sometimes central in the churches, present a grand array of wrought stone surfaces, soaring buttresses, double windows, triple windows, parapets patterned and crowned with pinnacles and crockets; noble creations, veritable triumphs of Perpendicular architecture (201).

Certainly we do not see human beings from Maesbury; but we look down on an expansive countryside that nurtured the sturdy and kind souls who made and inhabited stone houses, farms, and cottages near these churches they built, paid for, and worshipped in. They left memorials of themselves in fine interior roofs, screens, and many carvings, such as are found in naves, chancels, and churchyards at Weston Zoyland, Somerton, North Cadbury, Martock, Barwick, and frequent directions elsewhere. Descendants of this race thrive on. Among this earth's dwellers they are some of the best. That is one reason why it is always so nice to be in Somerset. The air is soft, contours and scenes are soft, and the people—well, if I say they are soft, it is only to pay them my highest compliment. Kind, good-natured, and good-mannered, their hospitality exactly corresponds with themselves, and many are the delightful experiences I could relate of courtesy and welcome shown to the stranger in their midst. For just one instance, particularly do I recall the benevolent squire who found me, unknown and unprovided for, sketching in his village; who would hear of no refusal to stay with him at his priory, told me of the Glastonbury Thorn on the lawn, one that of course blossomed at the appointed time, secretly mentioned the family ghost out of earshot of the servants, nobly acceded to my request to try the haunted chamber in the hope of encountering the midnight article, which, unluckily, failed to appear, and finally speeded the parting guest onward to more of his friends and more goodness. That is how one fares in homely, pleasant Somerset. Even ghosts move softly there and are unobtrusive.

And there is always a feeling of being under the mantle of old-time ways and traditions, very consoling in these days of steel and concrete, equality, and to hell with old fogies. The memorable past is always present in so much visible beauty, and is hinted at again by conversations heard in the full, round accents of local speech. Long ago an old man near Ilchester told me how his father, when a youth, remembered seeing the masons setting out patterns, and working and carving stone, by free and direct hand workmanship without the aid of instruments and mechanical contrivances—a simple statement which in one moment tracked straight into the Middle Ages, telling that while the horrors of the Industrial Revolution were being perpetuated, village craftsmen still preserved something of the spirit and fancy that made the glorious towers, the manor-houses, and Wells. Another recollection is of mummers who gave the well-known version of St. George and the Dragon in vernacular garble, an absurd and amusing performance, but punctuated with bangs and thwacks which nobody understood or could account for beyond saying, "It always had been done." A historian versed in such matters afterwards explained that the explosions undoubtedly were relics of effects produced in miracle plays, had been handed down from representations of the Nativity through generations, to at last become the alarums for King George, the Turk, Merrian, and their compeers. On that Christmastide night we had been transported from our own years into dim survivals of possibly the twelfth century. A wonderful county for escape is Somerset.

It is time to leave Maesbury Camp and the variety of thoughts it induces. My hot sketching ended, I descended the hill, feeling parched. Seeking a drink of water at a cottage, a good Samaritan said:

"Wouldn't you prefer orange juice?"

"That would be nice," I replied. "Thank you very much."

"And let me draw fresh water from the well to be sure it is cool," she added. Hospitable Somerset to the life!

Next, at the railway station—I had arrived by car, but was to return by train —nothing human was visible to offer a ticket or take money. The train drew in and stopped. Ticketless I climbed into it, reached my destination, offered the fare; but no, a smiling official could not think of taking it. Hospitable Somerset again! Yet I wondered if shareholders of the Somerset and Dorset line ever got, or even desired, dividends.

All that we have been contemplating, and a good deal more, is to be met with or discovered in this country stretching from the Mendip Hills. Stone manor-houses vie with the churches in adding sparkle to the scenes. Many of them are lovely; mellow walls and enrichments, often fine and always well wrought, give outward signs and intimate suggestions of a domestic life that flourished through Tudor and Elizabethan years to the times of the late seventeenth century and the Georges. Some of these houses are widely known, for the group includes Lytes Cary near Ilchester and Barrington Court near Ilminster, both Tudor examples; the Elizabethan houses of North Cadbury and Montacute; and Brympton d'Evercy, 2 miles from Yeovil, a wonderful combination of Tudor and Renaissance building. Almost every village, however, has a manor-house, a squire's home turned farm or cottages, or perhaps an old monkish dwelling to delight the eye. These often neighbour the churches and are embowered in gardens with smooth lawns where sundials tell the hours and stone ornaments stand against dark yews or regiments of tall hollyhocks. Bees hum among the flowers, and while the sun shines on gables and cornices, lights up oriels, stone doorways, windows, and chimneys, you want to stop and sketch everything (195). The regions of oolite stone in the borderlands of Somerset and Dorset show such features particularly well, yielding a manor-house at Ditcheat (196), the gatehouse and gables of Sandford Orcas (215), Hammoon's stone-work under a big thatched roof (216), a medieval group at Preston Plucknett

Old Guildhall, Stoford

(221), West Coker manor-house, an abbot's house and a priest's house in perfection at Muchelney, and other treasures in scores of places.

The stone towns dotted through this district never lack interest. All of them contain good things. They extend from Bruton standing over the valley to the hill of Chard, from the rare sculptured cross at Stalbridge to Ilminster's church tower (201) and grammar school hard by *The George*, the first hotel in which Queen Victoria ever stayed! The smaller places such as Somerton, the traditional capital of King Ine, would be difficult to match for an air of peace and tranquillity in this eruptive age. South Petherton, especially, seems to defy the inroads of time. It has Georgian houses, Tudor houses, an inn under the sign of *The Crown*, and an octagonal church tower on high, all apparently intent on holding time in check while upholding the ancient prestige of King Ine, though his palace, alas, noble fifteenth-century house that it is, could hardly have known the royal presence. Of the two larger towns, Yeovil may not be liked for its modern and busy aspect, yet for me it has the stately and lofty church in the wide square, interesting houses, and old inns. But Sherborne, not far away, is a town of towns, entrancing throughout (215). It would require pages to dwell on the abbey church, the marvellous fan-vaulting, the school with monastic buildings, castle ruins and the castle commenced by Sir Walter Raleigh, the wealth of domestic architecture in streets and by-ways known by time-honoured names, and other particulars of this fair haunt of traditions that still keeps fresh the English way of life.

Glastonbury, perhaps the cradle of our faith and civilization, is a place apart. Yet few towns can be more disappointing through having been so badly mauled, to reduce a rich heritage of legend, memories, and beauty to mere ghostliness. Certainly delights are not lacking. There are the impressive ruins of the abbey with the splendour of Norman masonry in the relics of St. Mary's chapel, the octagonal abbot's kitchen, vaulted in fifteenth-century style up to the stone lantern, and the great stone barn. Round and about are old houses, almshouses, gateways, the Tribunal for offenders built by Abbot Beere (1493–1524), a glorious Perpendicular tower at St. John's church due to the same abbot, and the celebrated *George*, the pilgrims' *hospitium* erected by Abbot Selwood late in the fifteenth century, in which we still can eat, drink, be merry, and go to sleep in original pilgrim surroundings without medieval inconveniences (210). But these sights are accompanied by furious thoughts of Henry VIII's plan for destruction in 1539, and by much that is dull and mean. After seeing all that is good I find consolation in going out along the road towards Meare. There you look back across the levels and dykes. The Mendip ridge makes a bold, distant line above Wookey Hole. In front Glastonbury nestles softly under the hill tower of St. Michael. The strange flat land, the horizon shapes, roofs of the town below green slopes ending in the point of the Tor, colours picked out mysteriously in sunlight—this scene, as I saw it on an

PRESTON PLUCKNETT. *A Somerset home and great barn erected in the early 1400's by the Stourton family in the ancient village of Alan de Plugenet.*

HINTON ST. GEORGE, *a notable Somerset village with stone cottages, a fine thatched Priory farm, and John the Baptist carved on the village cross. The church has a noble tower and wonderful tombs to the Pauletts, who lived in the great house.*

LYME REGIS, *Lyme Bay and the Dorset cliffs including the Golden Cap. The curved walls of the Cobb, or harbour, were first erected in the reign of Edward III. Here the Duke of Monmouth landed prior to the rebellion of 1685. This ancient and attractive town of steep streets had enthusiastic words from Jane Austen in "Persuasion," and in 1895 J. M. Whistler discovered "The Little Rose of Lyme Regis" and other subjects.*

autumn day, brought my truest impression of Avalon. Then it seemed to shine in the glamour of ancient fame and story. It revivified in the mind that holy spot known to primitive peoples and the lake dwellers of Meare in the Bronze Age, the green island in the marshes sought by Joseph of Arimathea and travellers over the hills from the east, the home of the oldest and one of the greatest of English abbeys, the jewelled shrine of Arthur and Guinevere, King Edmund and King Edgar, St. Patrick and St. Dunstan, and all those saints, kings, and untold hosts who trod, and sometimes ended this world's pilgrimage at, the hallowed acres of Glastonbury.

Another landmark comparable to Glastonbury Tor is Cadbury Castle, crowning its hill about a dozen miles distant in the south-east. If Glastonbury may disappoint, Cadbury need not. Nobody knows whether it was ever King Arthur's seat, so it is not necessary to shed tears on the demise of "many-tower'd Camelot." The crest of the height is ringed with great ruined earth-works of pre-Roman origin from which miles and miles of near and distant country are visible. Stacks of human bones, thousands of Roman coins, "a Horse Shoe of Sylver, with many other antique Thinges" have been unearthed round about. King Arthur's Well and King Arthur's Hunting Causeway are still marked on our maps. The villagers know, and have proved to their own satisfaction, that the hill is hollow and therefore must be full of treasure. Every-thing considered, this is just the kind of high spot to call on for exercise, fresh air, and views; for a chance of finding knights bounding about on steeds shod with silver shoes glistening in the moonlight; the exact elevation for ruminating on ancestors and tribes and whatever they might or might not have been up to; withal a tree-clad eminence diverting alike for walkers, naturalists, picnickers, lovers, romantic souls and archæological spades.

On a blue and white cloud day in June, the 15th of that month to be exact, I viewed this hill from afar, walked towards it, crossed the Cam stream, reached the turning for Sutton Montis, and saw Cadbury Castle crowned with trees rising above the buttercup fields. Three agitated natives here advised me to go to South Cadbury for the best ascent to the camp, and stated nothing was to be seen there. They added ruefully, "We have lost a cow." Some distance on I met that cow, hallooed at it, and with tactical success turned the animal about at a trot towards the ranks of the pursuers. At the corner of the lane into South Cadbury village a robust land girl awaited. She asked:

"Have you seen a cow on the road?"

"Yes," I replied. "I sent it back to the men who were looking for it."

"Then I shan't bother any more," she sang merrily, and went on her way rejoicing.

Following the directions given I found the *Red Lion* inn, the causeway beyond, read a notice "Beware of the traps," gingerly ascended the hill, spied out the grand views, explored all round the earthworks, and sat on one of them

Earthworks
Cadbury Castle

to sketch. It was very quiet and still. Only light breezes in the trees and occasional flutterings of birds could be heard. The sun shone now and again between high moving clouds, then faded. A magpie sailed down, settling so near to me that I could observe, better than ever before the lucent black colouring glossed with deep blue shining like velvet from slashes of white. At once this dull age brightened with the dramatic blazon of romantic pageantry. Could this bird, I wondered, be of the lineage "proud and pert" that chattered to King Arthur of Queen Guinevere's sly goings on with Sir Launcelot a long time ago?

Soft footsteps later made me aware of not being alone. Somebody approached from behind and stopped. Looking round, I quickly noticed a face of the modish pattern, a smile, youthlines trimly garbed, and the skimpy accoutrements of a modern fairy. This rival of the camp's leading lady did not fit the poet's fancy:

> A gown of grass-green silk she wore,
> Buckled with golden clasps before;
> A light-green tuft of plumes she bore
> Closed in a golden ring.

Decked with a permanent wave, lipstick, a brief skirt, and not much else, up-to-date Guinevere graced the aged turf of Camelot.

Profiting by my disadvantageous position of squatting with pencil and paper on an earthwork, she asked, "May I look?"

"Certainly," said I, without means or desire of escape, and exhibited my modest work, which obviously she thought little of while praising it. Next she explained her presence was due to being "on holiday" and revelling in the countryside round South Cadbury after the thrills of North Finchley.

"Lovely up here, isn't it," she added brightly.

"Very," I said, looking at her. "And so few people come this way. A romantic spot. Perhaps by now you know something about it? Arthur, I mean, knights, round tables, palaces, towers, ladies at casements accidentally dropping down handkerchiefs and rosebuds for masculines to pick up, and all the sorts of doings that used to happen here at Camelot."

"What!" she exclaimed, with wide eyes flashing. "I haven't seen anything, and I come here most days. Now you mention it, they did say something about Arthur where I am staying, but the gardener's called Arthur. And they also spoke of Cami-er-something—what did you say it was?"

"Camelot," I rapidly answered; "supposed to have been the home of King Arthur and knights in armour and helmets who rode great bouncing horses fitted with silver shoes and jingling bells to say nothing of singing ladies with braided ringlets and gold ornaments."

Amazed, Guinevere eyed me intently, perhaps doubtful of my brain in that lonely place.

"When you return to London," I continued, "you can read about them in William of Malmesbury, Geoffrey of Monmouth, and Layamon, and when you are tired of medieval Latin, make up to Alfred Tennyson."

This suggestion produced a chilly effect. Quite fleeting, it was followed by, "Anyhow, there's not much sign of life now."

"Ah!" I replied, and quoted,

> " Only reapers, reaping early
> In among the bearded barley,
> Hear a song that echoes cheerly
> From the river winding clearly
> Down to tower'd Camelot."

Guinevere blinked; she seemed to like the verse.

"There are the fields, down below," I pointed.

"But it's all grass. I can't see any barley."

"Oh, blow the whiskers!" I retorted. "Even barley is green in June. You cannot be matter-of-fact up here, want a bit of imagination. See where the willows and alders make a wiggly line? That's the Cam stream. The village round the bend is Queen Camel. So of course we must be standing on Camel-ot. Quite simple. Any old villager about here will tell you so. Well, I've done the sketch and must be going now."

"I must, too," she rejoined.

"Where are you going to, my pretty maid?" I asked.

"I'm going to Sutton Montis" (not sir), she said.

"That is also my direction," I ventured, "and then on to Sparkford. Shall we try to find the way? Some men in search of a cow said it was awkward."

We threaded downhill over mounds. All traces of a path fizzled out in masses of stinging-nettles, healthy and tall plants. Leading, I did not look round, for Guinevere was in the fashion of no stockings to the legs and therefore the prey of consequences beyond reckoning. More steep bumps, a highish stone wall with no exit, followed by two flying leaps deposited us in a field clear of King Arthur's private domains. We rounded an historic well, very muddy, found progress barred by more nettles and a stream; a bull quite near began to waggle his tail in token of welcome, and escape over the water by a providential plank just averted a tragedy. Trespassing past a farmer's back premises and open front door, where a dog barked madly, brought us at last into the public road behind the Norman archway of Sutton Montis church.

The conclusion of these exhausting feats at least suggested a consolation prize for Guinevere. Lacking a box of Cadbury's chocolates with the familiar trees of Camel printed on the lid, I proposed tea, a commodity not available until we had passed through Weston Bampfylde to espy with joy the words "Tea now being served" at the P.R.H.A. inn at Sparkford. Refreshed, we prepared to part. The maid of Finchley thanked me charmingly and with gratitude for the reviver, but resumed her holiday with, "Blow King Arthur, Queen Guinevere, and Camelot!" no doubt remembering the stinging-nettles.

I had asked Mr. Hurley of Yeovil to bring a car to Sparkford or thereabouts and look for me at a time uncertain. So there he was waiting. We quickly left, halted for the old manor-house and lovely fifteenth-century chapel at Marston Magna and next drew up at the *Manor Hotel* in Yeovil, where an excellent dinner awaited. After a glass of old port from a cobwebby bottle, solitary survivor of pre-war days, I went to bed quite convinced that the three men who said there was nothing to be seen at Cadbury Castle had lost a good deal more than a cow. With last waking thoughts of a gigantic Round Table piled up with King Arthur, Knights, Queen Guinevere—golden clasps and helmet feathers— gemmy bridles, silver horseshoes—a magpie and a wandering cow—a rampant bull, a barking dog—long nettles and a pot of tea—and Guinevere of Finchley North—I fell asleep.

Waking up in the morning at Yeovil, one is well placed for continuing the windings of the limestone belt by ambling along the byways to Crewkerne, and then heading south and east between the chalk hills and the Devon border. These tracks lead through a bit of real Dorsetshire, ample in green meadows, orchards, bright streams, little bridges, valleys, combes, and quite lofty heights which top 900 feet at Lew's on Hill and Pil's on Pen above the Marshwood Vale. Here are more villages for exploration; more Perpendicular churches, rising

CHURCH SCREENS

PILTON

DARTMOUTH

ATHERINGTON

SIDNEY R. JONES

DEVONSHIRE DETAILS.

BARNSTAPLE. *The crooked leaden spire of the parish church, and St. Anne's Chapel where John Gay went to school.*

The long bridge over the River Taw dating from the twelfth century.

especially well at Beaminster and Netherbury; more manor-houses, with the sumptuous Gothic masonry of Forde Abbey and the Tudor front of Parnham notable amongst them. Soon the fresh sea air blows in. Up and down we go behind the cliffs of the fine coastline. Chideock shows the lines of old cottages. Next comes Bridport with a Perpendicular church tower and the wide pavements for the rope-makers who supplied Henry VIII's navy. Up and down again past the church tower and monastic barn of Abbotsbury leads to Weymouth presenting Georgian fronts and Regency terraces above the heads of the holiday crowds. Out to sea juts Portland Bill, marking the southern limit of the grand sweep of limestone.

Across the bay from Chesil Bank is Lyme Regis, historic, literary, arty, and even the modern villas have not spoiled its quaintness, hilly streets, curly harbour, and pink and green cliffs (222). The harbour and jetty known as The Cobb, with a life dating back to the years of Edward III, is one of the oldest standing constructions of the kind on the south coast. In 1685 the Duke of Monmouth landed on it prior to reaching Taunton, Norton St. Philip, Sedgemoor and the eventual block at the Tower of London. Other famous visitors to this cosy town in Lyme Bay stormed it with mere weapons of peace. Writers had a fancy for the place, particularly the ladies who were led off by Mary Russell Mitford and Jane Austen in *Persuasion*. Innumerable wielders of paints and pencils have pounced on the picturesque bits that abound. In 1895 James McNeill Whistler arrived, produced " The Master Smith of Lyme Regis " and " The Rose of Lyme Regis " now in the Boston Museum, U.S.A., and gleaned the series of lithographs which notably included " The Smith's Yard." Plenty of attractions remain. All sorts of tastes are suited among the windows and doorways of the old town and along the little promenade to the harbour in view of the sea bounded by cliffs and the Golden Cap. The steep High Street is a very good street, flavoured Regency here and there, adorned with the *Royal Lion* and *The Three Cups* hotels, and bright in present liveliness. At the landslips beyond the harbour Devonshire begins and here end my speculations on the oolite and lias land of romance and golden tints, hills and blue distances, warm hearts, cheese, and bacon.

5. TO THE END OF ENGLAND

WEST SOMERSET, DEVON, CORNWALL

The seagirt strip of country, indicated by the map below, leads to the Atlantic and the end of my travels across Southern England. Shaped somewhat curiously, this piece of land might easily suggest a footballer's leg about to shoot the Scilly Islands into an Atlantic goal or over to Newfoundland. But England's one archipelago permanently retains its place. Sandstone beds and granite rocks —these are the principal geological accompaniments of this final pilgrimage. The sandstones begin at the Devon border around Axminster, at the Somerset vale of Taunton, and along the Bridgwater estuary below the Quantock Hills. These formations, bordered by culm measures and with bosses of granite interposed, occur through Devon and Cornwall, terminating at Land's End in nature's pillars of rock coloured by foam and spray. The earth surfaces thus piled up and surrounded by ocean waters afford famous scenes that are widely known and appreciated by holiday makers, picture makers, and others who make pleasure and profit in the far west. Inland there are the hills and vales of a rich countryside, glorious rivers, tors and miles of moors. The attractions of the broken coastline, broad estuaries, bays, harbours, and the wild grandeur of rocks and headlands, particularly in northern Cornwall and Devon, are not surpassed elsewhere on the English seaboard.

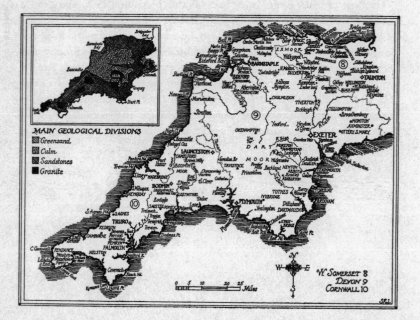

MINEHEAD. *West Somerset cob walls and thatching.*

At the Dorset border in the south, Devon may be entered in the neighbourhood of Axminster and Honiton. Or England's third largest county, justly called "glorious," can be approached in the north from west Somerset. This western wedge of Somerset, outside that county's belt of limestone and lias, has its Exmoor to correspond with Devon's Dartmoor, and contains light-faced cottages thickly shielded with roofs of thatch just like those in Devon. Because the geology, scene, and architecture are similar in both areas, I have bunched western Somerset with Devonshire.

We will then, if you please, arrive in Taunton, the thriving county and market town, pleasant for wandering in, but not showing a great deal to tell of a full historic past since King Ine founded it about the year 720. Superlatives from the dictionary are only demanded for explosions on the church towers of St. Mary Magdalene and St. James. These stand up so nobly·in Perpendicular finery that you need not worry about the evidences of restoration on both. St. Mary's has the most elaborate and tallest of all the Somerset towers (201); and these two Taunton features, with the neighbouring towered masterpieces at Staple Fitzpaine, Bishop's Lydeard, and Kingston, present a triumphant adieu to the crowning glories which are the pride of Somerset. Otherwise, as I have said, the town is pleasant rather than spectacular. The older house frontages vary from a few timbered ones to Georgian examples. Other things you might expect to find are represented by the old Grammar School, and three groups of almshouses in West Street and East Reach, the last mentioned being a picturesque survival of a leper hospital of the thirteenth century. The castle and the priory, ancient cores of the town, now merely signify partial or total eclipses. One small relic near St. James's Church marks the Priory of Austin Canons founded early in the twelfth century, and the gateway and restored walls of the castle bear little resemblance to the great stronghold of combined keep and hall that served Bishops of Winchester onward from Norman years. The glory that was but isn't hardly rouses to life the weighty movements and colour of West Country history centred round past Taunton. Full of incident, the town's story is highly lit with Perkin Warbeck's march in as Richard Plantagenet, followed by a midnight sneak out in September 1497 as nobody in particular; captures and recaptures in the Civil War by both Royalists and Parliamentarians; the siege of 1645, when the "sailor bold" Robert Blake, without ammunition or grub, told the Royalists "he would eat his boots before he yielded" and successfully sat tight; the Duke of Monmouth's entry to be proclaimed King at the market-place in June 1685, under a bombardment of welcome, green boughs, and merry maidens armed with a Bible and an embroidered flag, all much to the liking of the handsome progeny of Lucy Walters; and by way of gruesome conclusion, the Bloody Assize after the Battle of Sedgemoor held in the castle great hall, ominously draped in scarlet,

TORRINGTON. The old bridge over the Torridge.
From this point the river winds magnificently between
wooded banks to Wear Gifford. BIDEFORD. A section of the famous bridge of twenty-four arches known
far and wide through the words of Charles Kingsley.
Built over the River Torridge about 1350, widenings in
1793, 1810, 1865, and 1925, have partly marred its beauty.

EXETER. *Cathedral Yard surrounds the Cathedral Church of St. Peter, a masterpiece of Decorated architecture completed by 1400 to the east and west of the twin Norman towers of the transepts. Interesting domestic buildings border this green open space, notably Mol's Coffee House (shown at the extreme left) of Elizabethan date, and meeting-place of Armada heroes. The Cathedral suffered in the German raids, and vast areas of the beautiful City of the West were obliterated.*

EXETER, *from the lower riverside quarter outside the walls.*
The churches of St. Edmund-on-the-Bridge and St. Mary
Steps show the characteristic red sandstone towers. At this
point stood the West Gate (removed in 1815) through which
William, Prince of Orange, entered the city in 1688.

from which Judge Jeffreys sent two hundred victims to death prior to his own merited finale in the D.T.s at the Tower of London.

Not much in view is indicative of such happenings while standing in the wide, open space athwart the market house, a 1772 effort erected in brickwork. But the busy scene and the streets elsewhere, filled with nice Somerset folk of goodwill, carry a cheerful air, give just the sort of pictures that a stranger or a foreigner might like to remember for the typical pattern of the English county town. Over the way from the market hall stands the castle gateway. Hammet Street opposite ends with a magnificent elevation of St. Mary's tower. Ahead is North Street, agog with life and movement. You may decide to probe the castle gateway, see the museum, then find the *Castle Hotel*, and with calm philosophy sleep soundly in a comfortable bed without being troubled in the least by old Jeffreys' ghost at the spot of his infamous exploits. Or round the corner the long white front, the pilasters, and the cornices of the *County Hotel* may attract, may so shake up the coaching days and phantom horses that before you know it your footsteps are under the pillared porch and going inside.

The vale of Taunton Deane spreads out luxuriantly, bounded by the wooded slopes of the Quantock Hills, the Brendon Hills leading to Exmoor, and the Black Down Hills conspicuously marked by the Duke of Wellington's monument at the Devon border near Wellington. This rich vale between the hills, a land of plenty for people whose interiors appreciate the industry of cows and dairy farmers, is also amply provided with manor-houses to delight the eye. These old homes, charming outside and within, are dotted across the vale to the slopes of the hills. Among a full crop are those at Gerbestone near West Buckland, Cothay in perfect early Tudor, Greenham Barton also Tudor, Fitzhead Court, Cothelstone a prize for any county, Halsway, and Elizabethan Combe Sydenham.

Round about the manor-houses and near church towers are the cottages which introduce the type common to this district and prevalent throughout Devon. Bright and sparkling in their framings of leafage and flower gardens, characteristically home-bred, I have found and sketched them by the score across the vale of Taunton and onward near the coast through Williton, Dunster, and Minehead to the delicious collections tumbled at various angles in Selworthy, Allerford, Bossington, and Porlock. Old-time villagers made themselves cosy in these homesteads, thought them the best in the wide world; and the thick cob walls, plastered, buttressed, and lightly coloured, the big square chimneys, the roofs of sloping thatch projecting far out at the eaves, certainly evidence a cottage tradition unusually rural if not especially architectural. The buildings were made to last, even though the only damp-courses streamed down from the roofs and sanitation, as now glorified, did not worry the owners. Picturesque and rambling, tarred at the bases, walls rarely plumb upright, and with plenty of eyebrows that are never highbrow, these abodes have the vagrant charm which arose without conscious planning in times before rapid evolutions in England outstripped beauty's growth. They are harmonious in the landscapes, add a spice of quaintness to the rich natural scenes in west Somerset and through Devon. Following the contours of the ground, they might be actual growths of the soil. Their general family likeness is unmistakable. So true to type are they that a cottage expert suddenly deposited from the blue in front of any example between Bridgwater and Barnstaple Bays in the north and Tor and Bigbury Bays in the south might wonder more than twice whether he was in Dunster, Porlock, Saunton (11), Atherington, or had dropped into Buckland-in-the-Moor, Combe-in-Teignhead, or Thurlesstone (248).

The old red sandstone borders the Taunton vale with the Quantock Hills, the Brendon Hills, and Exmoor topped by over 1,700 feet at Dunkery Beacon. Lovely scenes belong to these heights. The Quantocks, especially, are a joyous combination of luxuriant combes, hanging woods, fresh hill-tops, and byways for contemplation and getting lost to the world. The eight miles or so from Cothelstone Hill and Will's Neck to Beacon Hill, where the Bristol Channel is seen extending to the Welsh hills, offer more than enough to souls athirst for nature's springs. Also in days of spiritual and material shortages every mile may arouse wistful musings on

> Water, water, everywhere,
> Nor any drop to drink,

and other Quantock inspirations. For here the ground is hallowed, prolific in memories of Coleridge at Nether Stowey and Wordsworth at Alfoxden Manor in 1796–1798 when *The Rime of the Ancient Mariner*, *The Idiot Boy*, and the *Lyrical Ballads* were born during

> That summer, under whose indulgent skies
> Upon smooth Quantock's airy ridge we roved
> Unchecked, or loitered mid her sylvan courts.

Here are Dorothy Wordsworth's "woods, smooth downs, and valleys with small brooks running down them." Local natives in the 1790's, not greatly interested in poets operating on fine raptures, thought their new neighbours a queer lot, called them "crack-brained, smugglers, or traitors." But the natives remained with their fleshpots, then died. The poets departed, to live for ever.

The expanse of Exmoor, which tumbles into Devon at the south and west, is an area of contrasts. Unlike the curate's egg, it is good in every part. The scenes in the hills that fringe the moor are glorious; for example, through the Horner vale from Porlock, in the steep combes by the sea around Culbone's tiny Saxon church, and up through Timberscombe after leaving Dunster.

Streams and infant rivers swiftly course from the moors down vales and glens of exceptional beauty. The Avill River and Horner Water swing along to Blue Anchor and Porlock Bays. Over by Oare, Badgworthy Water makes the Devon boundary and babbles over a rocky bed on its way to Lynmouth; but here, if you happen to have a copy of *Lorna Doone* in your pocket, it may be disappointing to notice the stream does not behave quite properly for a true version of the Doone Valley of a distinguished novelist and market-gardener. Best of all, perhaps, are the youthful strides of the Rivers Exe and Barle. I can picture them at this moment sweeping and curving from Exe Head and Goat Hill, winding round hill slopes, skirting woods and mossy branches of oak trees, ever chattering onward. High up extends the tableland of Exmoor Forest. The wide spaces of moorland, heather and bracken are lonely, wild, and grand, inhabited more by ponies and deer than by the two-legged species of animal. Once upon a time the ratio may have been otherwise. The crop of hut circles, tumuli, and barrows prove that quantities of people formerly favoured the hardy life without central heating. These miles are splendid for walking and driving exploits. With villages, houses, inns, and similar contrivances few and far between, adventurers need the accoutrements of solids and liquids about their persons for the sustenance of their bodies.

More than twenty years ago, and properly armed against hunger and thirst, I explored this district. And though my tracks over this area have been many,

Sydney R Jones

Winsford, Exmoor

that particular occasion now is mentioned because the route then covered indicates the general characteristics of Exmoor and its environs. My companion in the adventure, who lacked neither fame, knowledge, nor unconventional proclivities, possessed expert appreciation of scenery, architecture, topography and cats. Long experience had taught him the fallacy of travelling light or trusting to the gods for luck. Hence the enormous knapsack shouldered to his frame. This equipage rivalled the magic paraphernalia attributed to Arabian genii. Without the wave of a wand it could reveal soup, meat, and assortments of food in tins, in skins, and unadorned; out of the confusion would appear manuscripts, pyjamas, thermos flasks, a camera, spirit lamp and saucepan, pieces of fish to welcome stray cats, and a small library of books led by Horace's *Odes* in Latin, W. H. Hudson's specials, and Stanley Baldwin's *On England*. The recesses of his raiment disclosed a steel rule variously used in measuring fonts and memorial brasses and cutting up tinned fish; a piece of flexible wire for recording sections of mouldings or stirring coffee; and an electric torch to illuminate gloomy church interiors and chase snails or footpaths in the dark.

We began with building, house, and cottage hunting. This led to the ruined abbey of the Cistercians at Cleeve. Undeterred by the Latin inscription on the great gatehouse, "Never closed to honest folk," we passed through to the cloister garth, the Early English chapter house, the dormitory, and the refectory lit by splendid Perpendicular windows below a walnut roof, nobly carved and supported on angel corbels. Pangs of tragedy and for glory departed were roused by this wreckage of the spoliation of 1537 in the ancient "Vallis Florida" of Our Lady of Cleeve. Brighter thoughts prevailed after coffee and cake consumed under a hedge and an entry into Dunster. For this little town, previously known to us, is ever dear old Dunster, clustered round the yarn market of 1609, the medieval and modern *Luttrell Arms* and the manor-house. Many other delights were disposed feudal-wise in range of the eyepieces of the Elizabethan and older castle on the mound. A small squall next ruffled the serene horizon. A dull dinner in an atmosphere subdued by a butler of august shape and deportment reduced conversation to platitudes polite and proper. But the vagrant of the knapsack quickly regained customary poise on arrival at Minehead. A hearty lunch from tins and pots spread on a grave-slab in the churchyard, with pretty thatched cottages and Exmoor in view for the sauce, completely restored equilibrium. My lecture on seemliness in sacred places proved of no avail.

There, and onward, our quest centred on cottage cob walls and thatching. We found Selworthy attractive as ever and Porlock too. Cottages, cottages all the way, light plaster faces and brown thatch, decked the waysides and made a bright sequence on entering and crossing north Devon from Challacombe and Arlington to Georgeham, Saunton (11), and Hartland, where land and sea meet at Morte Bay, Braunton Burrows, and Bideford Bay. On every side the red earths, green fields, orchards, earthen hedgerows, wooded and steep valleys, and

DARTMOOR. *Powder Mill Farm, one of the lone homesteads shielded by trees in this wild upland region.*

EXETER. *Timbered and Elizabethan stone windows in High Street.*

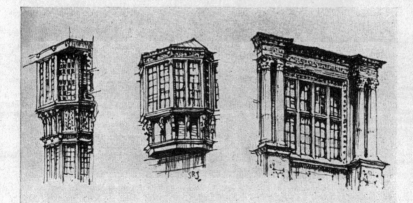

LYMPSTONE, *Devon, and the Exe estuary.*

sheep on hillsides, imparted full enchantment to luscious scenes. Nor could we resist heading to the coast, to Woody Bay, Hunter's Inn, Bull Point, Baggy Point, the grandeur of rocks and sea, and the cliffs onward from Clovelly that certainly are unrivalled in all England. At Clovelly we were not alone. Yet in spite of popularity it is a wonderful spectacle. The hilly ways, the gate, the bent arm of the harbour, boats, blue summer sea, houses and cottages seeming poised fantastically, the cleft in the hill, and banks of trees, offer nearly, if not quite, the most startling creation of nature and man to be seen in the south-west; it fully merits Charles Kingsley's description, "unique in its singular construction and beauty." My unconventional friend promptly wished to ride one of the donkeys, but could not accommodate his bulky frame to a pannier. Instead, we climbed to Temple Bar, curious, covered, facing a seaward view, and not in the least like the duplicate at the junction of the Strand and Fleet Street.

Back again on Exmoor, our duet continued with a walk down the course of the River Barle. As it was in the beginning, that is to say at Pinkworthy Pond, put us in touch with the beginnings of things, hinted all around by hut circles and barrows raised at draughty elevations up to more than 1,500 feet. These prehistoric relics doubtless kept their pots boiling in the sinister folklore of pixies, weird noises, dragons, wild men and beasts, that caused Exmoor farming and cottage natives to get the jitters round firesides on dark nights until the B.B.C. came to the rescue. No witches on view or phantom hunters of red deer upset our enjoyment of the magnificent wildness. Large visions extended beyond sight to imagination. Cloud shadows marched from hill to hill, chequered the valleys. The music of the stream cheered us along. We wound onward between rounded slopes, passed through Withypool, turned south under South Hill, met the oak trees, the woods, and the growing richness. Singing waters merrily played us to Tarr Steps Bridge. This we crossed and recrossed in respectful duty to our Celtic ancestors who had been there before us. The mounds of Brewer's Castle, in a delightful woody situation at the end of Hawkridge Ridge, called for a halt and the rites of the tins and thermos.

> Under an oak whose antique root peeps out
> Upon the brook that brawls along this wood,

we refreshed in a spot desirable enough for a banished Jacques, his "co-mates and brothers in exile." With packs heavily returned again to vertebral columns and scapulas, our trusty feet led to Dulverton in its green amphitheatre, crossed, at stream level, by the stone arched bridge. An ascent up Pound Walk, and a farmhouse discovered with roast chicken done to a turn preceded bed and sweet slumber without dreams after happy laborious hours.

We next crossed the River Exe, gained the 1,164-foot point on Haddon Hill for the view, marched between great woods along Hartford Bottom, admired the cottage scene from Bury packhorse bridge, where the Haddo stream babbled beneath. The last I saw of the cat lover, his *Odes*, tins, and miscellanea, was on Morebath station platform, bound for Taunton and London.

I continued to Bampton, the place of the October fairs for Exmoor ponies, but otherwise not exciting. Here the glorious weather that had been ours for days developed a depression. The drizzle at Bampton increased to a downpour at *Exeter Inn*, and rain cats and dogs damped my ardour for the wooded hills and green meadows of the Exe valley in plodding to Tiverton. The *Angel* being too much engaged for yet one more unattached male, my appeals for charity elsewhere at last ended with the opening of a basement window. A cheerful womanly voice called out, "Yes, all right: open the door and come down," which I did, to find myself in a cosy kitchen with a fire blazing, food already in sight, and the prospect of a bed up aloft. While steaming in front of the fire another arrival came in, a brave creature soaked like myself to the skin. "My line," he explained, was tailoring, practised that wet afternoon by measuring a farmer for a pair of riding-breeches in a windy field, made more draughty, the wag added, "because the gate had been left open." Such are the remarkable feats within the power of human beings on England's green and sodden land. The evening proceeded to the accompaniment of a harmonium and Moody and Sankey. It appropriately ended in a rousing chorus,

> All the storms will soon be over,
> Then we'll anchor in the harbour,

Next morning the lowering clouds had vanished. The sun shone. The ancient wool town presented its sights—the twelfth-century castle ruins reduced by the Cromwellians, the school of "Old Blundell, A.D. 1604" and John Ridd, the elaborate sculptures at the church and ornate Greenway chapel, the West Country Regency architecture in the streets, the scene from the Exe looking up, the view from the churchyard looking down. Leaving Tiverton, I next reached Bickleigh old bridge and castle on the road to Exeter. My thoughts roamed far and away to Widecombe-in-the-Moor, the homeland of the stirring Devonshire anthem "Old Uncle Tom Cobleigh, and all."

The mention of these places hints that we are now properly in Devon, the land of kind hearts and warm scenes, than which no county in England offers better. The very place-names ooze a nice softness, catch the character of the luscious land and its people. They ring kindly, sound courteous and good-humoured, fit the landscapes of joyous colours, orchards, watered valleys and deep lanes. Challacombe, Bishops Nympton, Yarnscombe, Yeoford, Ivybridge, Cullompton, Yealmpton, Chudleigh, Ottery St. Mary, Berry Pomeroy, and dozens of full-burred names plant just the right milestones for this land flowing with cream, jam, and splits, and scented with the smell of cider gratis.

Pointers such as the above add the commas and stops to the wide hill and valley country from the Exe to Barnstaple and Bideford, whither we are now bound. Often they mark locations of the cob cottages and thatched roofs mentioned on an earlier page. They also guide to the tall Devon towers, guardians of the church interiors rich in woodwork and screens for which the county is famous both in the north and the south. Tricked out with carving and finery either in wood or stone, of late Gothic or Renaissance periods, and spread in sweeps of arches and ribbed projections right across the east ends of aisles and chancel openings, the screens may cause an onlooker to gasp in wonder, so fine are they in craftsmanship and detail. Three of my notes of these features are given on page 227. Among many, examples at Chulmleigh, Atherington complete with a rood-loft, and at Swimbridge lie in the way to Barnstaple; and the seventeenth-century chancel panelling at North Molton need not be forgotten.

The names of Barnstaple and Bideford always tickle my fancy. They run to good swanking sounds; seem to be weathered and valorous; carry the savour of Elizabethan and glorious Devon, that led all England in merchant adventuring and sea exploits when the gallant men of the West, "the Drakes and Hawkins, Gilberts and Raleighs, Grenviles and Oxenhams, and a host more of forgotten worthies" laboriously endured to brighten the national fame and preserve the country's very existence. On a summer's afternoon at Bideford quay you can change to-day for the year of grace 1575 to picture a group of sailors and young Amyas Leigh listening earnestly to Mr. Oxenham's bold voice, oaths, "And hurra for the Spanish main, O!" Meanwhile the buses snort and turn for Westward Ho! and the golf links, and Kingsley looks down from his statue. Or in Barnstaple you may find the Renaissance Queen Anne's Walk, where the old merchants' walk was, sculptured overhead with devices, trophies, armorial vases, and a statue of the Queen in regal attire. Under the colonnade you can think of the year 1588, of the Great Quay in front brave with the tall masts, topsails curved to the breeze, the painted upper-works, the figureheads of *The Dudley*, *The God Save Her*, *The Tiger*, *The John of Barnstaple*, and *The Unicorn*, ready to join Sir Francis Drake's fleet at Plymouth and eager to put paid to the Spanish Armada. But here again the buses snort and turn; the West Gate opposite disappeared in 1852, and the place of the Great Quay is just unromantic railway lines.

Pre-eminently Bideford was Bideford by virtue of its bridge of twenty-four arches, built about the year 1350; and Barnstaple's capital B stood for sixteen arches, dating from the twelfth century (228). Structures so ancient and whose fame seamen carried far and wide, of course gathered wondrous legends, virtues, stories, and customs during hoary years. Now, alas, much of their glamour and beauty have been marred by widenings, made to accommodate ever-sprawling man. The overhanging parapet at Bideford so depressed me that I merely tried to sketch an old arch or two, crowded out, or rather in (233). Good fun awaited in the adjacent hilly streets in sight of the broad estuary.

There one can spot light Georgian fronts, bow windows out of which ancients had looked, and an exceptional ceiling of late Renaissance plasterwork at the *Royal Hotel*, Kingsley's spot for writing part of *Westward Ho!* If the day be a Tuesday, market day, jolly Devonian farmers and country types crowded in the streets and about the market hall, laughing and talking in round accents, bring joy to the heart. But little seen, either here or in Barnstaple, recalls the great seafaring past. Barum, an important Saxon stronghold before its first Norman lord ruled at the Conquest, has lost its castle, Cluniac priory, gates, and nearly a mile of walls that extended along the quay and Boutport Street. It preserves the church with the twisted leaden spire next to St. Anne's Chapel, where John Gay went to school (228), seventeenth-century almshouses in Litchdon Street, another picturesque group in Church Lane. The fashion of Georgian doorways and plaster frontages is hospitably led by the *Fortesque Hotel* and its generous bow windows. Very good plaster ceilings and chimney-pieces can be discovered in High Street, Cross Street, the *Golden Lion Hotel*, and elsewhere, specimens due to the virile school of Barnstaple's craftsmen in the seventeenth century. If you like *The Beggar's Opera* and happen to be rationed at the shop on the corner of High Street and Joy Street, something may be bought while standing on the floor of the house in which Gay was born in 1685. Always, both in this town and at Bideford, the broad expanses of the rivers, sparkling waters, sand-banks, boats, barges, and green uplands charm and endear.

These rivers, the Taw and the Torridge, beckon to enchanted landscapes. They and their compeers elsewhere wind through fairylands, flow gloriously, give foretastes of the sort of Arcadia we hope to reach hereafter and meet Pan, his pipe and his flocks, if we are good. The rivers of Devon! They are gems in the rich diadem of the county. The sweeps of the Taw between wooded heights past Bishop's Tawton, the valley of the Torridge from high Torrington's castle mound to the fifteenth-century hall and gatehouse at Wear Gifford (233), the Exe, the Culm and the Bovy, the Teign from Fingle Bridge to the estuary, the classic Dart below Totnes to Dittisham, the Tamer along the Cornish boundary, rivers big and rivers small in many places—what visions and magnificence do they bring to the mind! No wonder that artists innumerable have courted these scenes, or that Turner painted masterpieces for the National Gallery, amid the grandeur and luxuriance of the rivers of Devon.

A host of rivers and streams begin infant prances on Dartmoor. This granite fastness, where the air braces better than wine, is a 20-mile area of solitary expanses, space unlimited, tors, hollows, prehistoric remnants. It secretes dreadful legends of the Satanic Majesty, supernatural monsters, ghoulish packs of hounds and wolves, and it accommodates the flotsam of the broad arrows within sound of the little brooks a-gurgling, and the tune of the sweet Prince-town chime. When the weather favours, the Moor is splendid. You may see sixty tors at one go, tremendous views, and gleams of the sea. The Moor in the

TOTNES *mounts up a height commanding the River Dart. A castle, gates, walls, the quay, and covered walks under projecting gables in High Street, are features of this attractive town. The church, topped by a red sandstone tower, contains a magnificent stone screen glowing with old colouring and carving.*

THURLESTONE. *Devon cob walls and thatch.*

BOSCASTLE. *The Cornish harbour behind the rocks facing the Atlantic.*

rain is less nice; when mists come down suddenly it is the very devil. It also keeps vivid green but swampy places, capable of engulfing anybody and anything in less than a moment. Never shall I forget hopping rapidly from tuft to tuft haunted by the fear that the next step would be my last above ground. The high tors (High Willhays is the loftiest, at 2,039 feet) shape fantastically in exposed granite. Rising out of the mist or looming against the sunset, they can rouse creepy feelings, thoughts of gnomes, bogeys, and Edgar Allan Poe quotations. This ground for bright hours or gloomy moods does not specialize in architecture, for it is largely uninhabited. But the lonely farmsteads and cottages, roughly built, well fit the bleak expanses (241).

South and east of the Moor the red earths and greenery of Devon spread exuberantly, brightened with the light village walls and thatching that extend in sequence from Broadhembury, near the lace town of Honiton, and through amiable spots such as Newton St. Cyres, Lustleigh, Combe-in-Teignhead, and Thurlestone (248) to the neighbourhood of Plymouth. Here and there stand old houses of charm, fame, and interest. Of this variety are Sir Walter Raleigh's birthplace at Hayes Barton, the thatched Hall House at Lustleigh, fifteenth-century Bradley Manor with a hall and chapel tracery, the early Renaissance interiors of Forde House, Newton Abbot, once graced by Charles I and slept in by William of Orange in 1688 after landing at Brixham. Towns not too large or too small for pleasure, comfort, and homeliness, border Dartmoor and lie towards the coast. Okehampton, Sir Francis Drake's Tavistock, Moreton-hampstead, Ashburton, Ivybridge, and Totnes come into this capital collection. Notable churches are to be seen, streets often quietish, crowds on market days, bridges, rivers, streams, and trees in profusion everywhere. If you arrive in Okehampton on the right day, provided with good legs or a pony, you can join the gay throng in a 12-mile round to preserve common rights by beating the bounds in sight of Yes Tor's 2,028 feet. Or in Totnes on the hill above the Dart (247) you can explore the remains of the Norman keep, the north and east gates, the red sandstone church, containing one of the finest sculptured screens, the pillared market hall, the butterwalks beneath overhanging upper storeys like those at Dartmouth; you may find many a slate-fronted house in the steep streets and narrow byways, and wind up at the quay in a refreshing smell of Symons' cider issued free from a Methodist chapel whose hymn days are over. Reluctantly we must depart from these friendly towns. Each one merits those reams of paper that a benevolent Government reserves for forms. I must pass to their parent capital of Exeter.

Ah! Exeter of happy memories, what shall I say of thee now? The Germans wrecked many of thy charms. Of all war's tragedies that I have seen, and these are many, none have caused sadder pangs of heart than the ghost of this sacred, beautiful, lovable, kind, and faithful city of the West. The fabled British capital of Devon and Cornwall, Roman *Isca Damnoniorum*, the Saxon *Exanceaster* of

Egbert, Edward the Elder, and Athelstan, William the Conqueror's prize below the red Norman castle of Rougemont; the city of the sword and cap given by Henry VII (in the guildhall), Queen Elizabeth's "Semper Fidelis" (the civic motto), ever loyal to the Throne and to the shady Stuarts while that scoundrel Cromwell ransacked the shrines and smashed the maypoles; the goal of the great west road when merry England rang with tooting horns, rattling teams of mail coaches, and the celebrated Telegraph, speediest of the swift, bounded in from London; the centre of my first sketching expedition in the last year of the gay 1890's, and my periodical squatting place from then until this present year—old Exeter, or a great deal of it, is no more. While sketching in the ruins round St. Stephen's Saxon foundation a genial, elderly soul, without a suspicion of interrupting my doings, just whispered as he passed by, "How long do you think it will take to put all this right again?"

"The crack of doom," I called to him. "Centuries have gone, for ever."

But, as another genial native remarked, "We have a great deal to be thankful for." The *Royal Clarence* hotel, for example, is firm rooted in one of the happiest spots in England for ministering those hospitable contrivances of man so nobly eulogized by Dr. Johnson. To inhabit one of its rooms facing Cathedral Yard (No. 7 is mine), watch day change to night, sleep snug behind drawn curtains, to be awakened at 7.30 a.m. by the deep tones of that marvellous cathedral bell just when the door opens and early-morning tea comes in—well, this is all very nice. And to get up, look out, and go out means a good deal more; the promise of a small epitome of the English story, tracked from times lost in far-away mists to the present's emblems of motor cars ranked beneath the shady trees (234, 235). Round Cathedral Yard are the houses and courtyards of mixed domestic fashions; Mol's Coffee House, wherein Armada heroes met; the little church of St. Martin, dedicated in 1065. Hard by a rejuvenated *Ship Inn* stands for Sir Francis Drake's tippling fancy in 1587, "Next to mine own shippe I do most love that old Shippe in Exon, a tavern in St. Martin's Lane"; the old dogs liked their few draughts of sack under the eight! Over all the scarred cathedral of St. Peter rises in majesty. The site of the Saxon church, the towers of the Norman cathedral, and style, form, and sculptor's art, mounted up to the grandest expression of fourteenth-century architecture in England, transport the mind down the avenues of old time. The nave and choir inside represent the culmination of Decorated building, comparable to the later triumph of the Perpendicular period at Winchester, Wykeham's nave. Beyond the bishop's palace and the close are the walls, the relics of Athelstan's and later constructions that encircled the city from the castle to the line of masonry now standing above the lower town and the river in sight of the patterned green hills. Just across South Street the wreckage of war has opened up the story to A.D. 55–75 by revealing remains of the wooden houses of Roman *Isca*. Farther afield, though wide areas are vacant, inquisitive eyes can find ample rewards. What is left of the wonderful High Street shows the fourteenth-century guildhall with the Elizabethan projection over the pavement, the timbered, gabled, and square house skylines, the windows of assorted patterns (241). There are the Georgian houses in Southernhay facing the trees in the old south hay market; Northernhay and the great gate tower and castle ruins; characteristic red and high sandstone church towers; the medieval hall of the tuckers, weavers, and shearmen; St. Nicholas' Priory, founded in 1080 in The Mint; overhanging houses at Stepcote Hill; the curious lower town of narrow ways; a pretty Victorian lay-out at Queen's Terrace; reminders of Charles, Prince of Wales, in the town he finally had to get out of, and the place of the West Gate through which William of Orange marched in (236).

In fact, loving, hearty, and homely Exeter still has more than enough to keep feet busy, thoughts active, and for filling pages and pages of sketch-books. So much might be written on this high seat of many past monasteries and thirty-two churches, the stage of Perkin Warbeck's and more sieges than I can remember, on incidents historical and domestic, liveliness past and present, that my limits of space send me hastening away. The river leads down to artists' subjects at Countess Weir bridge, at Exeter's old port of Topsham, greatly celebrated in the years of wooden ships, and to Lympstone delightfully straggled by the estuary (242). The sea breezes blow in from the coast. They waft over the holiday resorts of Exmouth, Budleigh Salterton, Sidmouth, Dawlish, Teignmouth, and Torquay, surrounded by the marvels and colour of Devon's natural beauty.

The coast sweeps round, broken by the red cliffs of Sidmouth and Tor Bay, the heights of Start Point, Bolt Head, and Bolt Tail. Luscious estuaries of the south Devon rivers end in winding channels. Bays and coves, now enchanting, mark the landing-places of French marauders in the Middle Ages. There are delicious villages and fishing places within hail of the golden sands, and towns as well that have been there for centuries—Dartmouth, a port famed in Chaucer's time; old-world Kingsbridge; Brixham with trawlers, fish, damsels, and the statue of William of Orange at his point of welcome on the quay. Here and there houses date a long way back; others tell of the popularity of this coast in Georgian and Regency years, demonstrated at Budleigh Salterton, Torquay, and other points by light villas and terraces due to the birth of the seaside craze remembered by Cowper's lines ending with:

> And all, impatient of dry land, agree
> With one consent to rush into the sea.

And at the Cornish border is the scenic and historical centrepiece of Plymouth Sound, the beauty of which neither bombs nor anything else so far have destroyed. Great in sea traditions since Henry II made a naval base there; the port of the fleet that opposed the Armada; the birthplace for adventurous voyages of Frobisher, Gilbert, Drake, Raleigh, and their fraternity in old and new years; the Pilgrim Fathers' last of old England in the *Mayflower*, bound for Plymouth in the New World—these waters perpetually shine with the lights of glory and fame, and they lead to a capital P for the celebrated game of bowls completed on the Hoe. After Plymouth, those who enjoy a walk, ride, or drive, could rarely do better than explore the loveliness along the windings of the River Tamer. The parallel highway, from Bere Ferrers to Milton Abbot, drops through wooded country to Greston Bridge and enters—

CORNWALL

At this point the sands of my paper ration are fast running out. The few remaining pages for pictures and words could never do justice to the land of the courteous Celtic race. Yet writers of many good books already have told the Cornish tale; since the days of Stanhope Forbes, Frank Bramley, and Walter Langley's red pitchers, shoals of artists have worked industriously on the moods and graces of England's farthest county in the south-west. Our juveniles all know that the Conqueror's Earldom of Cornwall became the Royal Duchy for all Princes of Wales when Edward III turned the Black Prince into a duke. Centuries before Plantagenets appeared, Britons in possession claimed their kingdom far to the east of the River Tamar until pushed back by the Saxons, a state of affairs much resented by true-blue Cornishmen even to this day. Some early inhabitants specialized on barrows, tumuli, cells, and crosses now to be seen in good supply. Others put up the Pipers (at Boleigh), the Merry Maidens (near St. Just), the Hurlers (near St. Cleer), and similar stone effects to mystify archæologists. Traditional Phœnicians, British princes, Irish and Welsh missionaries of the fifth to the seventh centuries, and various known and unknown magicians waved spells of myth and legend over many scenes and points, and thereby caused funny feelings inside superstitious natives settled in the neighbourhoods. Nature piled up the wild and woody landscapes and impressive coastlines. Tin, copper, gold and china-clay, granite, sandstone and slate, furnished spices for history and story and gave means for past and present prosperity. Sunny hours, majestic cloud effects, full colours on land and sea, south-west gales, storms, gulls, weather-beaten fisherfolk, shining pilchards, flowers, cream, and ever so many things unite in making attraction and contrast in Cornwall.

Launceston, the ancient feudal capital of Cornwall, immediately presents itself beyond the Rivers Tamar and Ottery on leaving Devon (258). A high-placed Norman keep on a Saxon site, the square, *White Hart*, the south gate, and streets dropping steeply downhill, compose into pictures at every angle. The parish church, rebuilt with remarkable exuberance of incised and relief work in 1524, is a top-notch achievement in granite, a material of importance in the

Granite carving 1511-1524, St. Marys Launceston

St. George and the Dragon, St Martin and the Prince of Wales's feather

Cornish touring menu. It made the grey church towers and the interiors of clustered shafts, capitals, and arcades which most old churches in the county possess. Skill in tackling this hard local product led to the special type of sculpture and shallow ornamentation evident throughout the Duchy. Granite, with the prevalent sandstone and slate, together gave the components for domestic buildings in town and country from coast to coast. The bulky walls and low-pitched roofs of houses and cottages, justly schemed and simply devised, group in grey and cool colours. Roofs, frequently coated with cement to defy driving rain and wind, tell of heavy weather. Rougher walling here and there might be taken for nature's actual handiwork rather than constructed articles. Bulges and angular shapes of the big blocks can suggest just the settings for the impish pranks supposed to be played by gnomes and elves in wild and romantic regions (257). But these harmonies in grey and white exactly fit the leafy or bleak landscapes, the rocky coasts and the harbours; they have affinity with this fabled land of many saints, holy wells, hidden treasure, folklore, and bogey Tregeagle.

Beyond Launceston the landscape becomes bleaker. This promises Bodmin Moor and the long stretches of sandstone subdivided by granite beds that make the inland humps all down the county. These expanses of moors, rolling uplands, and undulations directing towards the coasts are not always at their best for dispensing warmth to the body and comfort to the mind, a circumstance doubtless responsible for Cornwall being likened sometimes to certain human beauties of ravishing exteriors but not much inside. Certainly it might be unpleasant on Brown Willy's 1,375 feet in Cornwall's special brand of driving rain and wind, or even uncanny to be caught in the dark at Dozmare Pool while fearful of "King Arthur's sword, Excalibur" coming up out of it.

Bodmin is an agreeable county town with a large Perpendicular church, but I for one should not choose long residence in the neighbourhoods of Redruth and Camborne for their charms of disused tin-mine chimney-stacks, or the district round St. Austell for the mounds of china-clay spoil. Nevertheless the moorlands and the environs have peculiar attractions. They offer features bleak, strange, and bright in lonely heights, long panoramas, and miles and miles of heather. Wonderful skies fresh from the sea gather and change shape overhead. Hundreds of streams run down from high places and reach many small and pretty valleys.

The River Camel, wild and picturesque, leads from Camelford to woods and Dunmere Pool. For gracious and romantic scenes nothing could be better than the River Fowey landscapes (259). The stream descends from Bodmin Moor to Red Gate, near the fine church tower, well, and cross of St. Cleer and the tower of St. Neot; it winds and hurries along past great steep woods, brightens long vistas beneath Glynn Park, prances in sight of the ruined Plantagenet stronghold of Restormel, and courses through the medieval arches of Lostwithiel bridge. Near stands Lanhydrock House, a notable achievement of the seventeenth century with a giddy pinnacled gatehouse. Two other famous Cornish houses lie in the borderlands of the River Tamar, medieval and Tudor Cothele and the Frenchy Charles II chateau at Botus Fleming, in which the castles of Pendennis and Plymouth were surrendered to the Prince of Orange in 1689.

This country of open spaces, big skies, atmospheric contrasts, and magnificent coasts, one that long remained isolated from the rest of England, imparts additional strangeness by its place-names. Visitors from afar, say Sheffield or Bermondsey natives, might find Clodgy, Bodiggo, Laity, or Perranzabuloe sound rather queer, or St. Issey, St. Feock, and other saints at least a bit curious to the palate. And jaunting through all the "Pen's," the "Pol's" and endless "Tre's," past Trewhiddle, Treloweh, Tregion, Trevarrick, Trevennen, Treveor, Tregavarras to the Dodman Point, for example, nobody could imagine being anywhere but in Cornwall.

The cathedral city of Truro, hilly within and hilly all round, gives a cheerful grey impression as you walk up, down, and along on pavements of Cornish granite, or look down from many good viewpoints (260–261). The place is old enough. It figures in Domesday with a frame divided in two pieces, one big and one little. The fortress of the Earls of Cornwall has changed itself to a mere mound by the railway line, and the earlier strain of "ye pride of Truro" on the Truro River is chiefly represented by the Perpendicular parish church incorporated in the cathedral, the grammar school, and a number of oldish houses. The city sets out its particular and regional character with rows and rows of eighteenth-century and Regency frontages of stone, granite, and plaster, roofed with slates. Doorways, quoins, white sash and bay windows, and walls hung with slates of quite small sizes, make distinctive and decorative effects in highways and narrow byways (262). These thoroughfares are full of years, and of courtesy too, for everybody says "Good morning" or passes the time o' day to strangers, a custom indicative of very many miles from London, West Bromwich, or Newcastle. But the streets also align to modern times; they offer waves and cuts of the hair with "all appliances sterilized by electricity," and dancing and the movies are on sale in the market hall. The cathedral mounts remarkably well from various vantage points. However much captious critics may groan at J. L. Pearson's imitative English and French Gothic features, the composition groups finely and is an outstanding example of the 1887–1910 period. The *Red Lion* in Boscawen Street tips the architectural theme back a bit, to "I I F 1671" in fact, as may be read over the doorway. This entrance well merits passing under, if only to see the staircase, black and antique, the elaborate doorways likewise antique and black, and for a sleep in a bedroom wherein, perhaps, Samuel Foote first squawked in 1720 at the former town house of the Foote family, prior to writing a lot of plays, launching witticisms at Dr. Johnson,

Polperro

and performing at the Theatre Royal, Bath, and the Haymarket. Not far distant, in the undulating country of stone walls and stunted trees, lies Helston, which also specializes in stone, granite, plaster, and slate-hanging in streets and byways (262). Its celebrated Floral Dance to the Furry Tune, due on May 8, hardly suggested immemorial antiquity and a Celtic origin when I beheld it tripped by merry men and maidens adorned with silk hats and fashionable dresses. A thatched cottage in the town nurtured Bob Fitzsimons, the world's champion eye-blacker for the year 1897; and at the other end of the county Stratton gave birth and buried Antony Payne, the 7 ft. 4 in. giant who helped Sir Beville Granville to trounce the Roundheads at Stamford Hill in 1643.

Towns small or large, villages, moors, hilly fields, rivers, and streams always hint at the never far distant sea-coast which holds scenic prizes of both Cornwall and England. No other county offers more of grandeur, solemnity, and delight than is presented here by majestic rock dispositions in headlands and cliffs, dark shadowy chasms, creeks, estuaries, rocky shores and sands, harbours protected by breakwaters curved fantastically, sturdy houses and cottages faced defiantly to the elements, and every shade of colour and movement in tides and sea. Nature's bulwarks down from Morwenstow, Boscastle (248), Tintagel, and Trevose Head to St. Ives and Cape Cornwall contain the ruggedness of the northern coastline, splendid on bright days, but "The Sailor's Grave" when storms blow in and breakers crash against the rocks. Onward from the split granite pillars of Land's End, St. Michael's Mount, and the Lizard, the river estuaries break the southern coastline. They reveal the loveliness of watery expanses leading far inland between green banks and woodlands of rare luxuriance, notable on the Helford River and the creeks of the Fal at Devoran (263) and King Harry's Passage. In north and south, facing sea and land, are the harbours, fishing villages, and curious towns—Port Isaac, Mousehole, Coverack, Mevagissey, Fowey, Polperro, Looe, scores of them, all set to words in noble prose, endless books, or sermons on holiday haunts.

My last bit of space is here. I can do no more than jot down a few coastal impressions remembered—thoughts on Parson Hawker and wreckers while perched on Henna Cliff; Rosy Bay and seals under High Cliff, the loftiest rock face, at 705 feet; a pursuit up the Valency valley behind Boscastle in a vain search for Endelstow Vicarage, which only existed in Thomas Hardy's *A Pair of Blue Eyes*; ? did King Arthur and his Knights really manage to get a round table on the perilous pinnacle of Tintagel, or on Cadbury Castle (page 224); coast views and tin-mine ruins seen from St. Agnes Head; St. Ives Island twinkling with lights at dusk; Land's End rocks, not so impressive as they should be for England's finale; artist hunting behind the coloured doors of Newlyn and St. Ives; brilliant sea colours under a blue sky at Kynance Cove; waves 50 feet high in a storm at the Lizard; the oddity of Upton Slip, Falmouth (264); Mevagissey and Polperro from the seaward angle; Fowey

Tintagel

St. Ives

Newlyn

Boscastle

QUAINT AND CURIOUS IN CORNWALL

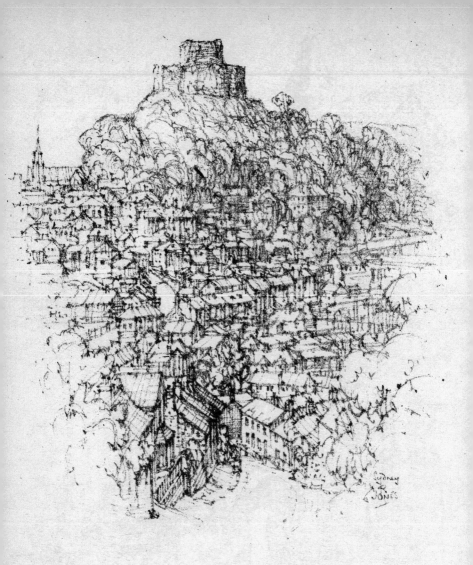

LAUNCESTON, *the old feudal capital of Cornwall, full of interest in up-and-down streets, a granite church enriched with carving, the South Gate, and the tower-keep raised high on a mound.*

FOWEY RIVER. *Its scenery compares with that of the Tamar and other notable rivers of the south-west. A view between St. Neot and Glynn, Cornwall.*

Sydney
R JONES
TRURO

TRURO, *the cathedral city of Cornwall. The modern Cathedral, designed by J. L. Pearon, R.A., consecrated in 1887 and completed in 1910, is a distinguished achievement of the Gothic Revival. It rises high over ancient streets of stone, slate, and granite buildings in the vale at the head of the Truro River.*

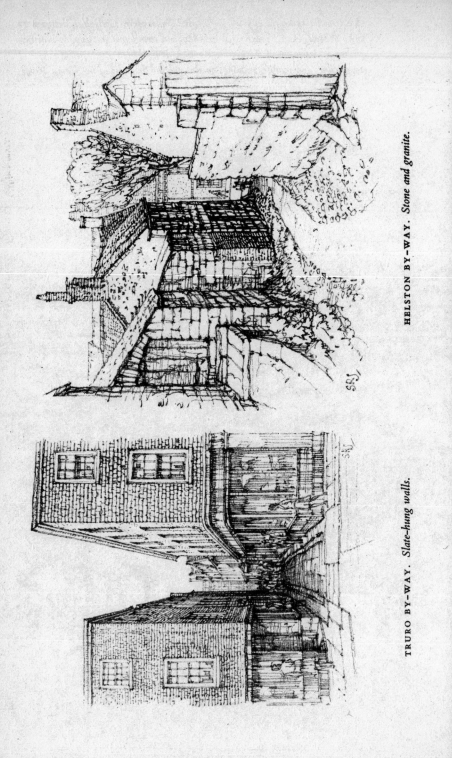

HELSTON BY-WAY. *Stone and granite.*

TRURO BY-WAY. *Slate-hung walls.*

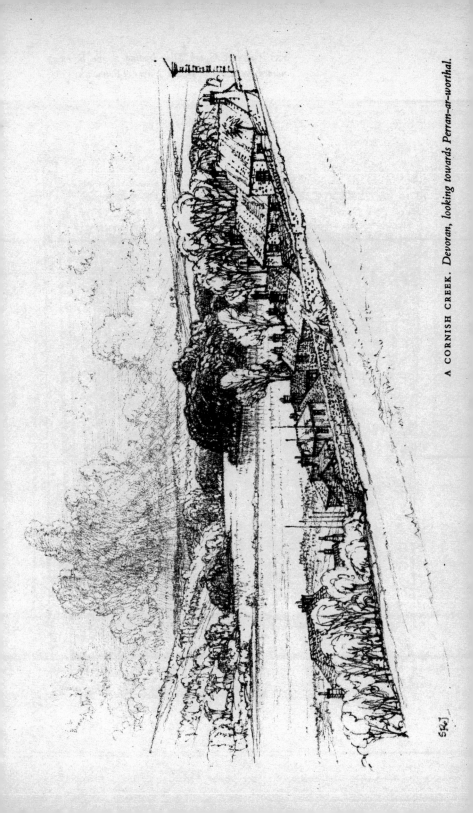

A CORNISH CREEK. Devoran, looking towards Perran-ar-worthal.

563

FALMOUTH. *Upton Slip, leading to the harbour; named after Captain Upton, Mayor of Falmouth, 1708.*

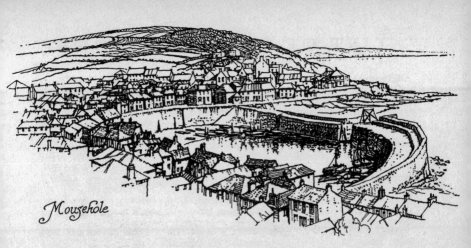

Mousehole

harbour and Quiller-Couch's *Troy Town* from Hall Walk; splits, real cream, home-made butter and jam in the lean war and post-war years; and in these times of triumph for the common man, bountiful courtesy everywhere. I add nothing on the flowered and coloured Scilly Islands, where Prince Charles sheltered from Cromwell, because my last passage in turbulent weather over fabled Lyonesse brought thoughts on the vanity of food and human life. And it is now the moment for good-bye, friendly reader, and a godspeed hope that you have enjoyed Southern England's scenes, ways, and storied past as much as I have done. Should you follow in my tracks, fare thee well.

LIST OF ILLUSTRATIONS

INDEX